OPERATION TIDAL WAVE

The Bloodiest Air Battle in the History of War

VINCENT dePAUL LUPIANO

Guilford, Connecticut

An imprint of The Rowman & Littlefield Publishing Group, Inc.
4501 Forbes Blvd., Ste. 200
Lanham, MD 20706
www.rowman.com

Distributed by NATIONAL BOOK NETWORK

British Library Cataloguing in Publication Information available

Library of Congress Cataloging-in-Publication Data

Names: Lupiano, Vincent dePaul, author.
Title: Operation Tidal Wave : the bloodiest air battle in the history of
    war / Vincent Lupiano.
Other titles: Bloodiest air battle in the history of war
Description: Guilford, Connecticut : Lyons Press, [2021] | Includes
    bibliographical references and index. | Summary: "The story of the
    bloodiest air battle in the history of war, when 1,700 American airmen
    set out to bomb the oil refineries surrounding the city of Ploieşti,
    Romania, on August 1, 1943."— Provided by publisher.
Identifiers: LCCN 2020010418 (print) | LCCN 2020010419 (ebook) | ISBN
    9781493053728 (hardback) | ISBN 9781493053735 (epub)
Subjects: LCSH: Ploieşti, Battles of, Ploieşti, Romania, 1943-1944. |
    Bombing, Aerial—Romania—Ploieşti—History—20th century. | World War,
    1939-1945—Aerial operations, American.
Classification: LCC D766.42.P56 L87 2021 (print) | LCC D766.42.P56
    (ebook) | DDC 940.54/21982—dc23
LC record available at https://lccn.loc.gov/2020010418
LC ebook record available at https://lccn.loc.gov/2020010419

♾™ The paper used in this publication meets the minimum requirements of American National Standard for Information Sciences—Permanence of Paper for Printed Library Materials, ANSI/NISO Z39.48-1992.

Dedicated to the air and ground crews who endured Black Sunday: the men of the 43rd, 44th, 93rd, 98th, and 376th Bomb Groups, who suffered hellfire and loss of life on that brutal date, August 1, 1943.

Greater love hath no man than this—
that a man lay down his life for his friends.
You served and died not in vain;
Our nation holds you dear and owes you much.

Dedicated to
Maj. Robert Warren Sternfels, pilot,
The Sandman—
No finer man, no finer pilot

For my children,
Elizabeth Alexandra Lupiano-Nocar and Paul Scheer Lupiano—
There when "there" mattered
I love you

For my parents,
Judge Vincent A. Lupiano and Roselle C. Lupiano—
for teaching me the craft and giving me an exceptional leg up

And my dear sister,
Paula Lupiano Conway—
for enduring

Contents

Introduction

Some say nothing good happens in bars after midnight.

On a late May evening, many years ago, I sat at a mahogany bar in the lounge of the Deepdene Manor Hotel in Hamilton, Bermuda, with my fiancée, Nancy Elizabeth Scheer. She was beguiling, as always. The midnight hour had drifted by, and what we faced was on the far side of our lives. The occasion on this clement evening was a life-changing moment that, sadly, is seldom experienced, or that presents itself with such velocity that the moment has no chance to thrive and plummets away.

Here and there were divans of dark oak and settees with pink linen tablecloths bearing flickering votive candles. The half-shadows on the walls reflected close friends and family sitting in small groups, chatting. And the air floating through the windows off Bermuda Harbor was enchanting—African violets and fresh-cut Bermuda grass. The renowned Bermuda Dark 'n' Stormy rum drinks were arriving on the linen tablecloths in multiples. The blue enameled seashell ashtrays had been emptied several times, and the air was dense with skeins of cigarette smoke, jolted every few moments with an outburst of laughter. Distant music played from years gone by.

If this was a black-and-white photograph, we would appear so young, so ingenuous and fresh, without artifice. We are fledglings. We are in love. We are holding the world in oh-so-hopeful hands.

Earlier that day, Nancy and I had flown down here from JFK International Airport in New York City aboard a Pan American Airlines Clipper, a now-long-gone Boeing 707 bearing the iconic Pan American blue and white "meatball" logo. It had left us here in a patch of civility, with expectations of embarking on a significant event the following day—our marriage. (I cannot look at that Pan Am logo without feeling a swell of sentiment and fond remembrance.)

From where Nancy and I sat, the candles' half-light could not dim the animated chatter at the opposite end of the bar: On the right of a small group, sitting on a barstool, was my uncle, Francis Sarubbi, handsome, with a smile that brightened the room. When he was born, my grandmother had told my mother, "This is your brother," and that would be his nickname forever. At this moment, Brother was forty-seven, and had already packed a large quantity of life's pain under his laughter, having served and seen combat in the US Marine Corps, in the Pacific Theater. In looking back, I sense that he had never had enough time to hammer out the horrors he had seen on those enemy-held islands. He was an artillery officer and had endured Guadalcanal, the Battle of Guam, and the Battle of Iwo Jima. At the unheard-of age of twenty-three, he was promoted to captain in the 3rd Marine Division, the "Fighting Third." There was still a lot of blood and sadness lingering in his memories, and he packed it up tightly and took it with him to an early death, just six years later.

To his right, tossing back his umpteenth Dark 'n' Stormy, was Robert Warren Sternfels. He was also forty-seven years old, and, similarly, an incomprehensibly young twenty-four when he was promoted to the rank of major in the US Army Air Force. (It usually takes about ten years to make major in the US armed services after you join up—these guys did it in three.)

This was the first time I'd met Bob, and at that moment I knew little about the historic mission he had participated in—the Battle of Ploieşti, aka Operation Tidal Wave. About the time of his promotion, Robert Sternfels had earned the Silver Star for a combat mission to Wiener Neustadt, in southeast Austria, in which he had led a disarrayed flock of B-24s to a successful bomb run over that charming city.

Bob, unlike Brother, had spent the bulk of his Army Air Force time up in the air, piloting the most produced aircraft of World War II, a Consolidated B-24 Liberator, which many thought was the ugliest airplane to ever get shoved off an assembly line. (It was.) The Germans called it a "moving van," and American crewmen said it was the plane that the B-17 was shipped in. Down below Bob and his B-24, hemispheres away in the slop and slime of the Pacific islands, Brother was humping artillery pieces in the jungles under tattered palm trees, Japanese bullets, and banzai charges from fanatical Japanese soldiers.

All in all, each thought their mode of fighting was the toughest, and what would win the war. Of course, neither would acknowledge that they could die just as quickly, just as painfully as the other—they did not want to admit that it was six of one, half dozen of the other. Dying was dying. Pain was pain. That's why it's called war.

And therein lies the genesis of the friendly argument they were having on this magical evening: The major, Bob, in his clean, fresh flying togs, dropped his bombs and shot the Germans down at 12,000 feet; and the captain, Brother, his shirt stained salty white from sweat, his camo helmet sitting angled with attitude on his head, slugged it out on Pacific islands with palm trees and seashells, and never enough letters from home. Which environment was the most perilous? Would one try to validate that ancient question that will never receive a conclusive answer? Especially on a night like this, at a bar in Bermuda with a boundless supply of Dark 'n' Stormys.

Both Bob and Brother fought their enemies at the same time in history, separated by multiple time zones. Bob expressed without hesitation that the air force was the best military organization in the world. He described his tour of duty in Libya as similar to living in a Hilton Hotel, sleeping in fresh sheets, enjoying gourmet meals, and occasionally flying on sunny days to drop a bomb or two; it was clean living, he said, tongue in cheek. Brother, lighting yet another Lucky Strike with a Zippo lighter from Bradford, Pennsylvania, that bore battle wounds from Guadalcanal, said directly to Bob's face, "If you want to win a war, call the marines." Period.

And so it went.

All this war chitchat had gotten the marine and the air force pilot riled up. But Brother's flank was not protected, because the man behind the bar, the bartender and owner of the Deepdene, had some contentious points of his own to make about a war he had lived through as a teenager in Berlin, with his father fighting the Russians. He tried occasionally to interject something prideful about the Wehrmacht between filling glasses with rum and umbrellas. He spoke English with a German/British accent that lent authority to his words, when he could slip them in. The bartender was also a proud member of the Hitler Youth, a quasi-military group in Germany during the war—like our Boy Scouts, but a bit edgier, with swastikas on their uniforms.

A framed black-and-white photo of the bartender stood proudly between a bottle of Johnny Walker Black and Hendrick's Dry Gin from Bulgaria, providing gravitas to what the bartender had to say to the former military officers at his bar, about how Bob's comrades bombed Berlin, many years ago. The conversation started to become uncomfortably prickly when Bob began a modified bomb run at both Brother and the bartender. Brother saw the bomb-bay doors opening and deftly changed the subject. (The marines came to the rescue.)

I breathed a sigh of relief. What this party did not need was World War II war stories upending a bar in Bermuda on the eve of my wedding.

So, there it was—bits and pieces from these two soldiers, having their Dark 'n' Stormys, telling their stories with typical military haughtiness, man-boys engaging in a "pissing contest" in the early-morning hours at a bar in romantic Bermuda. They were enjoying themselves, these former military men. After all, they had survived World War II. They had both helped win the war, each in his way. This was fun fighting they were engaged in. No blood. Both would survive, both would win. They were brothers in arms, even at this contentious moment at the bar. They both had faced the bullets and bombs of the foe. And what was the difference between them? Their commonality was that they had endured hell, and that kind of fire binds men forever.

I did not know it then, but this small, peculiar band of brothers was knitting together memories for me that would never unravel, never be equaled. I was looking at the real deal—not some blurry History Channel special, but two men who had come close to dying many times while I slept swaddled in a warm baby blanket in a blacked-out Manhattan apartment.

In essence, the gist of their friendly argument was who had the better army air force, who was better trained, who got shot at more, and, dare I say, who killed more. There was no pretense here; they all killed, and each of them knew this. That was one subject they did not dwell on this evening. One they wanted the Stormys to help them forget. They, collectively, had won the battle, and tonight's argument was just gentlemen jousting around glasses of dark rum while the perfumed air helped them forget the stink of battle. Booze and bars after midnight can, albeit infrequently, bring out some odd furtive magic.

Sitting on Bob's right was his wife, Nancy Barker Sternfels, born and raised in Vineland, New Jersey. The delicate-looking Nancy was the quintessential "girl next door," petite, with a cute raspy voice. Nancy, who shared my bride-to-be's name, bore a pleasant resemblance to June Allyson, the movie actress. When she laughed or smiled, her eyes disappeared, adding to her charm.

For me, the most notable of the trio, made up of Bob, Brother, and the bartender, was Robert Warren Sternfels, as of that moment, an executive at Kerr Dental Products in California. I loved aviation. I had taken flying lessons, and almost always looked up at heaven when a plane flew above, as Bob had in his youth. But meeting Bob that night was noteworthy. I knew he had flown *The Sandman*; I just didn't know the raw details. I realized there might be a compelling story here.

From that moment, Bob and I started talking about Ploieşti, how he piloted the big B-24 during the deadly minutes he and his fellow pilots flew over the Ploieşti refineries. Bob always had the patience to answer my questions until he was sure I had the facts stowed away clearly for future reference, if and when I ever put pen to paper.

That said, how a boy from New York City came to meet Bob Sternfels, who piloted a bomber over Ploieşti, is just a matter of reading on for the answer.

—◆—

Months before the Deepdene Hotel gathering and our marriage, Nancy and I were sitting at another bar, this one at Pam American International Terminal 3 at John F. Kennedy International Airport, in Queens, New York, the only airline terminal where I could linger and admire the architectural splendor as I might at the Taj Mahal. It was just that kind of building, a historic landmark. But this bar, situated on a balcony overlooking the main waiting room, is also the spot where this book, *Operation Tidal Wave*, took off on its journey. While historic journeys seldom spring from barstools, this landmark at JFK Airport led to the telling of bloodshed and sorrow on that Black Sunday, August 1, 1943, what some accurately call the Battle of Ploieşti.

Nancy and I sat there, people-watching, as we waited for a friend's overdue arrival. One sign at a gate announced the arrival of a Pan Am flight from Bermuda. We watched the people snake through the walkway coming off the Pan Am Clipper into the main hall, stopping, pausing to absorb the wonder they were standing in—*Yes, ladies and gentlemen, this massive airline terminal you are standing in is a huge, freshly baked Chinese fortune cookie, painted white.*

Then, Nancy leaned across the table and said, "Wouldn't it be wonderful if we got married in Bermuda instead of the Sherry-Netherland Hotel in New York City."

My glass did not drop from my hand because it was stabilized on my lower lip when I heard Nancy's proposition. My eyes were as big as the Pan Am "meatball" logo.

Wow. That was the only word that came to mind, and somehow, I couldn't enunciate it.

"Great, right?" she said, grinning like a Cheshire cat.

I nodded yes, while the line of people from Bermuda got thicker, and the word "Bermuda" and "married" became more prominent in my now-burgeoning fantasy.

"Just fifty of our best friends and family," Nancy said. "In Bermuda."

Wow.

"Have you . . . considered the cost?"

"No. I just got the idea. How could I consider the cost?"

"I mean," I said, with a two-foot-wide pause, "the cost could be a showstopper." Then, I had to ask—"Are you *really* serious?"

She nodded yes twice, her tiny gold earrings jiggling in rhythm to her affirmative response.

The passengers were still dressed in their Bermudian beachwear coming off the Clipper, even though the temperature in New York City was a chilly 32 degrees, and snow had started falling. I liked the idea of flowered shirts and sun and drinks with umbrellas and lots of British accents and real Bermuda rum and people exchanging "cheers." I wanted to be someplace where I could say "Cheers," and no one would do a double take.

We didn't have a calculator to crunch the numbers. There were no iPhones. No Internet to mine for answers. About thirty seconds drifted by, and that was enough to start serious discussion, and begin our financial due diligence, fueled by Nancy's imagination and enthusiasm.

"We would need to hire a travel agent," Nancy said.

"Could be a lot of money."

"I'll ask my mother."

"Sounds super," I said.

"We'll invite fifty people—friends and family, all expenses paid. We'll fly them down from . . . *this* airport!? All they have to do is pack and pay for their airfare from their homes here."

"Lucky people who live in New York and New Jersey."

She nodded.

"*All* expenses?"

"Airline tickets, hotel rooms, food, and a couple of extra days after the reception."

"Reception . . . church . . . priest . . . ?"

"I'll ask my mother."

My memory runs blank now, but I vaguely recall figuring that when you compared four hundred wedding guests at the tony Sherry-Netherland on Madison Avenue in New York City to fifty friends and family in Bermuda, all expenses paid, Bermuda somehow seemed less expensive. How could that be? In fact, to this day I don't know the answer.

Our friend, Hélène "Sophie" Solomon, arrived, and Nancy immediately told her about the Bermuda idea—what she was now referring to as the Fifty Guest Plan—to Sophie's quizzical, are-you-serious expression. Sophie looked to me for validation, and I nodded.

"Well, she sounds serious," Sophie said. She was probably thinking "Are you people nuts?" but gave us her subtle blessing nevertheless.

"When we get home, I'll talk it over with my mother," Nancy said again as we glided out the exit door of the fortune cookie and faced a developing blizzard and hazardous drive back into Manhattan.

When we arrived at Nancy's apartment, near midnight, she got on the phone, explained the Fifty Guest Plan as one would outline a significant military operation, and asked her mom what she thought. They were on the phone for three minutes. I suspect that at that hour, Nancy's mother just wanted to get back to sleep.

And that's how we wound up here at the Deepdene Manor Hotel, with African violets and the sweet scent of Bermuda grass and fifty of our best friends and family. And, most notably, how I met Robert Warren Sternfels and *Operation Tidal Wave* took off.

That simple.

Vincent dePaul Lupiano
Franklin Lakes, New Jersey

THE WRONG TURN

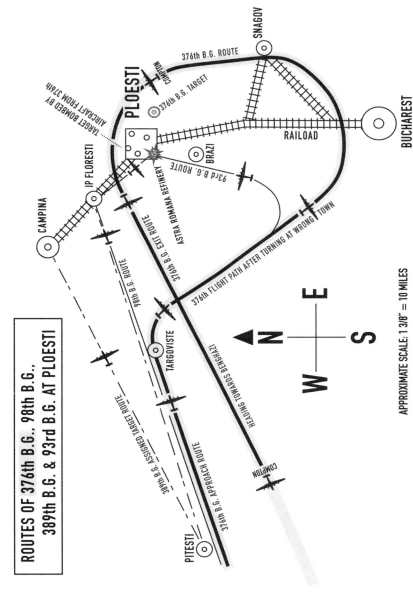

ROUTES OF 376th B.G., 98th B.G., 389th B.G. & 93rd B.G. AT PLOESTI

SNAGOV

376th B.G. ROUTE

COMPTON

PLOESTI

376th B.G. TARGET

TARGET BOMBED BY
AIRCRAFT FROM 376th

IP FLORESTI

CAMPINA

RAILOAD

BUCHAREST

BRAZI

93rd B.G. ROUTE

ASTRA ROMANA REFINERY

376th B.G. EXIT ROUTE

376th FLIGHT PATH AFTER TURNING AT WRONG TOWN

98th B.G. ROUTE

N
W — E
S

TARGOVISTE

389th B.G. ASSIGNED TARGET ROUTE

HEADING TOWARDS BENGHAZI

COMPTON

376th B.G. APPROACH ROUTE

PITESTI

APPROXIMATE SCALE: 1 3/8" = 10 MILES

Map data compiled by Maj. Robert W. Sternfels via crew members who flew the Ploiești mission, August 1, 1943.

CHAPTER I

Great Council of War

Anyone who has ever looked into the eyes of a soldier dying on the battlefield will think hard before starting a war.
—OTTO VON BISMARCK,
CHANCELLOR OF THE GERMAN EMPIRE
MARCH 21, 1871–MARCH 20, 1890

ON THE SEARING AFTERNOON OF JANUARY 14, 1943, AT THE LUXURIOUS Anfa Hotel in French Morocco, the Allied European strategy for World War II started to gestate under the orange trees at the Casablanca Conference, codenamed Symbol.

Prime Minister Winston Churchill and the thirty-second president of the United States, Franklin Delano Roosevelt, are captured in a historic photograph taken on the capacious lawn of the hotel's Moorish garden. Appearing both uncomfortable and apprehensive, they are seated, while a wall of military figures stands behind them—a tableau of vast implication.

Churchill, in the front row, is wearing his classic, three-piece, dark blue pinstripe suit, his distinctive Homburg hat nestled on his knee, his right hand relaxed atop his gentlemen's mahogany cane. His fingers are gripping an ever-present, prodigious La Aroma de Cuba cigar, one of his ten daily smokes, a cigar known by cigar aficionados around the world for its wonderful girth, prodigious length, and billows of blue smoke, and called thereafter a "Churchill."

Roosevelt, seated next to the prime minister, looks blue-blooded and presidential. He is in a light gray suit suitable for the sultry air. His nose is in the air, as it often was, his gray gentleman's eyes gazing into the mid-distance, as are Churchill's. Both leaders are surely scanning the horizon for a solution, a talisman, perhaps, to lead them to the victory line. Both men appear justifiably glum.

Behind them, a stunning flank of the highest-ranking military officers from around the globe. A war council of such stature, such bearing, such elegance, had never been grouped like this before. One wonders what skill it took to assemble them in this place, at this hour in history.

Standing in the front row behind Roosevelt and Churchill:

US Fleet Admiral Ernest Joseph King, sixty-five, the US Navy's second most senior officer after Fleet Admiral William D. Leah, the second admiral in the US Navy to be promoted to five-star rank, a tremendous achievement in American military circles.

US General of the Army—a five-star rank—George Catlett Marshall Jr., sixty-three, soldier and statesman, noted for his leadership roles during World War II and the Cold War, and Chief of Staff of the US Army; a Secretary of State, and the third US Secretary of Defense. Marshall was hailed as the "organizer of victory" by Winston Churchill for his peerless leadership of the Allied victory in World War II. A graduate of the Virginia Military Institute class of 1900, Marshall was the only man in US history to receive the Silver Star *and* the Nobel Peace Prize.

British Admiral of the Fleet Sir Alfred Dudley Pickman Rogers Pound, sixty-five, a participant in the Battle of Jutland and other notable naval successes. As captain of the HMS *Colossus,* Pound was a contributor to the sinking of the prestigious German light cruiser SMS *Wiesbaden* in May 1915, one month before the USS *Arizona* was launched in New York Harbor.

Marshal of the Royal Air Force Charles Frederick Algernon Portal, 1st Viscount Portal of Hungerford, fifty, recipient of The Most Noble Order of the Garter, founded in 1348, the highest order of chivalry and the third most prestigious honor after the lauded Victoria Cross.

Field Marshal Alan Francis Brooke, sixty, Chief of the Imperial General Staff during World War II, and promoted to field marshal in 1944. As chairman of the Chiefs of Staff Committee, Brooke was the foremost military advisor to Prime Minister Churchill, and the coordinator of British military efforts during the war, a hugely significant but little-known contributor to the Allies' victory in 1945. After retiring from the army, he served as Lord High Constable of England during the 1953 coronation of Queen Elizabeth II. Brooke's war diaries attracted attention for their criticism of Churchill, and for his plainspoken views on other leading figures of the war.

Field Marshal Sir John Greer Dill, sixty-two, who formed special relationships between Washington and London.

And, perhaps most notable because of his royal lineage, and one of the youngest on the committee, at age fifty, future Admiral of the Fleet, the regal Louis Francis Albert Victor Nicholas Mountbatten, 1st Earl Mountbatten of Burma, distinctly fetching and handsome both in and out of uniform, of unique elegance and grace and rare caliber. A favorite of Churchill's, Mountbatten planned commando raids across the English Channel, among other commendable achievements. On August 27, 1979, Mountbatten was assassinated by Irish Republican Army member Thomas McMahon while he sat aboard the *Shadow V*, a 30-foot lobster boat moored on Donegal Bay, an inlet in northwest Ireland. McMahon had placed a 50-pound bomb aboard the boat the day before and detonated it with a radio signal from the shore. Mountbatten suffered grievous wounds—his legs were severed—and he was pulled ashore, where he perished. The Admiral of the Fleet, the Earl of Burma, had a royal funeral of extraordinary grandeur and pomp at Westminster Abbey that none had been seen before, until the funeral of Princess Diana. The Queen attended. The entire Royal family was there, en masse. Members of the European royal household bid a ponderous farewell. A calamitous day for Great Britain.

These men set about with profound tenacity and verve to strategize and launch the death blow to world tyranny. A monumental task was before them, the likes of which had never been seen.

At the outer edge of this lofty flank, behind Roosevelt and Churchill, his head slightly cocked, was then US Army Air Force colonel Jacob "Jake" Edward Smart, thirty-nine. Smart was a native of Ridgeland, South Carolina, the son of a railroad conductor, and a 1931 graduate of the US Military Academy. A relative stripling compared to the upper-crusty group coiled around him, Jake Smart was a member of the Army

Air Corps Advisory Council and a former flight instructor, and, lest we forget, a future prisoner of war who was blown out of the sky and captured by the Germans. But at this historic moment, Smart was the primary aide-de-camp to Gen. Henry Harley "Hap" Arnold—a significant role to be realized later through his planning of the D-Day invasion of Europe on June 6, 1944.

General Arnold, fifty-seven, standing almost rigid at the opposing side of the photograph, and looking heavenward for strategic stimulus, was a US general officer who had the distinction of holding the highest grades of General of the Army *and* General of the Air Force. A feat never before achieved, and certainly not to be achieved again. Arnold, an aviation pioneer, was chief of the US Army Air Corps (1938–1941), Commanding General of the US Army Air Forces during World War II, the only air force general to hold a five-star rank, and the only person in US history to simultaneously hold a five-star rank in *two* different US military services.

If any military officers equal to or higher in rank or with more means than those conjoined on the lawn at Casablanca on this auspicious day could have been assembled anywhere in the universe at any moment, they would have to have been drawn from their graves or had yet to be born. When conclusions are drawn about the Allies' victory owing so much to America's ability to outproduce the Axis with materiel and men, they imprudently glide over the minds and experience of these prominent fellows—the power, the churning war engine that they were—gathered there near the brightly colored bracts and bougainvillea on this extraordinary day.

Did they know the full impact of their assemblage?

The *New York Times* had assigned a perceptive reporter to the historic meeting. Anne O'Hare McCormick wrote on January 27, 1943:

> *In a war without limits and without precedents, the reporters covering the action in North Africa cannot have been much surprised to be summoned to Casablanca and whisked into a tropical garden where they found the President of the United States and the Prime Minister of Great Britain. Perhaps they blinked a little to see a great*

council of war assembled under the orange trees and the purple bou-gainvillea vines—the general staffs of the Anglo-American armies, the commanders from the field, the entire dramatis personae *of the political performance in North Africa.*

"A historic moment," President Roosevelt commented to Churchill, the sun scorching their bare heads, sitting before a bevy of reporters and cameras.

"Do you want a hat?" Mr. Churchill asked the President of the United States.

"I was born without a hat," Mr. Roosevelt replied.

They did have cover, of course: Guards silhouetted on the hotel's rooftop bore weapons, and tight, droning formations of fighter planes circled like sullen eagles protecting their vulnerable young.

Roosevelt provided mostly vague answers to reporters' questions regarding the nature of the conference, saying that they had assembled to "discuss a variety of pressing issues"; specifically, that "peace can come to the world only by the total elimination of German and Japanese war power."

Summoning international reporters and writers to such a crucial conference attended by Churchill and Roosevelt received much serious attention. German intelligence, knowing the import of the "war council," hastened to their pens and notepads and maps and biographical write-ups. Their heads must have snapped up like voracious wolves smelling nearby prey when they caught a whiff of this gathering.

While Roosevelt's and the other participants' answers were elusive, the profound significance of the gathering, its intense reverberations and nuances, did not escape Ms. McCormick. She must have typed with white heat in her fingers. Her narrative voice signaled something porten-tous—not just to the Germans and Japanese, but to the entire universe:

Everything comes out of the blue these days—destruction and salva-tion, sudden attacks, and startling apparitions. When one follows in imagination the 5,000-mile hop of the President from hemisphere to hemisphere, it suggests something more than the dwindling and mutation of earth. It suggests that the planet has become so small that it cannot even contain itself, but must break a runway into the ether to make room and speed enough for the mighty business now afoot.

One runway from Casablanca went straight to Wünsdorf, Germany, an idyllic town 20 miles south of Berlin, and then down and down and down to the secret underground headquarters of the *Oberkommando der Wehrmacht* (OKW—Supreme Command of the Armed Forces), which consisted of four departments.

One, the *Abteilung Nachrichtenbeschaffung* (Division I, Secret Intelligence), gathered intelligence on the Casablanca participants and their supposed intentions. They even had a copy of that historic photograph taken on the pristine lawn of the Anfa Hotel in Casablanca showing the flanks of participants—after all, it had been seen all over the world.

In March, two months after the Casablanca Conference concluded, forty-year-old *Oberst* (Colonel) Georg Alexander Hansen was appointed Chief of Division I, Secret Intelligence Service. Since 1938, he had been aligned with the Resistance to eliminate Hitler, and one of the primary conspirators who had worked on plans to assassinate Hitler, coordinating the use of cars and aircraft, and the protection of his co-conspirators. His home in Rangsdorf, where his wife and five children resided, was often the site of secret meetings and covert intentions. He had strived to purge Germany of Hitler and achieve peace, either through the assassination of Hitler, or by defeating the Western Allies and working toward a conditional surrender in which he would have a central postwar position.

As group leader of Division I, Hansen continued to assemble intelligence on Casablanca, crafting profiles of all the well-known participants, devising theories and reports, and rightfully concluding that they intended to formulate a broad strategy to defeat his beloved Germany. During this time, he had had disagreements with the conspiracy's pivotal figure, *Oberst* Claus Count von Stauffenberg, over the post-assassination plans for the new German government.

Von Stauffenberg was the officer who, on July 20, 1944, at 12:42 p.m., a muggy day, would place a time bomb at Hitler's feet during a conference at the *Wolfsschanze* (Wolf's Lair) near Rasternburg, East Prussia.

But because of their disagreement, on July 18, 1944, Hansen had decided against his participation in the assassination attempt, and instead drove to Michelau to attend the baptism of his youngest daughter.

While he knew that Hitler had survived the July 20 attack—the coup had failed, and now his life was in danger—he drove back to Wünsdorf anyway, ignoring the chance to escape and save his life.

While Hansen was working toward eliminating Hitler, his division was working around the clock to crack the secret code of the US 9th Air Force. Further, Division I had already dispersed spies in and around the Benghazi airfields, where Bob Sternfels had been based before the Ploieşti raiders took off. They had been put to work on the assembled B-24s.

If Division I decoded the secret radio transmissions emanating from the 9th Air Force and collated it with the intelligence their spies were gathering, the information would deal a devastating blow to Bob, his crew, and the 1,760 airmen that would fly the mission. It's one thing to gather intelligence, and another to sift through the details for a lucid understanding.

Hansen possessed a profound love and allegiance to his Fatherland, and would do anything to prevent his nation's defeat. Even die for it, yes. He wanted peace for Germany, and without Hitler. One way or the other, Hansen wanted to end the war. The status quo, he was sure, could not last much longer.

Nor would Hansen.

On July 22, 1944, two days after the failed attempt to assassinate the Führer at *Wolfsschanze*, Heinrich Müller, chief of the *Geheime Sta-atspolizei* (Secret State Police, aka, the Gestapo), summoned Hansen to the *Reichssicherheitshauptamt* (Reich Main Security Office, or RSHA) at Prinz-Albrecht-Strasse No. 8, Berlin, where Hansen was immediately arrested in the vestibule for his involvement in the plot to kill Hitler. *Oberst* Hansen suffered through a prolonged, grueling interrogation by one of the masters of same, Heinrich Müller, during which he broke down and confessed to everything he knew.

On August 4, he was given a dishonorable discharge by the army's *Ehrenhof* (Court of Honor). Then on August 10, the day of his arraignment, in a show trial at the *Sondergericht*—a Special Court set up outside the framework of the German constitution—President-Justice Roland Freisler condemned Hansen to death. Almost simultaneously, Freisler, the notorious State Secrecta of the Reich Ministry, announced a death sentence for Berthold Alfred Maria Schenk Graf von Stauffenberg, an aristocrat, a naval lawyer, and the younger brother of the plot's key conspirator, *Oberst* Claus Schenk Graf von Stauffenberg. It was Claus who had placed his worn leather briefcase containing the time bomb with reliable British fuses next to the Führer's feet, during a crowded conference on that muggy July 20, 1944.

The explosion failed to kill the bastard, Hitler.

On September 8, *Oberst* Hansen was executed by hanging from a piano wire at Plötzensee Prison in Berlin, while cameras filmed his death for Hitler to watch.

After the war, hostility toward Hansen's family continued, and they were denied his pension because he had been dishonorably discharged from the Wehrmacht.

—✦—

Until the Casablanca meeting, neither Churchill nor Roosevelt knew much about the nascent state of strategic bombing. They had had little time to study and appreciate its merits; nor could they digest the myriad technical and scientific merits of what mayhem bombs dropped from the empyrean heights above the clouds could do to the enemy, and the effect such a strategy could have on victory, or defeat.

That's what Hap Arnold's purpose was—to plan the strategic daylight bombing of Europe.

Since Smart was Hap Arnold's aide, he was tasked at Casablanca with initiating three plans: the strategic bombing of Europe; the invasion of Europe; and, first and foremost, the bombing of those maddening refineries in Ploiești, Romania.

Arnold told Smart: "You get it done."

CHAPTER 2

The Ladder

There's nothing better than discovering, to your own astonishment, what you're meant to do—it's like falling in love.

—Unknown

On January 16, 1920, US citizens began enduring the national prohibition of liquor—its "noble experiment." After nearly "75 years of agitation," the Nineteenth Amendment gave women the right to vote. The telephone dial system was inaugurated. Transcontinental airmail service was established between New York and San Francisco. The Panama Canal officially opened on July 12, costing $366,650,000. On September 16, a massive bomb explosion on Wall Street in New York City killed thirty people, wounded one hundred, and caused $2,000,000 in damage. The population of the United States topped at 105,710,620.

And on October 31, 1920, Halloween, one more citizen joined the burgeoning US population: Robert Warren Sternfels was born to Harry and Anna A. Sternfels, in the fashionable neighborhood of northwest Detroit, Michigan. Bob was one of seven children, and their four-bedroom house was separated by four lots from their neighbors—"to make the neighborhood appear more occupied than it was," said Bob.

Until the Depression hit, his father's engineering company was doing well, but then he lost a bid on a proposed downtown post office building, and he had to close his offices. With nine mouths to feed, Harry Sternfels scrambled for a job. He had an advantage over most of the Detroit jobless: He was a licensed mechanical and electrical engineer, and also a part-time chemist, skills that Bob would inherit and carry through his life.

At the age of twelve, Bob's technical aspirations led him to a ham radio operator who took him under his wing. "But without money to buy tubes, wire, and solder, I had to junk everything. Instead, I did what a lot of twelve-year-olds did: Since I was in love with flight and aircraft, I began to build model airplanes—plastic ones, wooden ones."

It didn't take long for Bob's interest in aeronautics to expand toward loftier heights. Since he'd never actually flown in an airplane, he yearned for the thrill of flight, but his experiences were restricted to glancing skyward when a plane flew over, and wondering what flying might be like.

He could never imagine where his nascent yearning would take him, how it would engrave an astonishing page for him in the history books of military and World War II aviation. Impossible, yes, for the twelve-year-old boy to imagine that hands with model glue on them would one day grip the Bakelite control wheel of a B-24 Liberator bomber on the most historic, deadly bombing mission of World War II.

"Since our house had a separate garage," Bob said, "the most immediate way for me to experience the sensation of flying was to jump off the garage roof. Of course, I wasn't stupid enough to just jump. I knew I needed some kind of parachute. So, I got ahold of Mother's brand-new umbrella. In my twelve-year-old mind, it was logical and absolutely foolproof."

Bob leaned a wooden ladder against the garage's roofline and hooked the umbrella over his forearm. He looked behind him. He looked around the side of the garage.

The coast was clear.

He was alone.

He stepped on the first rung, gripped the rails, and glanced up. The sky was a vast cloudless blue, even more alluring than the looming rooftop.

He stepped onto the second rung, gripping the rails tighter.

The ladder started to shiver.

Then he saw it.

It sparked like a piece of his mother's flatware, distant and barely distinct—silver against brilliant sapphire.

The sound grew louder, a prominence up there that made him grin. It was flying away from him, toward the horizon, gradually masked by the dense tree line. He heard the hum of two engines, one of those new DC-3s Eastern Airlines flew, he guessed correctly.

Soon the hum faded beyond the trees, beyond the horizon. He assured himself that he had to get to the top of the ladder, then the garage roof, before he could ever fly one of those planes.

One step at a time, Bob.

Once on the rooftop, the breath he took was the deepest ever.

He jumped.

"First thing that happened was a bit frightening," he said. "I heard a ripping sound. A nail had caught my pants' cuff and ripped them right up to my you-know-what. There I was—the twelve-year-old boy pilot wanna-nabe, suspended in midair, with a tear right up to my crotch. What happened next was even more terrifying: The 'parachute' turned inside out. I dropped like a bag of potatoes and landed flat on my face on the grass."

Jumping off a garage roof—that was the beginning of Bob's flying dream. You couldn't compare it to flying a B-24 on a bombing run over Ploiești, Romania, but it taught him a lesson: "Before you start a flight, make sure your pants don't get caught on a nail."

Bob Sternfels's flying career began without injury. Or so he thought. "A few years ago, an X-ray technician asked me what I thought was an odd question," Bob recalled. "'Have you ever broken a bone?' I was a bit surprised, and I looked at him like he was crazy. 'No, never,' I said. But then he held up an X-ray that showed a slight but distinct fracture in my collarbone—the one that felt funny after jumping off the garage. Then, I remembered: the ripping sound . . . the garage . . . the roof . . . Mother's umbrella. It all came back in a flash."

Bob's dream came true a few years after his leap from the garage roof.

"Somehow, I managed to get my driver's license," he said. "The problem was, I needed a set of wheels to go with it. There was an old Model A Ford in the neighborhood not far from our home that needed some fixing. The engine was frozen, the tires were flat, and the body was almost all brown with rust. I asked the owner what he wanted for it, hoping he thought it was an eyesore and just wanted it off his property; however, I guess he saw the desperation in my eyes. He wanted ten dollars. How I managed ten bucks, I can't recall."

A friend of Bob's had a car, and they towed the old Model A back to Bob's house. "That's when all hell broke loose," Bob recalled. "My father came home from work. He must've had a bad day. When he spotted that pile of rust with four flat tires sitting in our driveway, he said, 'That piece of junk is not sitting on my property. Get it out of here!'"

Bob's dream had been crushed, but his friend's father was sympathetic, and offered him space in his garage to work in.

At that time in his life, nothing was too much for sixteen-year-old Bob Sternfels. He was occupied earning money as a delivery boy for a meat market, attending high school, and doing his homework. With the little money he was earning, the repairs and restoration to his car were proceeding, albeit slowly.

"I sanded all that rust off, then painted the body with a spray can attached to a vacuum cleaner. I picked a two-tone paint combination: silver and metallic blue. It started to look pretty spiffy. Then I pulled the engine out and carried it to an alley, cleaned it, and rebuilt it with a few new parts. Thank God Henry Ford made the engines from good castings. He'd cast the blocks and set them outside the foundry for months until they rusted and all the gases had left them. This made the block rock-hard, and they could take a beating. After the rebuilding process was complete, I drove it home, to show my dad. When he came home, he couldn't believe what he saw—an almost showroom-new 1929 Model A Ford. He was quite proud of me. I'll never forget that moment."

Bob's Model A could go 60 mph, regardless of whether he had two people or six inside. In the winter months, riding in it was a challenge: "Ford thought that anyone in the car would be wearing heavy clothes, so why bother installing a heater?"

Bob drove his car for four years, then gave it to his younger brother.

On June 22, 1941, Bob started taking private flying lessons in a Taylorcraft Cub, a small single-engine aircraft made by Taylor Brothers Aircraft Corp. Called a "Chummy," it sold for $4,000 ("Buy Your Airplane Taylor Made").

At the time, Bob was earning money as a delivery truck driver for the Kerr Dental Products Company in Detroit.

"There was one problem with that job," Bob said. "I always had an urge to see how fast that Ford one-and-a-half-ton truck could go without a full load. After a couple of weeks, my manager decided that I would be safer—less of a liability and a pain in the ass for the company—working as a trainee, sitting behind a desk in the research department."

So, with the blessing of Bob Kerr, the founder's son, Bob was transferred south to Lansdowne, Pennsylvania, where he took his mechanical skills and applied them to learning how to make dentures, gold inlays, and partials, and other minutiae of dentistry. His skills continued to serve him well, as his first gold partial was put on display to the entire sales department. He was almost nineteen years old. After the war, Bob returned to Kerr and remained until his retirement as a regional vice-president.

Two weeks after the Japanese bombed Pearl Harbor on December 7, 1941, twenty-one-year-old Bob Sternfels enlisted in what was then called the US Army Air Corps. (The name would change in 1941 to the US Army Air Force.) Bob figured that with his mechanical skills and his smattering of flying lessons in the little Chummy, he'd be a terrific pilot.

"Although I loved camping," he said, "I loved a real bed each night a lot more than a sleeping bag and mosquitoes. In the Air Corps, you had a bed every night and three decent meals, and no mud to slog through. I figured, too, that since I was a good swimmer, and working out every day carrying a ten-pound bag of sand, training would be a piece of cake. Nothing is easy."

When he enlisted he was asked if he'd had at least two years of college, the basic requirement for flight school. Bob said no, that he'd only had a year and a half of junior college Because he lacked a college degree, Bob had to pass a battery of tests before he could qualify for the Air Corps, when they would take him into the flight program. With books Bob's brother had on the required subjects, Bob studied every day for hours before he took and passed the tests.

A week later, he was on a train to Kelly Field outside San Antonio, Texas. But first, he had to take a physical. "I never had to undress so much in all my life. Every time I turned around somebody was testing me for hernias."

After a month of basic training, Bob was assigned to an Army Air Corps basic training base in Chickasha, Oklahoma, a privately owned field operated by the army, where he learned the arcane basics of military life: the chain of command, saluting, marching, and the mandatory prosaic rules and regulations. "The food was great," said Bob, "and the beds were even better. We were one of the first classes there, and started flight training in Fairchild PT-19As—a two-seat, open-cockpit plane built specifically to train pilots. It was user-friendly. You could make mistakes in it and recover without killing yourself."

Bob's first flight was more than memorable; it was a mess.

"First, they gave me a helmet made of sheepskin that stunk to high heaven—enough to make you sick," Bob recalled. "Same sheepskin for the chin strap."

His instructor took them up and put the plane through a series of stunning aerobatics—maneuvers Bob never dreamed of doing in the Chummy, and never thought an airplane or a human could endure.

"Between the stink from the sheepskin helmet and the loops and barrel rolls and the stink from the chin strap, I dumped that wonderful breakfast I'd just eaten all over the cockpit and side of the plane. Bombs away!? Next day, I left the strap off and had no more trouble with aerobatics."

Bob soloed after six hours, believing he was a hotshot pilot. Since the instructors wanted their students to get as much training as possible, they let them do almost anything they wanted with the PT-19A. Flying twice a day, doing loops, chandelles, snap rolls, and Bob's favorite, flying inverted, or upside down.

"Being a smart-ass, I ignored the explicit order not to fly the plane inverted for more than a few seconds—the instructors never gave us a reason. Well, I found out pretty fast why. I flipped that plane over on its back and held it upside down for more than a few seconds, until . . . dead silence!? The engine quit."

With the engine silent, Bob managed to skillfully glide the PT-19A back to the field, lined it up with the runway, and prepared for a tricky "deadstick" landing. The "stick" here does not refer to the control column and rudder pedals, which in 1942 (and in some planes today) worked through cables and pulleys, not electronics. "Deadstick" here refers to the traditional wooden propeller, which, without power, would be just a "dead stick."

(One of the most successful deadstick landings ever occurred on August 24, 2001, over the Atlantic Ocean. Air Transat Flight 236, a twin-engine Airbus A330, flying from Toronto, Canada, to Lisbon, Portugal, suffered a complete power loss to both General Electric A330 engines due to a fuel leak caused by improper maintenance, turning the passenger plane into a burdened, massive glider. There were 306 people aboard. All were lucky that day to have Captain Robert Piché at the controls, as he was an experienced glider pilot. Piché and his co-pilot, First Officer Dirk de Jager, "flew" the A330 for 100 miles with no power, to a successful emergency landing in the Azores. The incident stands today as a world record for a commercial passenger jet. Captain Piché and First Officer de Jager are national heroes and recipients of the Superior Airmanship Award, given by the Air Line Pilots Association.)

As soon as Bob parked the plane, he heard his name over the loudspeaker.

"Cadet Robert Sternfels, report immediately to the operations officer!"

The announcement made him smile.

"I felt kinda good walking away from that plane in one piece," said Bob. "Matter of fact, I was grinning from ear to ear. I thought, Wow, they're probably going to give me a medal for that great flying without engine power."

Instead, what happened almost cost him his flying career.

"I soon learned that flying inverted drained the oil from the engine. The instructors, in their infinite wisdom, had failed to tell us that. No oil, and the engine freezes up. The clue was, when that happens, oil sprays along the sides of the plane, something I thought no one could have seen, because it happened a few miles from the base. Of course, the operations officer had a pair of binoculars and saw the oil stains as soon as I landed; he knew exactly what I'd done. It didn't take a rocket scientist to deduce that I was flying the plane upside down, against orders."

Guilty of disobeying an order was the first declaratory bark from the operations officer. Second, Bob was ordered to clean the oil from the fuselage. And, third, he had to march "tours," as they were called, up and down the parade grounds for an hour. Since there were no surplus rifles at that time, and there was no need for pilots to have them, they gave him one made of wood to march with, and he almost laughed in their face. "It was undignified, marching in a uniform with a fake rifle," said Bob.

After fifty-three hours of basic training, Bob found himself in Waco, Texas, with a fresh aeronautical challenge: a bigger, heavier trainer.

The Vultee BT-13 Valiant—pilots nicknamed it the "Vultee Vibrator"—was the second phase of the three-phase training program for student pilots at the onset of World War II. After flying the PT-19A trainer, the student pilot stepped up to the more-complex Valiant for continued flight training. The BT-13 had a more-powerful 450-horsepower engine and was faster and heavier than the primary trainer. The student pilot was required to use two-way radio communications with the ground and to operate landing flaps and a two-position Hamilton Standard controllable-pitch propeller. It was without a retractable landing gear and did not have a hydraulic system. The flaps were operated by a crank-and-cable system. Pilots nicknamed it the "Vultee Vibrator" for good reason.

Bob said, "The Vibrator was extremely noisy but extremely tough. You couldn't beat it to death if you tried. And try, I did."

He took it up to 4,000 feet one bright afternoon, pushed the nose straight down, and watched until the airspeed hit the red line, at which point he pulled the stick straight back, held it there for about five seconds, the 450-horsepower engine screaming, until it shivered, shimmied, and stalled—like a car coming to a sudden stop. Then, it slid back onto its tail for a couple of seconds and dove down into a spin.

"Never did break that plane."

On the last flying day before graduation, Bob and a group of five other student pilots decided to do their own "low-level" flying exercise. "We were the guys considered to be the best pilots in our class," he said, "which was a judgment we made among ourselves." So they took off, agreeing to meet over a huge patch of flat fields outside Waco. They watched as Bob indicated his intentions: Ahead, he'd spotted a farmer on a tractor, plowing a field. He aimed directly for him. The other planes quickly followed behind in trail formation.

When the farmer saw them approaching, he stood on the tractor and waved his big straw hat—*Hello, boys!* As Bob's plane narrowed the distance, he descended lower and lower. Through the Vibrator's windscreen, the little tractor sat on the nose of Bob's airplane, a speck, then, blooming larger and larger. At the last second, Bob pulled back on the stick and slammed the throttle into full power. The farmer jumped, a big, high leap, hit the dirt, and rolled under the tractor. All five planes followed Bob's path, thundering over the tractor, wagging their wings, waving, their prop wash and blue exhaust smoke making big swirling clouds of dust. The last thing Bob saw was the farmer dusting himself off; then, he raised his hat and gave them another big wave. The most excitement he'd had in a long time.

When the group landed, their radios ordered them to the operations officer.

Bob knew what was in store; he'd been through this once before. After a vigorous chewing out, the group received punishing tours deferred to their next assignment to Houston, Texas, where Bob would spend the next fifty-two days learning to fly "the ugliest twin-engine plane ever made."

❦

The time had arrived for Bob to start learning the intricacies of twin-engine aircraft, and the Air Corps had the perfect plane for the task: the Curtiss-Wright AT-9 Jeep. It was bulbous in appearance, an all-metal, twin-engine, low-wing, cantilever monoplane design with retractable landing gear and two Lycoming radial engines. But it served its purpose well: to provide a gap between single-engine trainers and twin-engine combat aircraft. Curtiss-Wright, anticipating a European war and the inevitable requirement for this type of "high-performance" aircraft, produced 792 AT-9s between 1941 and 1943.

"It was rather slow," said Bob, "but no one crashed, and we learned to fly instruments day and night."

After flying a total of 578 hours, an average of 5.5 hours per day, over 52 days, on October 4, 1942, Bob Sternfels received a clothing allowance, purchased a set of officer's uniforms, and graduated a second lieutenant in the Air Corps Reserves.

CHAPTER 3

HALPRO

The Kingdom of Heaven runs on righteousness, but the Kingdom of Earth runs on oil.

—ERNEST BEVIN,
CHURCHILL'S MINISTER OF LABOUR AND NATIONAL SERVICE

IN JANUARY 1942, WHILE BOB STERNFELS WAS PACING THROUGH BASIC flight training, President Roosevelt approved a plan to shove *Generalfeldmarschall* Erwin Rommel off the tumultuous North African map.

Until now, the war in North Africa had been going well for Germany's most popular soldier. Rommel (aka, the Desert Fox), at fifty-one, was a German national hero with a cult following equivalent to today's sports stars. One of the most skilled military commanders of World War II, he was the recipient of the Knight's Cross with Oak Leaves and Swords and the esteemed *Pour le Mérite* (For Merit), two of the highest decorations conferred on German soldiers.

On August 23, 1939, Rommel, one of Hitler's favorite generals, was promoted to *Generalmajor* (major general) and assigned as the commander of the *Führerbegleitbrigade*, a battalion-strength unit guarding Hitler and his field headquarters during the invasion of Poland, which began on September 1, 1939, and considered as the starting point of World War II.

Germany had never been a country with natural resources of crude oil, the crucial element missing from Rommel's strategy to sustain a successful campaign in North Africa. Germany had gone into the war with meager reserves of gasoline, a dubious position. Without food and ammunition, armies are immobilized. Without oil, troops stand fallow.

Germany needed the oil supplies flowing from Ploieşti to be plentiful, not only for Rommel's *Afrika Korps*, but for the entire German war machine. If oil production coming from the nine oil refineries nestled around Ploieşti was cut off—they amounted to 30 percent of Germany's crude oil supply—Rommel's campaign in North Africa would break down and likely fail.

To achieve this result, President Roosevelt agreed to bomb the oil refineries around the city of Ploieşti, Romania. The action, if successful, would affect the *Afrika Korps* and the entire German Wehrmacht.

Col. Harry A. Halverson, a forty-two-year-old US Army Air Force officer, was chosen to lead this bombing mission—albeit, through an odd turn of events. Initially, Harry was selected to bomb targets in Japan, as Doolittle had done earlier; instead, at the last minute, Harry would be sidetracked and ordered to bomb Ploieşti.

At the start, in May 1942, Halverson was given the task of leading twenty-three factory-fresh B-24s of the First Provisional Group (Heavy), Middle East Air Forces, from Fort Meyers in Florida across the Atlantic Ocean, and eventually, to Chekiang, China. There, the raid would be staged—even though the crews were not bombardment-trained. Few had B-24 experience; in fact, according to the unit's after-action report, they became "teachers who had to teach themselves."

From Chekiang, after refueling and freshening up, Harry and his boys would fly 1,000 miles, drop tons of bombs on the unsuspecting city of Tokyo, and return, hopefully unscathed—this, an encore of the raid that had made Doolittle a household name and had the potential of doing the same for Harry and his airmen. A reprise, too, of the morale booster for the American people that Doolittle had provided a month earlier.

It would be an ambitious, exhilarating journey of larger-than-life proportions that had the potential to produce headlines around the world and show the Japanese that, once again, their shores were not impermeable. Harry and his crews would be able to taste the sweet fruits of fame—promotions, publicity, medals—even though those fruits were out there on the end of the high and flimsy branches of a perilous military mission.

By accomplishing this mission, Harry unwittingly and historically initiated the bombing campaign for all of World War II Europe—an obscure fact that the world has overlooked, and something for which Harry has barely received a nickel's worth of credit.

The covert mission was officially called Project 63, codenamed HAL-PRO, an abbreviation of the "Harry Halverson Project," which made Harry quite pleased; US military missions were seldom named after living men.

But like so many war plans, HALPRO did not go as conceived.

After Harry and his boys touched down at Fayid, a Royal Air Force field in Egypt, and alighted from their bombers, he was handed orders to stand down.

Because the fall of Chekiang was imminent, the bombing raid was taken off the boards.

The big mission to Tokyo was aborted.

And so were Harry's dreams; at least, for the moment.

Instead, Harry—despondent, and seeing his chance to make history, and perhaps earn a general's star, flit away—got top secret orders to bomb the Astra Romana oil refinery in Ploiești, Romania.

This presented an immediate conundrum to Harry and his boys. The crewmen knew the location of Chentu—it is in Szechwan province, near Chungking—and they certainly knew where China was, as they were standing on it. But no one in the group, Harry and all his young first-cut savvy navigators and wannabe famous airmen, had any notion where this Ploiești place was located; they could hardly get the name off their tongues.

So, to the charts and maps the boys went, to find their bearings. And there they saw it—in a relatively obscure country called Romania, the grudging oil-producing ally of Nazi Germany, and just a hop, skip, and a jump from Bucharest, the Romanian capital. Matter of fact, it was 37 miles north of Bucharest on the snaky Autostrada-Bucureşt-Piteşi highway, the blue-veined Route E81, just in case they got lost along the way and had to pull out their careworn National Geographic maps, which they relied on heavily.

On June 11, 1942, about 10:30 a.m., with a beckoning pilot's sky, bright blue and glimmering with hope and adventure, away Harry's crew flew with renewed spirit, unwavering faith, and a resolute promise to themselves and to their country, to do their best to engrave a mark on army air force history, and to do something impactful to help win the damned war.

But only the best thirteen of the twenty-three US Army Air Force B-24s that had arrived in Egypt a short time ago had enough huff and puff to take off on this 2,600-mile round-trip, historic mission. Twelve of the birds were sick for a variety of mechanical reasons: the long, laborious flight from Florida over the Atlantic and North Africa, for one thing, and the harsh sands of Egypt that had worn down aircraft components and wreaked havoc on cylinders and fuel pumps and oil filters and a variety of complex items that bedevil intricate airplanes and make them ill-tempered and cantankerous. What pilots call "war-weary birds"—even though Harry's planes had not seen a puff of gun smoke, or ducked a single morsel of lead since they had left the balmy Florida weather.

HALPRO, the force that set out to bomb Tokyo in the footsteps of Jimmy Doolittle, arrived furtively over Ploieşti the next day, at dawn, June 12, a pristine day, golden sun rays dappling the target area with shades of dazzling orange. A day that would scribe its own signature and remain indelibly marked on the pages of military history, Harry and his boys interwoven in the accomplishment.

When the HALPRO bomb-bay doors swung open, twelve planes were at the Astra Romana refinery, as directed by the battle order.

One B-24, olive drab with a belly the delicate blue of a bird's egg, was off target and precipitously loosed its entire bomb load over the port area of Constanta, the third-largest city in Romania, rich in archaeological lore and treasures, historical monuments, ancient ruins, a grand casino, museums and shops, and within close proximity to beautiful beach resorts. Certainly not a military target. As such are the errors of war—sometimes innocuous, infrequently monumental, mostly sad, and often deadly and extremely woeful.

An account in *The Army Air Forces in World War II: Combat Chronology, 1941–19 From the Office of Air Force History Headquarters USAF 1973* noted Harry's soon-to-be historic attack on June 12, 1943, in a terse and truncated tone:

HALPRO: *13 B-24s of det under cmd of Col Harry A Halverson en route from US to China take off during 11/12 Jun from Fayid to bomb oilfields at Ploesti. Only 12 attack at dawn. 4 of the 13 land at a base in Iraqi which was designated for recovery of the flight, 2 land in Syria, and 4 are interned in Turkey. Though damage to tgt is negligible, the raid is significant because it is the first AAF combat mission in EAME, and the first strike at a tgt which will later be famous.*

Post-mission, the crews from two of the B-24s scratched their heads and had no idea what the hell it was they had bombed. Overall damage to the Ploieşti refinery caused by HALPRO was negligible. No US airmen's lives were lost.

And so, it was that on June 12, 1942, Ploieşti was the first target in Europe bombed by American aircraft flown by American crews. Many, many more would follow.

Despite this relatively benign foray, General Order No. 17, dated September 23, 1942, from headquarters US Army Forces in the Middle East, awarded Col. Harry A. Halverson the Silver Star for his actions. But sadly, for Harry, that was about as far out on the branch of fruits he would go; he received no promotion.

The Silver Star is the third-highest military decoration. According to the official award criteria, "[T]he Silver Star is awarded for gallantry not justifying the award of one of the next higher valor awards—the Distinguished Service Cross, the Navy Cross, or the Air Force Cross. The gallantry displayed must have taken place while in action against an enemy of the United States, while engaged in military operations involving conflict with an opposing foreign force, or while serving with friendly foreign forces engaged in an armed conflict against an opposing armed force in which the United States is not a belligerent party."

At that moment, Harry had no notion of the groundwork he had established, which later in the history of World War II, would be a high honor in itself.

Not that Harry didn't deserve *some* recognition, but his bombers had almost wholly missed the target. Constanta sustained some damage, particularly the lovely casino.

Often in military operations, when the mission planners and all those involved recognize their poor judgment, they pull out the decorations to mask their decisions and failures. It would appear that the award was given because it was a bombing mission into German-occupied Europe, a feat of airmanship in itself, and also to cover up the lack of results at the target—which might have indicated that the whole idea was harebrained, from its inception. HALPRO having been planned 6,000 miles away didn't help apply precision and accuracy to the mission.

If nothing else, HALPRO was a historical footnote of World War II that got the entire world spinning on its head. It was at least a start. (Brushing off HALPRO, textbooks would later claim that the August 17, 1942, 8th Air Force raid on the marshaling yards at Rouen, France—six months *after* HALPRO—was the "official" start of US daylight bombing in Europe.)

Nevertheless, on the plus side, Harry's boys showed remarkable flying skills, even though they were mostly unfamiliar with the B-24 and had little bombardment experience. After all, it made a mark on history, although it was not recognized as such at the time.

After the war, Colonel Halverson summed up his effort with a laudable dose of humility: "We were headed to China and hoped to hit Japan. You know the result. We were put to work against Rommel. We did all right."

In the end, when their moment arrived, the men of HALPRO got it more than all right.

Soon after Harry's trek across the Atlantic and the HALPRO bombing mission, planning began for more-precise, aggressive strikes against the Nazis. Until this time, Churchill and Roosevelt had had little understanding, no appreciation, and not much enthusiasm for the myriad technical and modern mechanical aspects of high-altitude, strategic bombing, and little cause to know what questions to ask about what was then an almost new format of contemporary warfare—unlike the strategic value of naval and ground operations that had endured for centuries.

But with the war in Europe growing more pervasive, a new strategy needed to be designed by the Allies, a strategy that had the potential to eventually destroy Nazi Germany. And, if fortunate, to set a precedent in a variety of ways for the future of the air force.

More-precise war objectives would amalgamate six months later, formulated by some of the most brilliant minds and influential leaders in the world, who would gather at a noteworthy venue unknown to most of the world.

CHAPTER 4

"The Smart Plan"

A good plan violently executed right now is far better than a perfect plan executed next week.

—GENERAL GEORGE S. PATTON

THE JANUARY 1943 CASABLANCA CONFERENCE WITH PRESIDENT ROOSevelt and Prime Minister Churchill initiated the planning stages for the August bombing that year of the seven oil refineries that encircled Ploiești, Romania. The order to disable the refineries had been handed to Gen. Henry Harley "Hap" Arnold, US Army Air Corps, one of the towering military personalities and tacticians of World War II, the commander of all US air forces during the war.

"Hap" was short for "Happy," a nickname he either picked up while moonlighting as a stunt pilot or got from his wife, who started to use the nickname in her correspondence to him. And the nicknames did not stop there: He was called Harley by his family during his youth, and "Sunny" by both his mother and wife. At West Point, he was known to classmates as "Pewt," or "Benny." Later, his immediate subordinates and headquarters staff referred to Arnold as "The Chief." But the nickname of "Hap" eventually won out, and that's how he was known throughout the war, and afterward—as Hap Arnold.

Hap holds the distinction of being the only US Air Force general to hold a five-star rank, and the only US military officer to hold a five-star rank in *two* different US military services—the air force and the army—an unprecedented, monumental achievement that will most certainly never be equaled again.

Hap Arnold never retired; those who hold the five-star rank never do. They receive full pay for the remainder of their lives. (George Washington, 177 years after his death, was awarded a five-star rank effective on July 4, 1976, the bicentennial of the United States, and with the title "general of the armies." Washington's appointment stated he was to have "rank and precedence over all other grades of the Army, past or present.") Hap is in lofty company.

Further, he has the historic and unparalleled distinction of being taught how to fly an airplane by the Wright brothers. He was one of the first military pilots worldwide, and one of the first three rated pilots in the history of the US Air Force—and all of this despite an early fear of flying. Arnold was also the founder of Project RAND, which evolved into one of the world's largest nonprofit global policy think tanks, the RAND Corporation. He was also one of the founders of the prestigious Pan American World Airways, the largest international air carrier in the United States from 1921 until its collapse in 1991. He is regarded as one of the pivotal American generals of World War II, and a primary facilitator of the US tactics that helped to defeat Nazi Germany.

His order to organize a plan to bomb Ploiești landed in the capable hands of Colonel Jacob "Jake" Smart, thirty-nine at the time, an experienced pilot himself. Smart, if you recall, was the youngest officer posing among the leaders in the now-classic photograph of the historic 1943 Casablanca meeting that January. He was partially cut off by the right frame of the famous photo, in the background, as it were, but very prominent in the plans for the Normandy invasion, the bombing of Europe, and planning the raid on Ploiești. Smart had a full plate. Ploiești, however, was most imminent, and thus a high priority. As such, Jake Smart's black-and-white image is a metaphor for his involvement in the D-Day as well as the raid on Ploiești. Although he is barely visible in the famous photo, he nonetheless made it into the history books.

Jake Smart, a "fast track" young officer with a patrician manner, had many positive attributes that made him a rising star in the US Army Air Force, eventually carrying him to a four-star rank in the US Air Force. Smart was born and raised in Ridgeland, North Carolina, the son of a railroad conductor, and a graduate of West Point. In 1931, he graduated as a second lieutenant and served in Panama. He became a flying instructor and was chief of staff for flight training at air force headquarters in Washington, DC. Later, when the United States entered World War II, he was appointed to the air staff in Washington, DC, which led him to a significant staff position on General Arnold's Advisory Council. As a participant of the Casablanca Conference, Smart was later awarded the Distinguished Service Medal for planning not only the Ploieşti raid, but also for his involvement in the highly secret plans for the invasion of Europe.

Colonel Smart may have had shortcomings, but they didn't hold him back from being selected by General Arnold as the principal strategist for Ploieşti. He had no combat experience at that point in his career, something that bothered him, and that he would try to change later on; and he was unfamiliar with North African operations, the area of the world where the Ploieşti mission would stage and take flight. After Ploieşti, these would be marked as limitations—someone should have been chosen with combat experience and full knowledge of the B-24 Liberator, the aircraft chosen to bomb Ploieşti—a thought expressed many times by Bob Sternfels.

But, wisely, Smart chose to surround himself with a group of experienced staff members, some senior to himself, including an engineer from the British Army who had eight years' experience managing the Astra Romana refinery that Bob Sternfels would be assigned to bomb; a senior intelligence expert; and several Royal Air Force bomber crews with experience in North Africa. Oddly absent, though, and curiously inexplicable, he had no B-24 aircrews who had prior air combat experience in North Africa and who would eventually fly the Ploieşti mission. No explanation has been found to elucidate this omission. Smart had never flown a B-24, and he had yet to fly a combat mission (something he wouldn't do until the following year). Many—Bob Sternfels, in particular —thought Smart's lack of experience in both areas was preposterous.

In March 1943, Smart and his staff began honing the details of their new assignment. Their research quickly determined—through conventional thinking—that bombing Ploieşti would take 1,370 bombers and would produce a 90 percent chance of hitting the seven significant refineries encircling the city. This was unacceptable. Initially, Smart's plan indicated that the bombing would be done from a traditionally high altitude—a conservative approach—at more than 20,000 feet. He had yet to think outside of the box. But after studying preliminary data and making extensive calculations, the results were not satisfactory. Their conclusion: It would take four to six weeks to fly 120 missions with nine planes per mission—and there were insufficient numbers of B-24 bombers available. (The main force of American bombers was occupied almost daily, weather permitting, dropping ordnance on European targets, mainly Germany and France; and the USAAF commanders that had them were not eager to lend them out.)

Either way, the idea would blossom, incubate, change, and then, finally, resolve into a large number of bombers—approximately 200—that would fly a single, en masse raid in formation at a never-before-done, dangerously low-level altitude—practically at ground level. The planes would take off from several bases around the sandy Benghazi area, fly over the Mediterranean, bomb Ploiești, and then return to their bases.

Since there were seven refineries—there were actually nine, but two were deemed too small for the risk—each refinery would be a target for a specific section of bombers that would separate into groups before reaching Ploiești. Bob Sternfels flew with the 98th Bombardment Group, a component of the 9th Air Force Bomber Command, selected to bomb the Astra Romana refinery, codenamed White IV to make it easier to remember (and less of a tongue-twister). Smart and his staff felt they had an intelligence advantage, because originally eleven refineries had been built, financed, and operated by US, British, Dutch, and French companies before 1940, the year Hitler took them for himself. The refineries were confined to an area 5 miles wide. As such, high-altitude bombing would have been ineffective.

At this point, Smart's theory—the Smart Plan—became the crux of the mission.

It was quickly evident that the standard practice of high-altitude bombing—the conventional approach—was mathematically impossible for the Ploiești mission to be, at best, marginally successful, and would likely be an unachievable and a wholly impractical tactic resulting in an unnecessarily high number of crews killed, wounded, or captured. Smart knew, too, that bombing from altitudes between 20,000 and 22,000 feet, even with the then top-secret, state-of-the-art Norden and Sperry bomb-sights, would not make much difference. Unlike today's precision digital "smart" bombing with laser-guided weapons that can sluice a bomb through a window frame, World War II bombs were "dumb," without guidance, and fell to their targets in a haphazard wobbly pattern, with only fins on their ends to stabilize them. Gravity did the rest, and they were also subjected to prevailing winds. Accuracy was often further determined by cloud cover, flak, and the persistent menace of enemy fighters hell-bent on bringing down as many bombers as possible.

As such, some targets were often missed by miles, killing civilians who had no idea that a 500-pound bomb was about to wreck their lunch that day. And all too frequently, a disabled bomber with severe battle damage would jettison its bombs with impunity in order to stabilize altitude. To make up for this inaccuracy, Smart concluded the need for multiple missions. But this would mean more exposure to flak and enemy fighters, and put aircrews at incremental risk.

Smart started searching for another tactic, something radical, something entirely fresh that would surprise the Germans and provide an advantage—something other military minds had either overlooked or rejected, that would satisfy his superiors and indeed the whole chain of command he would have to schlep through for final approval. At this time, lingering in the background of his mind, were two exemplars: the Japanese attack on Pearl Harbor, which was conducted by numerous fighters and bombers flying to the target at low altitudes, and Jimmy Doolittle's attack on Japan, which was also flown to the target at less than 100 feet.

Sometime in April, serendipity sparked possibility: During a visit to Eglin Air Force Base in Florida, Smart witnessed something that turned his thinking on its head.

A group of Douglas A-20 Havoc attack planes was practicing impressive low-level, "down on the deck," bombing runs, often referred to as "buzzing," a word in aviation that instantly connotes a "stunt." Such a daredevil maneuver, wholly disallowed then, and now, would often ground a pilot—or worse, end the pilot's career. This low-level flying Smart was witnessing gave him the idea of flying to the target at 150 feet or less.

This could be the core of the plan, the lynchpin for a successful mission. It would keep the aircraft below enemy radar and would be a major surprise. And when the German and Romanian gunners saw, heard, and felt the B-24s thundering just above their heads, almost at arms' reach, it would have a shocking effect—or so they thought.

Smart took an objective look at the relatively small Havoc. He needed something more than a bomber that could fly at low altitudes; almost any aircraft could do that. The Havoc, a twin-engine attack, light bomber (not appealing), an intruder aircraft (not a plus), had a top speed of less than 200 mph (also not a plus) and a bomb load of 1,200 pounds (unimpressive).

Pilots summed up the Havoc, stating that "it has no vices and is very easy to take off and land . . . the airplane represents a definite advantage in the design of flight controls . . . extremely pleasant to fly and maneuver."

While "an extremely pleasant plane to fly and maneuver" might be an apt description for a private plane, it had unappealing attributes for the military aircraft needed for the Ploiești mission: It lacked the range, fuel capability, and the essential bomb-load capacity to get the job done in one single, massive, devastating raid. Smart thought the little Havoc had the personality of a lightweight boxer, and could not reach the target and hit it like the heavyweight he sought. He quickly deduced that the Havoc would be seriously deficient for the Ploiești mission. It was "too pleasant to fly."

Then he had a eureka moment, bright and clear, a notion that brought the whole raid into focus.

Whether it is apocryphal or not, it is interesting to note how Smart's plan evolved from a simple scribble, or so the legend goes, into a complex low-level, historic bombing raid.

There are two stories about the plan's birth: first, that Smart woke from a dream about the raid and doodled the details on a piece of paper on his nightstand; and second, that he was having cocktails in a bar in Washington, DC, one evening when the idea popped into his head, and he noted it on a cocktail napkin and stuffed it into his tunic.

However it came about, what Smart wanted would start to come together through due diligence and perseverance, and, yes, trial and error.

He needed a bomber that could hold a lot more than 1,200 pounds of bombs—a long-range bomber that could destroy the forty-one critical elements of the refineries; one that could be assembled into a powerful strike force; one that could fly the 2,100-mile round-trip mission from Benghazi; and one with the muscularity to sustain heavy battle damage.

Smart believed it would be possible to destroy the forty-one key elements at Ploieşti if such a bomber could be found.

The first candidate considered for the mission was, naturally, the B-17 Flying Fortress.

The dashing, ubiquitous, soon-to-be-a-legend centerpiece of movies, then and now, the B-17, a "Flying Fortress," bristled with .50 caliber guns and could carry between 4,000 and 8,000 pounds of target-busting bombs, depending on the fuel load. Movie star Jimmy Stewart piloted a B-17 through twelve combat missions over Europe (he flew many more as a crewman, and would eventually attain the rank of brigadier general in the US Air Force Reserve). Americans loved their B-17, and still do; it's as American as baseball and apple pie. A movie star. The blight of Nazi Germany. And it sat with its tail on the ground and nose in the air for good reason; she was a proud bird.

But Smart didn't have to ponder too long; as much as he loved the B-17, and would eventually fly one in combat, the Flying Fortress did not have the fuel capacity to fly 2,100 miles to Ploieşti, even when configured with a lighter bomb load; that was a significant negative. This almost automatically took it off Smart's shopping list. It was loved, yes, a legend in its own time, yes. But it did not meet Smart's bombing criteria, so it was scratched.

Next, the B-29 Superfortress was immediately eliminated, because it was still in development. It would later be headed to fight in the Pacific Theater. (The B-29 *Enola Gay* dropped an atomic bomb on Hiroshima, and Nagasaki was bombed by *Bockscar*, another B-29.)

What remained was the unsightly B-24 Liberator, a long-range heavy bomber, the most unattractive aircraft in the air force inventory. The "Lumbering Lib," as many referred to it, squatted on its landing gear like a cumbersome bullfrog, the sumo wrestler of airplanes. It looked like a boxcar with wheels and wings. Or, an overgrown eggplant. Soon, the

B-24 came to be known as "the crate the B-17 was shipped in." There were so many jokes about the B-24 at first that no one took it seriously. Until they took a closer look. After Bob Sternfels flew one, he compared it to the B-17: "The B-24 flew like a Ferrari, the B-17, like a Buick. It was a first-rate aircraft to fly."

But was the B-24 capable of a low-level, "down on the deck," "balls-to-the-wall," fearsome attack?

Coming over Ploieşti "in the grass"—the flying boxcar, the eggplant, the sumo wrestler would have to fly in formation just above chimney height—less than 150 feet. This low-level flying was now a top priority in the Smart Plan. It had never been done before, and many looked at it as totally suicidal.

In reality, they weren't half wrong.

It became apparent that through some reconfiguration, the Liberator would be the near-optimum long-range bomber for the job. The Liberator was indeed the only aircraft at that time that could fulfill Smart's criteria. (It went into production before the bombing of Pearl Harbor and was in production in 1944 at the implausible rate of one B-24 every fifty-seven minutes, a rate as plentiful as manufacturing canned soup, which, in that year, exceeded the military's ability to use the aircraft.)

Despite the snide remarks and jokes, there was nothing else out there that could do the job. And the added plus was the new Davis Wing design, which had been used for a while on a variety of World War II aircraft, most prominently, the B-24. The Davis Wing design provided higher speeds and allowed significant lift at low angles of attack. For some time it had been used on seaplanes, too.

One of the most significant changes would be increasing the B-24's fuel capacity for the long flight. The B-24 offered Smart a sufficient bomb load, and, when retrofitted with extra fuel tanks capable of holding 3,100 gallons, it could fly the tedious round-trip from Benghazi to Ploieşti and back, a flight of approximately 2,100 miles that would consume 2,280 gallons of fuel, depending on how deft the flight engineers were in calculating their fuel consumptions. This was an assurance of a safe margin. By replacing the forward bomb bay with Tokyo fuel tanks, extra fuel capacity and range could be achieved; this, however, would also reduce the bomb load. Because of its size and construction, the Lib could sustain massive battle damage and still limp home, or at least hold on until the pilot found a relatively safe place to put it down.

At some point, Smart and his mission planners had to disregard a cold fact: The B-24 was, first and foremost, an aircraft that flew off the design boards as a high-altitude, long-range bomber. It was a species that preferred empyrean heights above 15,000 feet and relished cold, thin air. But somehow they were going to make it work; close enough it was, and there was nothing else left in the showroom for Smart to evaluate.

Presently, the Washington brass was steadfastly fixated on bombing the oil fields around Ploiești, and were relying on Smart's thinking to achieve their unswerving goal during this time of crisis: They wanted the knockout blow Americans were looking for to end the war—a miracle, yes—and Smart, understandably mindful of his career, was determined to give it to them, simultaneously reaping accolades as quickly as possible. This "knockout" notion was the impetus for their planning.

By destroying the oil refineries around Ploiești, the United States would cut off 30 percent of the oil supply to Nazi Germany and cripple a formidable German war machine. There were additional and perhaps more significant benefits for destroying the refineries: It had been estimated that such destruction would reduce Germany's capacity to produce precious aviation fuel by 95 percent, an impactful number that could indeed strike a death blow to Germany's war effort. Such damage could incapacitate Ploiești's cracking towers, steam plants, and essential pipelines. German aircraft would be grounded, military vehicles would stand down, and tanks would not clatter along (a lack of gasoline would cause them to lose the critical Battle of the Bulge). Two key elements can bring an army to its knees: a lack of oil and a lack of food.

But knockout blows in wars seldom provide intended results. Smoothly.

Washington planners and politicians were chasing the elusive "magic pill"—a "panacea target"—an abstract holy grail that could end the war and provide victory in one stroke that never actually transpires except in planners' daydreams, before they make presentations to politicians and the upper echelons of their respective branches. The analogy of one boxer punching another and knocking him out with one punch is often used to no avail in military matters.

Nevertheless, Smart's knockout "magic pill" was at the forefront of his mind: Bombing Ploiești was an evolving reverie he and his staff pursued, which would eventually ensnare them in a calamitous trap, with disastrous results for the young aircrews that would fly the mission on that day.

In the weeks ahead, Smart pursued what came to be known around the new Pentagon building as "the Smart Plan," soon anointed with a codename, Operation Statesman. But this was almost immediately rejected because it was in use by another project. It was quickly changed to the peculiar Operation Soapsuds, and wallowed as such for a short time. Throughout the process of planning and preparing for the raid, the Smart team would ultimately overlook key details, either purposely, or as a result of just plain bad luck.

One key detail that was overlooked was the fact that up to this point in time, pilots, military or otherwise, had not been trained to fly 200 miles per hour, skimming over treetops like airshow flyboys; in fact, pilots—military *and* civilian—were, and still are, forbidden to fly at those levels. Such flying is often derisively referred to as a "stunt." The one distinct advantage to this on-the-deck, treetop tactic was that it brought the bombers low enough to avoid detection by German radar—at least, part of the time. This was not a significant advantage for the Americans, because the Germans had spies on the ground at Benghazi who reported large numbers of Liberators taking off—another fact that Smart and his planners missed or, for the sake of expediency, disregarded.

And there was another overlooked fact, probably intentionally unheeded.

The lower an aircraft flies, the more difficult it is for pilots and navigators to navigate, the landscape blurring into a Jackson Pollock painting. Down low, they have a minimized bird's-eye view compared to what they have at higher altitudes, where the topography passes in "slow motion," giving the observer a chance to identify landmarks. At 200-plus miles per hour, landmarks at treetop level blur past with stunning speed. Also, the lower the aircraft, the less observable distance you have available.

Maybe Smart considered this; maybe he did not.

Smart's plan was starting to show chips and fissures from top to bottom, and, up to the day of the mission, more would ensue. Maybe luck would patch the walls, or pull the drawbridge up? Perhaps the bravery of the boys flying that day would overcome and anneal the evolving weaknesses? Ploieşti was a predicament of the first rank, a quandary too often seen in the days of warfare.

Smart and his staff, and all those privy to the details, knew that the strike plan had an abundance of challenges and plentiful weaknesses—problems that would lead to the deaths of many Americans, but would nevertheless have to be undertaken. After all, war crushes timelines and restricts comprehensive, leisurely planning; it necessitates immediacy and expediency—often at a terrible cost.

Smart pressed on.

Another option, outside variations of multiple low-level raids, could have been a large-scale attack by enormous numbers of Allied ground forces, but this would have taken many months and caused hundreds of deaths, even among civilians. To consider this now would be reckless and irresponsible.

During the planning stages, Smart's courage rested in the comfort he took from the possibility of some coveted chance, a "best choice" among many to be plucked from a landscape of bad alternatives. He was in a pickle, facing only one direction—forward.

The words of Johann von Goethe resonate here:

Then indecision brings its own delays, and days are lost lamenting o'er lost days. Are you in earnest? Seize this very minute; What you can do, or dream you can, begin it.

Go forth, young colonel; face your troublesome conclusion with what you have at hand, and take God's speed as your sword. May your choice be the best you can realize. God willing, of course.

George Brinton, a second lieutenant, and co-pilot of *Vagabond King* from the 98th Bomb Group, encapsulated the overall feeling of the plan that had been presented to the airmen:

The comment was made by one of the briefing officers that the mission was of such importance that if 75 percent of the group failed to return, it would still be profitable, which really made you feel like you were expendable, period. It was very frank.

Smart was convinced, surely, that the enormity of the mission's purpose, the potential "to still be profitable," despite the obvious evolving risks and mounting weaknesses inherent in the plan, would transcend the challenges and be worth the effort. But, as the plan evolved and layers of strategies and tactics and procedures and opining piled up, there would be more details overlooked, or simply unknown, more options disregarded—bits and pieces that would cloud and befuddle the mission, and that would enforce deadly penalties paid by the valiant aircrews who flew that historic first day of August 1943.

Surprises would be plentiful, yes.

Outcomes calamitous, yes.

And there would be one other element overlooked, but inescapable— bad luck.

Always something to contend with, dwelling forever on soldiers' shoulders, vultures waiting their turn.

The Smart Plan would go forward.

Two months before the raid, on May 21, 1943, at the newly completed Pentagon building in Washington, DC, Jake Smart packed folders containing his research and set off to seek a round of approvals. At this stage, the mission still bore the absurd codename Soapsuds. (What aircrew would be emboldened flying a deadly combat mission with such a cartoonish codename?)

He motored not far to the newly convened Anglo-American Trident Conference—codenamed Trident—held at the Federal Reserve Building on Constitution Avenue, with the main delegations again headed by Roosevelt and Churchill.

The prime minister had arrived in Washington that same month for the fourteen-day conference on the speedy HMS *Queen Elizabeth*, the world's largest troopship (a converted ocean liner). He met with Roosevelt every other day in the White House, while various British and American military leaders met almost daily in the Board of Governors' room. Both Roosevelt and Churchill had time between discussions to escape the blistering 90-degree temperatures that month to do some light fishing and casually enjoy cigars, cigarettes, and the other's company.

The primary purpose of the Trident assemblage was to discuss and plan the Allied invasion of Sicily, including the extent of military force necessary; the date for invading Europe (which Smart helped plan); and tactics for the war in the Pacific. During this meeting, Smart deployed his Ploieşti pitch, which was low on the agenda. However scant the attention was, the central question among the assemblage regarding Soapsuds was where the necessary aircraft for the raid would come from. Solutions for this would be reached later.

Despite its brief appearance on the agenda, Soapsuds was approved. Privately, most thought the mission was a stupid concept, particularly the low-level-flying aspect of the mission.

Gen. Gordon Saville, on the staff of Gen. Carl Spaatz, commander of Strategic Air Forces in Europe, reportedly rolled his eyes and had critical words for Smart's plan, calling it "ridiculous and suicidal."

—•—

Whether Smart felt confident or not is moot: The Smart Plan was in hand, as such. The thirty-nine-year-old colonel stuffed his files into his briefcase again and soon descended upon Algiers, the capital city of Algeria, nicknamed "Algiers the White," because the buildings, seen from the sea, glistened silvery and lustrous.

There, at the plush St. Georges Hotel, he presented the Smart Plan to Gen. Dwight D. Eisenhower, at the time the commander of all Allied air forces, a man who knew how to weigh the pluses and minuses of a military plan. When Smart left, he had Eisenhower's endorsement, which was not wholeheartedly approved by the general's doubting staff.

The next day, Jake Smart flew to London for a private meeting with Prime Minister Winston Churchill and made one of the most important pitches of his air force career. Not many thirty-nine-year-old colonels got to present privately to a British prime minister. Churchill, attentive, liked the idea, mostly the surprise attack aspect of the mission (which, even before the first bomb fell, would not be a surprise at all). It was a direct assault on Churchill's nemesis, Adolf Hitler, and seemed to have the potential to seriously curtail the oil supply to Nazi Germany.

In that meeting, Churchill was beneficent, offering Smart two British Lancaster bomber groups—approximately 140 Lancaster bombers— which Smart tactfully declined, citing the comparative variances in performance characteristics of the Lancaster versus the Liberator. The meeting ended on a typically cheery British note—Churchill saying it would be a "good show," and giving the plan a thumbs-up with his famous "V" sign.

Now Smart needed only one more round of approvals, which he was confident he would obtain.

By the end of June 1943, the Smart Plan for Ploiești was finally presented to the commander of the US 9th Air Force, Maj. Gen. Lewis Hyde Brereton. Not only did Brereton give his approval, but he would also later erroneously claim credit for the plan. And, he yearned to fly the mission in one of the B-24s.

Simultaneously, Brereton's chief of staff, Brig. Gen. Uzal Girard Ent, the overall mission commander, also gave his blessing, albeit reluctantly, and with a caveat—he would have to fly the mission as mission commander. As a brigadier general, Ent outranked twenty-seven-year-old Col. Keith K. Compton (a whippersnapper in comparison, known as "K. K."). Compton would be at the controls of the aircraft the day that Ent flew, and would have significant and controversial results during one of the most crucial stages of the mission.

At this point, Smart assumed he would fly the mission, despite knowing extremely sensitive details regarding the invasion of Europe—details that if pried from his mind could change the course of the war in Europe, and lead to a major loss for the Allies.

Other commanders questioned the mission's potential effectiveness because it was a single-strike attack, and anticipated a 40 percent loss rate. They also regarded it as a "panacea target." Nevertheless, all endorsements were finally signed.

Except, thankfully, for one more piece of housekeeping.

Prime Minister Churchill, a man who knew his way around a sentence and valued the precise meanings of words, soon voiced his disapproval and inclination for a better code name, which was no surprise at all. He summed up his feelings about the Americans' choice in a memo to his old friend, President Roosevelt, dated June 26, 1943:

On reflection, I thought Soapsuds was inappropriate for an operation in which so many brave Americans would risk or lose their lives. I do not think it good for morale to affix disparaging labels to daring feats of arms. I am very glad that the United States Chiefs of Staff agree with ours to substitute Tidal Wave for Soapsuds. I wish all our problems were so quickly settled.

So, the codename came from the British, not the Americans. It was appropriately renamed, too, since the mission would be flown in several "tidal waves" of bombers over the targets.

With approvals and endorsements in place, the battle lines had been drawn.

The colonel from Ridgeland, North Carolina, the West Point graduate who purportedly doodled an outline for the mission on a piece of paper (or a napkin), the thirty-nine-year-old air force officer who had presented his strategy to Pentagon leaders, the prime minister of Great Britain, and a future president of the United States, now had to face the most formidable challenge to Tidal Wave—his nemesis, *Generalleutnant* Alfred Gerstenberg, the Protector, the Luftwaffe's most capable air defense general.

Tidal Wave was less than two months away.

CHAPTER 5

Lumbering Lib

You love a lot of things if you live around them. But there isn't any woman and there isn't any horse, nor any before or after, that is as lovely as a fighter plane. And men who love them are faithful to them even though they leave them for others.

—ERNEST HEMINGWAY

BOB STERNFELS'S NEXT TRAINING ASSIGNMENT—LEARNING TO FLY four-engined bombers—was at sunny Hendricks Army Airfield, not far from Sebring, Florida, a city noted since 1950 for the 12 Hours of Sebring, an annual motorsport endurance race for sports cars held at the Sebring International Raceway.

On October 15, 1942, when Bob arrived, Hendricks was a Heavy Bomber Training School for potential B-17 Flying Fortress and B-24 Liberator pilots. When Bob saw his first B-17, it set him back on his heels. He shook his head, thinking there was no way a plane that size would ever get off the ground.

Indeed, the $99,620 B-17 was massive, especially compared to the small trainers Bob had been training in. The B-17's four powerful Pratt & Whitney engines and the 103-foot wingspan presented a daunting impression; it sat on its tail, nose held high, imperious, mighty. And it bristled with armament, a "flying fortress," with seven Browning .50 caliber gun platforms: a gun in the nose, two in the chin turret, two in the ball turret on the belly, .50 caliber guns at two waist positions, an upper turret with two .50 caliber guns, and a .50 caliber tail gun. It was an American masterpiece proudly crafted, engineered, and hand-assembled by men and women at the Boeing plants in Seattle, Washington.

The B-17E that made Bob grin in awe on that humid October morning would eventually be the primary bomber used by the US Army Air Forces in the daylight precision strategic bombing campaign of World War II—primarily flying against German and French industrial and military targets in Europe. The B-17 was touted not merely as a bomber, but as a strategic weapon, a potent, high-flying, long-range bomber that was able to defend itself and return home, even with extensive battle damage. In countless, mostly black-and-white images and films of the era, the B-17 can be seen in flocks of gray specks, bombing German targets while being attacked by darting Luftwaffe fighters camouflaged in shades of gray and blue. The B-17s were often surrounded by puffs of deadly gray-black flak; and, too often, falling, devastated, aflame, crewmen bailing out, or going down, trapped in their ship by centrifugal force.

Initially, Douglas, Martin, and Boeing competed for a contract to build two hundred B-17s. But the Boeing entry outperformed both of its competitors and exceeded the air corps' expectations. Although Boeing initially lost the contract because the prototype crashed and killed its two test pilots (several onboard observers survived), the air corps was so impressed with Boeing's design that it ordered thirteen more B-17s for further evaluation.

After Harry Halverson's Ploiești mission and the first bombing of Europe began, the B-17's reputation swiftly ascended, taking on a mythological, heroic hold over the American public—some say overblown when compared, side by side, to the B-24 Liberator, the bomber Bob would eventually fly in fifty combat missions. (For an idea of how terrible the August 1 Ploiești raid was: When asked how many combat missions he had flown, Bob said, "I'm credited with fifty. The Ploiești mission was so long and rough that we were allowed to count that single mission as five.")

The Flying Fortress that surprised Bob that day was an E model, a four-engine, heavy bomber aircraft developed in the 1930s for the US Army Air Corps, designed for bombing from high altitudes. Because it would be produced in large numbers, and in several versions, it was the most publicized American plane of the war. Frequently featured in *Life*,

Time, and *Collier's* magazines, and in newspapers and newsreels from Pathé News, it swiftly became a revered emblem of the country's industrial prowess and might, a reputation the aircraft maintains today. Total production amounted to 12,731, far less than the B-24—the bomber Bob would fly on the Ploieşti mission.

Intact existing airframes are increasingly rare; only ten complete, flyable B-17s are known to exist today. Restorers are now seeking out airframes that were previously considered unrecoverable. Restored models, whether they are flyable or on static display, draw millions of enthusiastic aviation buffs from around the world. (One B-17, the renowned *Memphis Belle*, represents fifty missions flown over Europe during World War II, and is presently memorialized on permanent static display at the National Museum of the US Air Force, located at Wright-Patterson Air Force Base, near Dayton, Ohio.)

———

Almost every B-24 that flew combat missions during World War II had a name painted on its nose, and the names varied according to the crew's partialities. Often, the choice of a name, slogan, caricature, or motif came from the collective minds of the entire crew—or the command pilot, if he had a strong notion of what he wanted painted on the nose of his plane.

Ideas popped up from every possible source that sauntered through the minds of the red-blooded American boys who crewed the planes: magazines, movies, matchbook covers, comics, songs, girlfriends, mothers, cities, cartoon characters. Walt Disney Studios would often donate an artist's time and have him send a crew a rough drawing based on the crewmen's ideas. Alberto Vargas, premier pinup artist and the leading artist for *Esquire* magazine at the time, provided many drawings, mostly of voluptuous women in colorful poses, tastefully drawn. Vargas's artwork would come to be the most copied for caricatures on airplanes. Anyone in a squadron who had the slightest talent for drawing was put to work painting what would later become known as "nose art." Often, the drawings were caricatures of half-naked or fully naked women with conspicuous breasts and picture-perfect rosy nipples proudly displayed on the bomber's olive-green or beige fuselage, just under the cockpit windows.

Many of the captions were blunt, leaving nothing to the imagination: *Patched Up Piece, Just Once More, SHEDONWANNA, LAKANOOKI, Innocence A Broad.* Almost any subject was allowed—as long as it wasn't too vulgar or profane—the brass figuring that ten young men flying combat missions in a bomber whose odds of dying on any given mission were reasonably high had the right to paint whatever the hell they wanted on the nose of their airplane. Imagine going to work every day and facing better than a 50 percent chance of getting killed or wounded before dinner that night.

Of course, occasionally the brass had to put their foot down. David Perry, a pilot from the 390th Bomb Group, recalled:

> *We had a crew chief named Delorenzo, an Italian from New York, very tough. Everything to him was a douchebag; this was a douchebag, the airplane was a douchebag. Everyone around us was naming their airplanes* Sweet Sue *and stuff like that. We named ours* The Douchebag. *We thought that was a sacred thing—you could name your airplane anything you wanted. But the CO and everybody got on my tail and made it very difficult for us. We had to change the name. A favorite name of the bombardier at that time was a "dull tool," that guy's a dull tool, and so on, like saying he was an asshole. So we renamed the airplane* The Dull Tool, *and that's how we went through our tour.*

Some of the names were intensely personal, while others, according to today's standards, were outright sexist and over-the-top politically incorrect: *Little Pink Panties* showed a lithe, wholly naked woman slipping on a pair of pink lace panties. Then there were the double entendres: *Miss "B" Haven, Jamaica?, Daddy's Delight, Mis-Abortion, Pregnant Portia, Screw, Shack Bunny, Virgin's Delight, Impatient Virgin, Stud Duck, Iza Vailable Too,* and, most transparent of all, *Big Dick.*

Miss Slipstream had a flamboyant drawing of a naked woman with her lingerie being blown off. One of the main subjects on the minds of the young crewmen were women who gave them inspiration, love, and a profound yearning for the home fires. Many of these drawings today, if painted on military aircraft, would be cause for courts-martial (they've been banned by regulations).

There were names that inspired and emboldened the crews: a picture of Mickey Mouse holding two pistols and a bullet-laden gun belt around his waist had a caption that read, "Let Them Come, Gang, I'll Take Care of Them." *Lightning Strikes* showed a lightning bolt pointed at a comical-looking Adolf Hitler. *Can Do* bore a shield that showed a shattered swastika. Below *Exterminator* had a large V with Hitler's face squeezed in the crux of the letter. Hitler's head was seen in another on the body of a rat, and above was lettered *E-RAT-ICATOR*. Another was inspired by beer and whiskey, something most young men eagerly sought, second only to the female touch: *Dry Martini—The Cocktail Kid* displayed nineteen little bombs and accurately drawn swastikas, indicating missions the bomber had completed.

These names and caricatures inspired their crews, gave them a strong sense of proprietorship and oneness; it diverted them from the mayhem they faced in the sky on each mission they flew; it made them laugh, feel proud and hopeful, more able to bear up under the anxiety of flying through death's clouds on nearly every mission. No wonder they were never asked to remove them.

Such nose art had been a tradition since World War I on all types of aircraft—military vehicles, tanks, and guns, too—until such naming slammed up against the mighty rampart of political correctness. Then the ax fell with cold sharpness:

The British banned the use of pinup women in nose art on Royal Air Force aircraft in 2007, as commanders decided the images (many containing naked women), were inappropriate and potentially offensive to female personnel, although there were no documented complaints. In 1993 the United States Air Force Air Mobility Command ordered that all nose art should be gender-neutral. [Assuming, too, that the US Navy and Marines soon followed.]

Many of these aircraft would be blown out of the sky, badly damaged, or simply vanish, the names, the crewmen that inspired them, lost forever—except for grainy black-and-white photographs and the waning memories of those who knew and loved them.

After their duty was done and the smoke of battle had thinned, some bombers were sent to salvage and scrapped. Only a few survive today, with a few more sitting fallow, waiting for restoration.

From the co-pilot's right-hand seat, Bob spent twenty hours flying the B-17E. He flew day and night landings, cross-country flights as far as Washington, DC, and gained valued instrument flying time. Then, after 20 hours, it was time to solo.

"That's when the fun began," he said. Because the B-17E was considered a high-altitude bomber, Bob couldn't resist finding out for himself just what "high altitude" meant, and how far up the bird could go.

"Alone in the co-pilot's seat, I got it up to 25,000, then 28,000, then 29,500, and, bingo, one of the engines just gave up," he said. "That one engine didn't want me to push her anymore, so she called it quits. Made my head turn a bit. I had to land with three engines. It was a good teaching experience."

Between October 18 and December 16, when Bob's B-17 training ended, he had racked up nearly 100 hours of flying time. A short time later, the Boeing B-17G would go into production; this model would have more power and could climb to 30,000 feet.

By Christmas 1942, Bob was at Davis-Monthan Air Force Base, near Tucson, Arizona, for training in the aircraft he would go to war in, the B-24 Liberator. He had started to develop a discerning eye, and this plane was a revelation, despite its outward appearances.

"Compared to the B-17," said Bob, "the feeling was that the B-24 was an ugly, slab-sided bird. People called it the Flying Boxcar, the Lumbering Lib, because it looked like something that belonged on a pair of railroad tracks hauling freight, not in the air. It was a much more demanding airplane than the B-17. It cruised much faster, could go as high, and carried twice the bomb load. All these aspects were reasons it was chosen for mass production."

The B-24 might have been ugly, but it was effective, and a remarkably large aircraft. It would take Bob to war, fly him through many battles, and then bring him home whole. She was a lovely bird. Before the war ended, nearly twenty thousand B-24s would be produced. Most of them were chopped up after the war, and today just a handful exist.

———

The B-24 Liberator, designated a heavy bomber, was designed by the Consolidated Aircraft Co. of San Diego, California. Over eight thousand B-24s were manufactured by the Ford Motor Company at the Ypsilanti, Michigan, Willow Run plant alone, and were coming off the assembly line at the rate of one aircraft every one hundred minutes. The B-24 holds the distinction of being the most produced heavy bomber in history, the most produced multi-engine aircraft in history, and the most-produced American military aircraft, period. In the end, nearly nineteen thousand B-24s were manufactured.

In January 1939, the US Army Air Corps invited Consolidated to submit a design study for a bomber with longer range, higher speed, and greater ceiling than its more aerodynamically curvy cousin, the imperious, ubiquitous B-17. By comparison, a B-24 on the ground might seem like a boxcar because it doesn't sit like a B-17; instead, it seems to squat, its bulky bluntness like a cannon shell, all shoulder and muscle—a horizontal fireplug, thank you very much. The front landing wheel is barely visible, the wing is high-shouldered, and the tail has twin rudders.

Although it was eventually admired, respected, and revered, the B-24 was not a perfect plane, as Ira Eakin, crew chief of the 92nd Bombardment Group, recalled:

I guess the B-24 was a reasonably good airplane, but they had a bomb bay fuel tank in them and an electric landing gear right close to that tank, and I've seen those things blow up on takeoff. You'd get a leak in the tank, see, and when you flipped your gear switch, an arc from the electric motor would set it off. You didn't want to be in it when it went off.

At its inception, the B-24 featured a modern design, including the Davis Wing, an unusual and highly efficient shoulder-mounted, high-aspect-ratio wing named after its inventor, freelance aeronautical engineer David R. Davis. Davis had approached Consolidated, intending to get them to license the wing for use on their sizable flying boat designs. After wind tunnel tests at the California Institute of Technology, the results showed that the design was the most significant of the time: It would give aircraft the ability to generate lift at low angles of attack, making it especially beneficial for flying boats because it would reduce the need to pull up the nose for takeoff and landing. The wing gave the Liberator a high cruise speed, long range, and the ability to carry a heavy bomb load. It was only later that the reason for the Davis Wing's excellent performance became clear. In retrospect, the cross section shows a strong resemblance to another iconic American plane's wing, the famous P-51 Mustang. As you will see, the Davis Wing played a pivotal role in the 1943 Ploieşti raid.

In a survey taken two weeks before the Normandy invasion, researchers questioned three thousand enlisted officers and crew members of B-24s and B-17s. Seventy-six percent of B-24 crews said they had the best type of aircraft, and a solid 92 percent of B-17 crews stated that their Flying Fortresses were better.

Bob Sternfels, like almost all the pilots who flew the B-24, stated that flying it and keeping it in formation was difficult; one had to strain to keep control—it needed a strong hand. In the survey, a Liberator pilot wrote: "Men who are picked to fly the B-24 should be picked for their physical abilities; there should be no pilots under 160 pounds, because the physical strain of formation flying is too much."

After flying both bombers, Bob said, "The B-17 was like flying a Buick; the B-24, like flying a Ferrari. In the end, both were the best of what America had."

On Christmas Eve, 1942, Bob Sternfels stepped off a train in Tucson, Arizona, at Davis-Monthan Air Base, where he would be introduced to his first B-24 Liberator.

"Many of us," he said, "thought we were being punished when we saw the bomber they were giving us. After the wonderful experience with the B-17, we thought we were being assigned to a lesser plane. No one liked the looks of it, and the B-17 had most of the good publicity up to that point. But that's what they gave us, and that's what we had to learn to fly, and learn to love."

It turned out to be a positive experience for Bob and all of his fellow student pilots. "The B-24 was a much more demanding airplane, true," Bob recalled. "It cruised faster, could go as high, and carried twice the load of a B-17. It wasn't as pretty, but all of these things and much more were why the B-24 had been chosen for mass production."

There would be many variations of the B-24 Liberator before war's end. The bomber Bob was assigned to, the ship he would fly through the end of the war, was the B-24D. The "D" designation denoted the latest model, and the first variant that went into mass production by Consolidated Aircraft. The initial batch was delivered to the army air corps in January and February of 1943, so the B-24 that Bob was staring at was a brand-new airplane; "I could even smell the fresh paint," Bob said.

It had a wingspan of 110 feet, was 66 feet long, 17 feet high, and was powered by four Pratt & Whitney engines rated at 1,200 horsepower apiece. Armament consisted of eleven .50 caliber machine guns. Maximum speed was 303 mph, and it had a service ceiling of 32,000 feet, a bit higher than Bob's engine-busting journey to 29,000 feet in the B-17.

———

At the beginning of 1943, while Bob was training in the B-24, back home the cost of World War II had hit a staggering $8 billion a month. The Pentagon—the world's largest office building, covering 34 acres outside Washington, DC—was completed, at a cost of $64 million. The most popular books were Ayn Rand's *The Fountainhead*, William Saroyan's *The Human Comedy*, and Martin Flavin's Pulitzer Prize–winning *Journey in the Dark*. Americans were rushing to see Humphrey Bogart and Ingrid

Bergman in what would become an all-time classic, *Casablanca*. Gary Cooper and Ingrid Bergman were starring in the popular *For Whom the Bells Toll*. Big songs on the radio were "Besame Mucho—Kiss Me Much," "Comin' in on a Wing and a Prayer," and some soon-to-become American standards: "I'll Be Seeing You," "People Will Say We're in Love," and "Do Nothing Till You Hear from Me," and from the musical Oklahoma, "The Surrey with the Fringe on Top" and "Oh, What a Beautiful Morning."

Otherwise that year, Benito Mussolini resigned as prime minister of Italy, and that country ended hostilities with the United States. Gen. Dwight D. Eisenhower was appointed Supreme Commander of the Anglo-American forces for the invasion of Europe, and was promoted to a five-star rank.

Perhaps most significant of all, the Casablanca Conference was held, with President Roosevelt and Prime Minister Churchill conferring on the "unconditional surrender of Germany, Italy, and Japan." Commenting on the war effort, British observer, D. W. Brogan remarked, "To the Americans, war is a business, not an art."

January 27, 1943, three days after the Casablanca Conference ended halfway around the world, marked another, more personal landmark: One of America's own, a product of Detroit, Michigan, Robert Warren Sternfels—a boy who'd jumped off a garage roof with his mother's umbrella to pursue his dream of flying—had concluded another phase of his flying career and soloed successfully after forty-eight hours and five minutes of training.

And this time he didn't rip his trousers.

On February 6, with a new crew that would mostly remain intact through the raid on Ploiești, serious training with the B-24D began. First, gunnery school at Alamogordo, New Mexico; then, on to Clovis, New Mexico, for night flying and instrument flying, as well as cross-country training. Finally, after nearly three months' training, on April 13, 1943, Bob and his crew were assigned a brand-new B-24D in Topeka, Kansas, one that would bear them throughout the rest of the war—or almost.

Bob's factory-fresh B-24, to be named after they arrived in Benghazi, started her historic World War II journey in Dallas, Texas, as a series of cold figures: Serial Number 42-40402-55-CO, at a cost of $297,627—equal to approximately $4,541,692 in today's dollars.

The Ford motor company built her. Her birth was partially completed on a dreary Friday afternoon at around three p.m., when the workers pushed her out onto the flight line where she joined a bevy of other B-24s impatiently waiting to bolt off to war. From Dallas, Texas, where she arrived without battle colors, in plain shiny metal that sparkled like Bob's mother's polished silver, soon to be painted not the typical flat green of a fresh olive, but the dull rouge of desert sand, almost pink (officially, Shade 49 Sand over neutral grey). Then more quickly, another flight to Hamilton Field, California, and, finally, to completion at Topeka, Kansas, where Lt. Robert W. Sternfels and nine other crewmen, all young men without combat experience, walked out onto the tarmac early in the morning to look up at her and say hello.

There they pulled away her chocks and took her to a taxiway for their first test drive. A bunch of American boys, well-trained, so eager, bursting with the same glee and anticipation that other young men might have felt, taking the keys to Dad's new car, yearning for the adventure of their lives and wondering, of course, what fate awaited them. But mostly, would they survive and come back to Mom's home cooking and the girl next door?

It was a bright, sunny afternoon of high expectations, and the hope that someday, at the war's end, they would wind up back where innocence began, older and more prudent, and, above all, whole in soul, body, and mind.

Bob said, "The ramp where all the planes were parked was filled with planes painted the usual dark, dull green paint. Not ours—it was beige, almost *pink*, and I hated it. I thought of asking Maintenance to repaint it, but then I had second thoughts."

Their first flight was not encouraging.

"One of the engines started to show signs of failure as soon as we got it up in the air, so when I brought it back I asked the crew chief to check it out. He did, and the next day we went up again, and the same problem was showing. I took it back up again. This time, I had to feather the engine and landed with only three engines working. I told the crew chief what happened, and he looked at me like I was nuts. So, I said, 'Grab your flying clothes, we're going up for a ride.' I didn't have to say anything after we got up. When we got back on the ground, he gave me a new engine. It took three days to replace it."

With this new engine, up they went for a test flight.

"My logbook shows we got up to 240 mph," Bob recalled, "which was beyond what the B-24 could do. I finally had a new airplane and wondered what our assignment was."

It quickly became apparent what that would be.

"Green planes went to green areas—such as England," said Bob. "Pink planes went to the desert areas. So, off we went on our trip to the desert. First, we flew to Miami and then to Trinidad. We heard that there was a lot of rum in Puerto Rico, and because we had 'mechanical problems,' we had to stay there for a while and have them checked out. The cases of rum were for 'medicinal purposes.'"

Over the next month, they flew thousands of miles: Belan, Natal, Ascension Island, Accra, Mandarin, Khartoum, and on to Cairo.

"We spent a few days in Fayit, Egypt, and then finally got assigned to Benina, Libya, twelve miles outside of Benghazi. We were in the desert, our new home. And that's where our war began."

CHAPTER 6

Black Gold

Oil they would buy from anyone. From Satan.

—CHRISTOPHER BUCKLEY

GERMAN CITIZENS IN 1943 HAD A GROWING SENSE THAT THE WAR WAS not going the way Adolf Hitler had promised. The notion of lives lost and hopelessness showed in the indelible anguish Germans were enduring and suffused the entire population with unyielding despair.

As a journalist in Berlin that year, Ursula von Kardorff, a fervent anti-Nazi, was better informed than most citizens about the condition of Germany and the state of the war. In her book, *Diary of a Nightmare: Berlin, 1942–1945*, she wrote an incisive entry on January 12, 1943, succinctly articulating the feelings of many Germans:

> *I sometimes feel like a candle burning at both ends. At the front, my brothers and my friends are fighting for a victory, the very prospect of which fills me with horror. To think [of] Hitler as the Master of Europe!? But I suppose it must be some kind of perversion to hope that one's own country will be defeated. Anyhow, it is something utterly beyond the comprehension of the worthy citizens who glory in their power and possessions. Klaus turned up yesterday from Meiningen, and I asked a few people in to meet him. The sirens went at the beginning, and after the all-clear, we got into a mood of rather sinister merriment. Papa, returning from a memorial service for E. R. Weiss, had passed burning houses on his way home, and was shocked at us. But for some reason, I was bursting with vitality and*

cheerfulness. It was really dreadful to feel like that . . . to feel that the thickness of a wall could shut out all the horrors, that they were nothing to do with me at all.

For von Kardorff and millions of Germans, new, devastating military setbacks in 1943 accentuated the feeling of portent, of sinister things to come. Terrible things.

Two weeks after von Kardorff's penetrating diary entry, the Soviets declared that they had finally busted a road through the spine of the Wehrmacht's defense and were able to hump copious loads of supplies to Leningrad (also called the 900-Day Siege) along the shores of Lake Ladoga, ending one of the bloodiest, most prolonged sieges in history—872 brutal, pummeling, blood-spitting days. Of the 91,000 men who surrendered, only some 5,000–6,000 ever returned to their homelands (the last of them a full decade after the end of the war in 1945); the rest died in Soviet prison and labor camps. On the Soviet side, official Russian military historians estimate that there were 1,100,000 Red Army dead, wounded, missing, or captured in the campaign to defend the city. An estimated 40,000 civilians died as well. Only five thousand Germans returned to Germany after the war.

On that same day, January 27, another Third Reich calamity descended upon the Fatherland: the first daylight bombing raid by the US Army Air Force. Fifty-five American B-17 Flying Fortress bombers from the 8th Air Force, led by the 306th Bomb Group (H) churned out of England, Brig. Gen. Frank A. Armstrong in command, and bombed Wilhelmshaven in northern Germany: 137 tons of America's premium, meticulously handmade, Tritonal-packed bombs rippled from their bellies onto warehouses, industrial plants, and docks, leaving the area pocked and aflame, as nightmarish as an Edvard Munch moonscape.

As if that was not bad enough, four days after the Battle of Stalingrad ended, newly appointed German general field marshal (*Generalfeldmarschall*) Friedrich Wilhelm Ernst Paulus, fifty-three, surrendered his entire 6th Army, a staggering, tattered 280,000 men, half of them already dead, the other half, centimeters from death; 91,000 German soldiers died from starvation and exposure on a forced march to a prison camp in one of the most pitiless winters in Russian history. Paulus surrendered on the same day Hitler had promoted him to field marshal, to spur him on, to deviate the newly made field marshal from capitulation; it was for naught. After Paulus's white flag caught an ill wind, Hitler ruthlessly rebuked him because he did not put a bullet in his head—"No German field marshal has ever been captured alive!" Paulus's response to Hitler's disaffecting sentiment was succinct and smartly phrased: "I have no intention of shooting myself for that Bohemian corporal."

No, the beginning of 1943 was not a good time for Germany and its citizens.

To add to their burden of grief and heartfelt misery, Joseph Goebbels, the Third Reich's Minister of Public Enlightenment and Propaganda (*Reichsministerium für Volksaufklärung und Propaganda*) gave his "Total War" speech (*Sportpalastredein*) at the Sport Palace (*Sportpalast*) in the tony Schöneberg section of Berlin on February 18, 1943. It was considered to be the first public admission by the Nazi leadership that the war was going badly. Large black-and-white Nazi banners and swastikas hung everywhere. Behind Goebbels, an immense sovereign eagle with ominous outspread wings was displayed, guarding and glaring. Part of the audience sat above Goebbels's lectern on a balcony with a massive sign that read ***TOTALER KRIEG—KÜRZESTER KRIEG*** (*Total War—Shortest War*). The enthused crowd of 14,000 carefully culled by Goebbels, listened, mesmerized, to the speech. Herculean in length and packed tightly with energy and pacing, it called for "total war" (*Totaler Krieg*), and was Goebbels's most famous, most animated.

While he fed the hand-picked audience with the tone and strength they needed, he deftly circumvented, veiled, and diluted the realities their nation was facing; this was Goebbels at his best. The last line was the title of the speech, the power punch: *"Nation, Rise Up, and Let the Storm Break Loose!"* His exhortation was strident and lengthy and sweaty. In part, he said:

> *It was a moving experience for me, and probably also for all of you, to be bound by radio with the last heroic fighters in Stalingrad during our powerful meeting here in the Sport Palace. They radioed to*

*us that they had heard the Führer's proclamation, and perhaps for
the last time in their lives joined us in raising their hands to sing the
national anthem. What an example German soldiers have set in this
great age! And what an obligation it puts on us all, particularly the
entire German homeland! Stalingrad was and is fate's great alarm
call to the German nation! A nation that has the strength to survive and overcome such a disaster, even to draw from it additional
strength, is unbeatable. In my speech to you and the German people,
I shall remember the heroes of Stalingrad, who put me and all of us
under a deep obligation.*

After the speech, Albert Speer, Reich Minister of Armaments and
War Production, said Goebbels told him "that it was the best-trained
audience one could find in Germany." Millions listened on the radio, and
soon a "whisper joke"—a joke one dared to repeat only in a whisper—
spread throughout the country:

> Dear Tommy, fly further
> We're all mine-workers here.
> Fly further to Berlin
> there they've all screamed Yes!

It was another parcel of despair that made the mountain of desola-
tion reach higher toward the gray clouds of inevitable ruin. Woe filled the
masses, threw cold water on waning hope. So grew their misery. Emboldened their enemies. And, mounted further obligations and challenges on
the German people. Faith was spiraling away with the speed of falling
bombs. After all, Germans could only have so many bombs fall on their
heads and continue to believe the swastika was a cross.

These calamitous newsflashes slammed the German people with
the force of a malicious hailstorm. An unruly virus of doubt continued
to spread wider, deeper. Things were getting worse, not better. And to
underscore their misery, before Goebbels's speech the government had
taken the first of many drastic measures for all-out mobilization: They
closed restaurants, clubs, bars, theaters, and luxury stores throughout the

country, to divert the civilian population toward contributing more to the war effort.

But the German population was astute. They knew grievous losses like Leningrad and Stalingrad and the bombing of Wilhelmshaven and the "total war" speech meant further deprivation and tremendous loss of life, on German soil and on faraway battlefields. They knew that if the Führer was to keep his promises, he desperately needed petroleum and the benefits it would provide against the backdrop of these ominous events. All depended on petroleum. Without it, more defeats were certain, and victory, less so.

While the German people worried about shelter and food on their tables, Hitler worried about oil in the veins of his vehicles. This dire situation was emphasized in Hitler's own words at a secretly recorded meeting. On June 4, 1942, Hitler met with Baron Carl Gustaf Emil Mannerheim, commander in chief of the Finnish armed forces, to honor Mannerheim's seventy-fifth birthday, and for informal talks. Actually, it was a surprise for Mannerheim, who did not want to meet at his headquarters or in Helsinki; he wished to avoid the appearance of a state visit. Hitler flew to Immola Airfield in Imatra, Finland, aboard his private plane, a gray-green camouflaged four-motor Focke-Wulf Fw 200 Condor, nicknamed *Immelmann III*, after the World War I German ace Max Immelmann. (Oddly, the registration number on Hitler's Condor was D-2600. The aircraft President Kennedy flew to Dallas on November 22, 1963, had registration number 26000 on its tail.)

From Immola Airfield, Hitler, accompanied by Finnish president Risto Heikki Ryti, was driven to a railroad siding. There, Baron Mannerheim greeted Hitler and his entourage outside his private train with the clicking of polished heels and a flock of stiff Nazi salutes. To memorialize the details of the secret meeting, a Finnish sound engineer, Thor Damen from Yle, the Finnish Broadcasting Company, had been assigned to record the event. After Hitler gave his short, official speech and birthday greetings—and more heel-clicking and *Sieg Heils*—he took a table in Mannerheim's salon car for drinks and light lunch. Seated opposite Hitler was President Ryti; to Hitler's left, Finnish prime minister Jukka Rangel, and Mannerheim across from him.

Instead of stopping the recording, Thor Damen surreptitiously continued taping the group's conversation through a microphone hanging from the ceiling above Mannerheim's head. This is probably the only known existence of a recording of Hitler speaking in his natural, conversational voice—ad-libbing, as it were. At first, no one at the table, most notably Hitler, knew that Damen was recording their conversation. But eleven minutes into it, Hitler's SS bodyguards from the *Begleitkommando des Führers* (the Führer's Bodyguard Detachment) realized Damen was still getting the conversation down on his elaborate tape machine; they ordered him to stop immediately, with a "cut across the throat" gesture, and asked for the tape. At first, Damen refused; later, he relented, but only after making a full copy for himself. (Damen gave this historic copy to Kustaa Vilkuna, the head of the state censors' office. It was returned to Yle in 1957, and made public several years later.)

What were Hitler's pertinent comments on that tape?

The usually long-winded Führer dominated the eleven-minute conversation: He spoke of the failure of Operation Barbarossa, and commented on Italian defeats in Africa, Yugoslavia, and Albania. He seemed particularly enthralled by the Soviet Union's ability to produce thousands of tanks, many more than the Third Reich; he found their production numbers unbelievable.

Most revealing during the eleven minutes, he spoke about the petroleum in Ploiești, and the disaster the German nation would certainly face if oil stopped flowing. In part, these are Hitler's exact words:

Hitler: Already in the fall of 1940 we continuously faced the question, uh, shall we consider a breakup [in relations with the USSR]? At that time, I advised the Finnish government, to negotiate and to gain time, to act dilatory in this matter—because *I always feared that Russia suddenly would attack Romania in the late fall and occupy the petroleum wells [in Ploiești]* [emphasis added], and we would have not been ready in the late fall of 1940. *If Russia indeed had taken Romania's petroleum wells, then Germany would have been lost* [emphasis added]. It would have required just 60 Russian divisions to handle that matter.

In Romania, we had of course—at that time—no major units. The Romanian government had turned to us only recently—*and what we did have was laughable. They only had to occupy the petroleum wells* [emphasis added]. Of course, with our weapons, I could not start a war in September or October . . . It would have been impossible to attack before the spring of 1941. *And if the Russians at that time—in the fall of 1940—had occupied Romania—taken the petroleum wells [in Ploesti], then we would have been helpless in 1941* . . . [emphasis added]

Unknown Voice (interrupting): Without petroleum—

Hitler (interrupting): We had huge German production; however, the demands of the air force, our Panzer divisions—they are really huge. *It is a level of consumption that surpasses the imagination. And without the addition of four to five million tons of Romanian petroleum, we could not have fought the war—and we would have had to let it be. And that was my big worry* [emphasis added].

The thought of invading Romania and grabbing the oil fields by force before 1940 was out of the question. Colonel Smart had the same tactical notion—it would take months and months and cost thousands of lives, and probably inflict severe damage to (or destroy) the refineries.

Between 1941 and 1944, Hitler maintained close contact with Ion Victor Antonescu, Prime Minister and Conducător of Romania, the first non-German to receive Germany's coveted award, the Knight's Cross of the Iron Cross, which he received from Hitler at an August 6, 1941, meeting in Ukraine. He proudly wore the coveted decoration suspended around his neck as prescribed by German regulations. Antonescu was the self-proclaimed, brutal "General of the Legion of the Archangel Michael for the Christian and Racial Renovation of Romania," aka, the Iron Guard—an over-the-top title with not-so-subtle tones of egocentricity and irredeemable self-importance. Without Germany's formidable protection and military resources, Antonescu and Hitler knew the Russians would swoop down from the north and take over Romania and its oil fields.

Antonescu was happy with Hitler's offer for both military and economic aid, which Hitler was more than pleased to provide. A puppet government was formed. To legalize the takeover, a German oil company was established, *Kontinentale*; the majority of ownership went, of course, to German industrialists and the German government. In turn, well-trained, hardened Wehrmacht troops, mostly Luftwaffe, along with 250 first-rate Messerschmitt fighter planes, occupied Romania. They focused on the seven oil fields surrounding the city of Ploiești, staving off, at least for that moment, any potential Russian attempts to take control of the refineries.

On August 23, 1944—ironically, almost a year (to the day) after the Ploiești raid, King Michael I of Romania gained the support of several political parties and put together a coup d'état and deposed Antonescu. At war's end, Antonescu, was prosecuted at the People's Tribunals on charges of war crimes, crimes against the peace, and treason. He was found guilty for the deaths of as many as 400,000 people, most of them Bessarabian, Ukrainian, and Romanian Jews, as well as Romanian Romani—and the regime's complicity in the Holocaust's combined pogroms and mass murders, such as the Odessa massacre. He was pressed against a stone wall and executed by a firing squad of enthused Romanian boy-soldiers in Jilava, Romania, on June 1, 1946. Like Hitler, Antonescu's tenure did not end with a sugary song.

Through that moment in history, and up to the end of the war, the petroleum fields remained under German control. It wasn't until the day the war ended that control took a different turn.

Chapter 7

Eine Falle

La plus belle des ruses du diable est de vous persuader qu'il n'existe pas.
(The devil's finest trick is to persuade you that he does not exist.)
—CHARLES BAUDELAIRE, *LE SPLEEN DE PARIS*

THE LUFTWAFFE ATTACHÉ AT THE GERMAN LEGATION IN BUCHAREST, Romania, since June 1938, was the portly *Generalleutnant* (lieutenant general) Alfred Gerstenberg, age fifty, a personal friend of the more portly and portentous *Reichsmarschall des Grossdeutschen Reiches* (Reich Marshal of the Greater German Reich), Hermann Göring, second in the Nazi hierarchy to the Führer. Because he was the de facto German official in Romania, and liked by Hitler, in February 1942 Gerstenberg was assigned the additional responsibility of Commanding General and Commander of German Luftwaffe (*Kommandierender General und Befehlshaber der Deutschen Luftwaffe*). Above all, he was in charge of German and Romanian forces and the defense of Romania—both air and ground—most notably, those sweet oil fields and refineries around the city of Ploieşti that the Allies and Russians were thirsting after. His loyalty to Führer and Fatherland had been absolute (even though at one time, he had refused to wear the sovereign eagle and swastika on his uniform); Gerstenberg's vow to protect Ploieşti at any cost was not a hollow, sanctimonious, heel-clicking loyalty. He took the responsibility very seriously, with a profound sense of duty. Back in Berlin, he had been a highly respected German officer, among Germany's best. Beyond that, hardly anyone knew him—unlike the Rommels and von Mansteins and Guderians.

He was the devil the Allies should have known, but knew little about. His mostly clandestine military career gave him good cover. Perhaps if the Allies had penetrated his mind, they would have had access to some of his secret defenses and had better results on August 1, 1943.

While in Romania, an inactive theater of war, Gerstenberg had been cut off from the whims and impulses of Hitler. (Ploiești was a nineteen-hour drive, located over 900 miles from Berlin.) Also, he was detached from the meddling of the Luftwaffe High Command (Oberkommando der Luftwaffe), located at Wilhelmstraße 97 in the heart of Berlin, a unique and envious position. He was only beholden to his benefactor, Hermann Göring, his former World War I "Flying Circus" squadron mate, who allowed him free rein, fulfilling practically any requests he made: 250 of the best Messerschmitt fighter planes, seasoned troops, technicians and administrative personnel, and an essential range of the latest antiaircraft guns. Göring gave him the new low-UHF band Würzburg radar, the primary ground-based radar for the Luftwaffe and the Wehrmacht, named after the German city of Würzburg. Gerstenberg also received numerous 88mm antiaircraft artillery guns, one of the deadliest and most respected guns of World War II. And by July of 1943, one month before the Ploiești raid, Gerstenberg had 75,000 Luftwaffe troops, plus an unpaid corvée of Russians laborers, who worked intermittently and for limited periods. Since Romania was an inactive theater of war, it was considered cushy duty by the German troops—no land battles, no flying bullets or bombings, plenty of women, alcohol, nightlife, and good food. This kept the troops in line and maintained good discipline—otherwise, they would be shipped off to the Eastern Front.

⚊⚊

At five-foot-eight, in his blue-gray bespoke Luftwaffe uniforms, silver and gold epaulets, white and gold rank gorgets on his collars, and constantly smoking a cigar, *Generalleutnant* Gerstenberg stood out. He wore the distinguished neck order, the House Order of Hohenzollern (*Hausorden von Hohenzollern* or *Hohenzollernscher Hausorden*), an enameled and gold, dynastic order of knighthood of the House of Hohenzollern awarded to military commissioned officers and civilians of comparable status. When Gerstenberg walked into a room, he sparkled. He had an aura—the beribboned award that hung from his neck, the silver and gold insignia of his high rank, lit up a room like a floodlamp; the cigar and billows of blue smoke added a disarming insouciance—perhaps a deliberate affectation. The right man for the job, and aptly nicknamed the Protector (*der Beschützer*). Altogether, including his brilliant strategist's mind, endowed him with the respect he would require for the problematic, deadly task of protecting Ploiești from destruction, whether it be Russian or American. He had been attending to this, devising and implementing a defense system since he'd arrived in Romania as air attaché in 1938. Two years later Hitler took hold of Romania through a cunning combination of military offense and diplomatic purpose.

— —

Alfred Gerstenberg was born in 1893 in Grainau, a municipality in the district of Garmisch-Partenkirchen, in southern Bavaria, Germany. (The two cities, Garmisch and Partenkirchen, were merged into one for the 1936 Winter Olympics and have remained as one.) At the age of seventeen, in 1912, he began his army service and was sent to the Eastern Front. Later, he transferred into the German air force and flew as an observation aircraft pilot. By 1916, he met good fortune and his name rippled with distinction throughout the Luftwaffe: He joined the famous Richthofen Squadron, *Jagdgeschwader I*, led by one of the best-known fighter pilots of all time: Manfred Albrecht Freiherr von Richthofen—the "Red Baron," a national hero in Germany. (Freiherr denotes a rank—literally, "free lord." In English it means "baron," a title of nobility.) Before his death on April 21, 1918, the Red Baron had been officially credited with eighty air combat victories. The death of such a revered young man was mourned throughout Germany; thousands of young girls' faces glistened with tears over the loss of their handsome, young hero. His fame lingered, however, beyond the Great War to the year 1966, when the Royal Guardsmen had a hit novelty song about the Baron, "Snoopy vs. The Red Baron."

Manfred von Richthofen was the ace of aces in World War I. One of the planes he flew was a Fokker Dr I, a triplane (*Dreidecker*) with three wings, one of the first produced and assigned to Richthofen's

Jagdgeschwader I (abbreviation: *Jasta I*). Von Richthofen had nineteen victories in this aircraft. The plane had been painted a mundane greenwash like all the others from the factory, but von Richthofen's had the upper wing, nose, wheels, and tail painted red—thus, the "Red Baron," a name given to him by British pilots who had much respect for his aeronautical and tactical skills. Why red? In his own words: "For whatever reasons, one fine day I came upon the idea of having my crate painted glaring red. The result was that absolutely everyone could not help but notice my red bird. My opponents also seemed to be not entirely unaware [of it]." Other pilots in his squadron followed his example and painted their planes a variety of bright colors. Because of this, and the squadron's itinerant schedule, *Jasta I* became known as "The Flying Circus."

In October 1917, Gerstenberg's observation plane was shot down, and he suffered a prolonged injury. A year later, after rehabilitation, he returned to the Flying Circus as a non-flying officer.

During this time, Hermann Göring was a fighter pilot in *Jasta I*, also gaining international recognition for himself as a flying ace. He had twenty-two aerial victories and was awarded the esteemed *Pour le Mérite* (For Merit). The award was famously referred to as the "Blue Max" (*Blauer Max*), because of its dazzling gold and blue enamel, and was worn around the neck of the recipient (it is also known as a "throat order"). Göring revered his *Pour le Mérite* more than any other decoration, and he had many. A skilled pilot, handsome and slender at that time, decorated and grandiloquent, the future *Reichsmarschall* of the Third Reich started a long friendship with Gerstenberg at this time. Like Gerstenberg, Göring endured a prolonged recovery from a hip wound during a dogfight. This led to a drug addiction that followed him throughout the Nuremberg trials, where he committed suicide using poison the day before he was to be hanged.

After von Richthofen's death on April 21, 1918, *Hauptmann* (Captain) Wilhelm Reinhard became *Jasta I*'s commanding officer, but his command was short-lived. Reinhard was killed in a flying accident on July 3, 1918. *Oberleutnant* Hermann Göring, on July 14, became *Jasta I*'s third and last commander of the war. From here, the Gerstenberg–Göring relationship grew, and others significant to his career burgeoned.

Another member of *Jasta I* and friend of Gerstenberg's and Göring's, Ernst Udet, was the second-highest-scoring pilot, after von Richthofen, with sixty-two victories. Udet was a squadron commander under von Richthofen and Göring. After the war and through the 1930s, Udet became a stunt pilot, a well-known international barnstormer, a manufacturer of small aircraft, and, most notably, a handsome and charming playboy with dozens of stories to tell the ladies. By 1939, with help from Göring, Udet had risen to the post of director-general of equipment for the Luftwaffe (*Generalluftzeugmeister*), with the rank of colonel general (*generaloberst*), equivalent to a four-star general in the US Air Force.

Udet had many disagreements with Göring and the Nazi party.

On the evening of November 17, 1941, while speaking on the telephone with his girlfriend, Inge Bleyle, Udet shot himself in the head. He left two suicide notes scribed on the headboard of his bed in red grease pencil: one to his girlfriend that said, "Ingelein, why have you left me?" and one to his longtime mentor and squadron mate, Hermann Göring: "Iron One, you are responsible for my death." The world was told Udet died in a flying accident. It is believed his suicide was a result of his contentious relationship with Göring, friction with the Nazi Party, and the loss of his love, Ingelein.

Later, Hitler had unforgiving words for Udet, blaming him for losing the Battle of Britain: "Our defeat [at the Battle of Britain] was caused by Udet. That man concocted the most nonsensical state of affairs ever seen in the history of the Luftwaffe." It had been common knowledge at the time that Göring made Udet the scapegoat for Germany's Battle of Britain's loss.

Ernst Udet is at the *Invalidenfriedhof* (Invalids' Cemetery) in Berlin, established in 1748, one of the oldest, most historic cemeteries in that city. His gravesite rests beside that of his former commanding officer, Manfred von Richthofen. Richthofen had been buried there for years beside *Oberst* Werner Molders, the first pilot in aviation history to shoot down one hundred enemy planes. *Oberst* Werner Molders was killed in a transport plane crash the day he was flying to Udet's funeral. (Because von Richtofen's grave had been on the boundary of the Soviet Union during the Cold War, it was pockmarked by bullets shot at escapees trying to flee from East Germany. In 1975, his family decided to move his grave to a family plot at the *Südfriedhof* in Wiesbaden, Germany.) Now, Udet and Molders are in repose side by side, brothers in arms forever.

⚊ ⚊

In 1919 the Treaty of Versailles stated that Germany was forbidden from ever again having a full-time air force. In 1926 Gerstenberg retired from the air force and was fortunately presented with an invaluable career opportunity. That year, Joseph Stalin allowed Germany to establish a secret flying school at Lipetsk, a city on the banks of the Voronezh River in the Don basin, 272 miles southeast of Moscow. For the next seven years, Gerstenberg wore a Russian uniform, and learned fluent Russian— he already spoke Polish, and would soon learn Romanian—and would eventually turn out some of the leading German aces of World War II. When Hitler came to power in 1933, Stalin gave the boot to the German air school. A year later, Gerstenberg became chief of staff of the German Air Sports Association (*Deutscher Luftsportverband*), or DLV, a deceptive organization, what had been called a "sport flying club," with members spending sunny days "learning to fly." It was a well-known secret that the DLV had been training fighter pilots for the-soon-to-be-formed Luft- waffe. In March of 1933, the DLV was officially blessed by the Nazi Party to bring uniformity, discipline, and professionalism to the training of the nation's future German pilots, a task Gerstenberg knew well. The chair- man of the DLV was his benefactor, Hermann Göring, who appointed him to the position, and the notorious Ernst Röhm, vice chairman and leader of the ruthless *Sturmabteilung* (Storm Battalion), or SA. The DLV served the country—Hitler—as the forerunner of the most intimidating air force in history, the Luftwaffe.

Gerstenberg's command and administration of the DLV taught him, undoubtedly, the art of not being seen but being felt. That was the whole purpose of the DLV: to hide its intention from the world, to "conform" to the Treaty of Versailles, something Gerstenberg would effectively apply through the end of his command in Romania—an act of prestidigitation, a magic act of mental tricks that only a devil could efficiently perform to fool the enemy.

During the time Gerstenberg served in World War I, and up to his chief of staff position in the DLV, he remained inconspicuous; it was his nature. The Allies had their eyes on many military leaders in Germany during this period, but Gerstenberg was not one of them. Consequently, he was able to go about the business of setting up defenses around Ploieşti, the scope of which was almost overlooked. It appears Gerstenberg had many tricks up his sleeve, many strategies, and little effort by the Allies had been made to learn what those tricks were, what his capabilities were. Particularly, how could his proficiencies affect the results of the August 1 raid on Ploieşti? Until his position as air attaché in Romania in 1940, he had been a cipher, and between that time and the raid on the oil fields, he remained discreet, a semi-mystery, much to Colonel Smart's disadvantage. Not knowing who his nemesis was put Smart and the airmen who flew the mission on August 1 in a lopsided position. If the Americans' minds had been focused more on Gerstenberg's proclivities and career history, perhaps the raid on Ploieşti would have had a different result.

Meanwhile, the Germans continued building a phone-book-thick dossier of detailed intelligence on the Casablanca Conference, beginning with the day it first convened. *Oberst* Georg Alexander Hansen, Chief of Division I, Office of Foreign Military Intelligence (*Amt Ausland / Abwehr*), in Wünsdorf, Germany, took control of the dossier. He had been collating bits and pieces on all the critical Casablanca attendees—those personages in the black-and-white photo on the lawn of the Anfa Hotel—including, of course, Col. Jacob Smart, standing there on the outer edge of the historical picture.

Gerstenberg had also been studying the roster of relevant US Army Air Corps personnel. He kept adding to his dossier on Gen. Lewis H. Brereton of the 9th Air Force, who would command the main component of the raid, the 9th Bomber Command. He knew Brereton had been a controversial officer: During 1927, the year Lindbergh crossed the Atlantic, Brereton experienced a stressful amount of friction with his wife and his superiors, who thought he spent too much time working on technical boards and not enough time on his command duties. He also had a reputation for hard drinking. Returning to Langley, Virginia, from maneuvers in Texas in May 1927, Brereton was the co-pilot of an aircraft that experienced engine failure over Reynoldsburg, Ohio, and crashed, killing a passenger. Soon after, Brereton requested and received a medical leave because of "incipient fear of flying." Simultaneously, his wife left him and filed for divorce. All of this, Gerstenberg observed, caused "nervous anxiety, insomnia, and nightmares." To add to his stress, a misunderstanding led to a reprimand for being AWOL for leading an aerial escort for Charles A. Lindbergh's return from France. It was Brereton who initially outlined the Tidal Wave mission in his orders: "To destroy installations in the PLOIEŞTI area, which will deny the enemy of the petroleum products produced and distilled from the Rumanian [*sic*] oil fields."

Also of interest to Gerstenberg was Bob Sternfels's commanding officer, Col. John Riley "Killer" Kane, commander of the 98th Bomb Group, who reported to Brereton, and would lead the third wave of bombers over Ploieşti.

~~~

The Americans had no idea how predictive HALPRO was, or how accurately it had telegraphed to the Germans—Gerstenberg—what their long-term strategy foreshadowed. Gerstenberg viewed the mostly ineffective raid as an "excellent forecast," a prequel of sorts, of what would undoubtedly come to pass. He studied HALPRO; he applied pieces of it to his defense for Ploieşti. He wisely acknowledged that there would be no strategic value for the Americans to attack the city of Bucharest; they wanted to destroy petroleum production, and there was nothing like that in or around Bucharest. He was sure they would try to stay away, too, from the city of Ploieşti itself; they would focus their resources, their main force majeure, on the oil fields located miles outside the city. And that's where he would concentrate the bulk of his defense system.

HALPRO also alerted the Protector to what would soon descend on him with certainty: the routes the Americans would fly to the oil fields, their egress routes, and, undoubtedly, the use of their long-range bomber, the B-24 Liberator—what Germans condescendingly referred to as a "moving van." The Americans, he knew, would adjust, correct, and fine-tune the B-24's range and operative bomb load and overall weight. And, too, the Protector would continue to analyze the young, thirty-nine-year-old colonel, Jacob Smart.

Nothing in the war right now mattered more than the petroleum fields Gerstenberg had been ordered to protect. He knew the Americans would be back, yes, but he did not know when. Unlike other less-effective strategies, he chose to set up his defenses in the south, southwest, and southeast, the routes the Americans would use. This meant that they would be flying from North Africa; he guesstimated Benghazi.

He knew the Americans had the resources, a fire in their belly, to reach out thousands of miles and drop tons of bombs. The Protector would have fourteen months to sharpen his pencil and strategically spread his multifarious guns, fighter planes, and antiaircraft platforms in a strategic perimeter around the hills and valleys and roads and railroad tracks of Ploieşti.

After all his plans and fighters were in place, after all the guns were in situ to bring down the American attack, the Protector had amassed a more significant defense than what was currently situated around his nation's capital, Berlin. At this moment, Ploieşti boasted the world's most critical defense system. Although Gerstenberg was unquestionably the master of defense, "the air defense genius of the war," he has never received his due, nor has there been much written about him—until now.

The Protector was not going to allow a thirty-nine-year-old American colonel's strategy involving a bunch of damned ugly moving vans to blow through his air defenses and wreck his refineries without a massive, dazzling barrage of corrosive hellfire. The Protector would be ready. Any nibbles or large bites at his defenses would trigger him and his strategy, full force.

The American boys who took off on that first day of August in 1943 would be leaving the Smart Plan and its deficiencies behind, flying into Gerstenberg's crafty mind, sharpened to a deadly point.

All of them, every one of them, flying headfirst into *Eine Falle*.

A trap.

CHAPTER 8

The Sandman Would Live Forever

The sadness will last forever.

—Vincent van Gogh

On May 24, 1943, Robert Sternfels and his crew landed in Benina, their new desert "airfield" not far from Benghazi.

"Airfield" here is a misnomer, as it connotes a traditional, paved runway, and a variety of functional buildings, like hangars and living quarters for sleeping and taking meals, and comforts, like running water and toilets. No such amenities existed in Benina. Nothing existed at Benina. Benina was biblical. Benina was a vacant desert area—sand, scrub, a vast searing, blue sky that would scorch the camouflage paint on the B-24s and sauteé it to a homely pink. The sun suited itself. The average temperature hovered at 95-plus with a daunting lack of humidity. When it rained, it was a hallowed event that could cause flash flooding. But it never rained. Blue sky and reddish-pink sand extended to the horizon and shimmered a gossamer veil of heat haze, scribing a path to an unknown alternative hell.

The "runway" was a hard-as-cement tract crafted level for B-24s to land and take off. There were no hangars. There were no "sleeping quarters." There were pup tents set up randomly to obscure a discernible target for bombing and strafing by Luftwaffe fighters stationed 250 miles away, should they come. Friends were the kangaroo rats, because they were cute. Landlords were lethal scorpions, beefy tarantulas with glittering eyes and fangs the size of billhooks. You shook your boots before you put your toe in, oh yeah. And then you did it again. Sometimes it was better to fly through killer flak than slip into a boot and have a toe nuzzle up against an aggrieved scorpion.

Benina could only be pleasant and lovely if you were not in Benina; if it were a "back there" memory.

Benina was primeval.

Benina stunk.

For Bob Sternfels and the crew, it would be "fun and exciting" for who knew how long, and they would make the best of it. Soon, with the onset of reality, dark clouds would descend, grow bleak, and bring a reflective ambiguity—which, despite their youth and their life's experiences, they knew would lead to unrelenting anxiety as long as they flew in this war.

Stink or not, Bob and his young crew would tolerate their desert home, the venomous landlords and discomforts, and go about the perilous business of making war as best they could. They started by getting down to the dull business of housing, setting up their "living quarters." Bob recalled:

> We were ordered to report to the 98th Bomb Group, and they placed me in the 345 Squadron. The first thing they handed us was a shovel, a tent, and a hammer. We dug into the sand only to find it was solid rock just below the surface, but we pitched the tent which had a standard English type double roof. It was much better than the GI tents for desert living. Later, we got the armament guys to blow up the rock. Then we could step down into the ground, which was cooler and gave us more headroom. Temperatures were over 100 every day, and without any ice coolers of any kind, living wasn't what I expected from the Air Corps.

Although it might not have been what he expected, Robert Warren Sternfels was built for the desert. Built for flying bombers. Built for combat, skillful and deft. He was the quintessential "all-American boy," a charter member of Tom Brokaw's "The Greatest Generation." And he would remain the all-American boy to the end of his blessed life. Bob could make you laugh, but not cry. He would not want to do that.

Bob was born and raised in the middle of America in a manicured Detroit suburb, when America's growth and force began to flourish with good fortune and potential. He was built for flying a complicated, hand-made American, albeit ugly, bomber with a million parts crafted mostly by American women.

Not too many people had Bob's skill. At an early age, he developed an inborn mechanical ability and mind-set to learn flying, to master its complexity, its mystery, its nuances, to blunt its surprises. He had the square-jawed presence of William Holden, confident but not overcooked. The quiet strength of Gary Cooper, handsome but in a traditional way. The charm of Jimmy Stewart, the smile of a trickster. He smoked a pipe, and this meant he looked bookish or collegiate. He was fun to be around. He was an easy guy, a guy's guy, and a girl's guy, too, always with a smile on his face, and you wanted to share that. When Bob walked into a living room, a bar, an office, you knew there was "Bob in the air." You saw Bob, you wanted to talk to him. And he would take you in, in a soft, easy, approachable way.

You wanted Bob on your side. You trusted him. You admired him. You could put your life in Bob's hands, as his crew did, without doubt of heart or flesh or mind. When you flew into hell, you wanted to look behind and see Bob the angel leading the way with the reins in his hands, saving your back with the skill of a combat-tested, multi-missioned, bomber pilot. America's best up there in the cockpit, thank you. You would want him piloting that complicated bird you were strapped to, because, damn it, you knew Bob Sternfels would do his best to get you back to the scorpions and tarantulas—maybe not whole, but he'd get you back.

Bob was built to endure the enemy's hellfire and suppress his fear; he wasn't afraid to admit that he was just as fearful as you, but you wouldn't know the difference. Bob was a leader. Bob was the boy every American mom would love to bake a Sunday apple pie for, or have marry their daughter. He just knew his way to wherever he was meant to go. And he got it right almost all of the time. He was not perfect. He could raise hell above his head. But this he was built for, this flying stuff—this living. And everyone in his crew felt it, and they slept well with it every night.

And that was Bob. There were no other Bobs like him anywhere else.

After a few weeks at Benina, the air force decided to move Bob's squadron to Herglia, a little west of Benina—another former Italian air force base. The only difference between Herglia and Benina was the name. Herglia was set in a dry lake bed. "The Luftwaffe had used it before for their Messerschmitt fighters," said Bob, "but the hard-sand runway was long enough to take a big bird like the B-24."

That would soon change.

"One night, during a rainstorm, I woke up," Bob recalled, "and my tail was soaking wet, and I thought I'd lost it. But when I reached down, my hand was in water up to the edge of the cot—that's about a foot and a half of water. So much for a dry lake bed. Almost everything was floating. The Luftwaffe knew when to use the lake bed, and when not to use it, all right, but they weren't courteous enough to tell us Americas—that's why they left the place. Our bombers had water up to the bomb-bay bomb holders, and of course, we could not start or move any of the aircraft. It was a real mess. I lost a new camera, and everything I owned was wet. It was days before the water receded, but the rust caused many problems with the bomb-release mechanism, and bombs would hang up even after the bombardier released them. I had this happen to us."

What do you do with 500 pounds of Tritonal that would not fall after the bombardier actuated the release button?

Not much.

"First thing, you politely ask the bombardier—his name was Dave Polaschek—'Dave, do you have time to come up from the nose and kick the bomb loose, because it could hurt somebody?' You tell him all on board would be most grateful. Once there, Dave has to stand in the narrow walkway between the nose of the plane and the tail. Of course, the bomb-bay doors must be open. Dave's not a happy guy at that moment, because he's looking down to earth from about 12,000 feet without a parachute, which, of course, he left back in the nose, kicking away, cursing at that damn bomb. A bit exciting, no? No wonder Dave objected. But he tried and he failed.

"At the same time that Dave was grunting, cursing, and kicking, we also had a damned engine failure, so I elected to land in Sicily with only three fans turning," said Bob. "The runway was short with a stone wall at the end. It was just dirt and not unusually rough. I decided to land short, and when the bird touched down, that 500-pound baby did what she wanted to do for a long time, and finally cut loose and hit that damned runway with a stunning sound—for one second, the scariest sound I'd ever heard in my entire life. All the guys were forward, but of course, the bomb did not explode. Polaschek had replaced the safety pins so the detonator would not revolve. The next day some poor soul drove out onto the runway and removed the bomb. Luck was shining on us."

As soon as the water receded," Bob recalled, they moved back to Benina.

Bob's tent at Benina was the only one that had an indoor wash sink with running water. "Also, an outside shower that I made using the rear section of an old German biplane that we found in the graveyard," Bob noted. "I had a 50-gallon drum welded on top of the 'A' frame from the biplane. Each day the water truck guys would check the level of the tank. During the day, when temperatures were in the 100s, our water would warm up, so returning from a mission we were able to take hot showers—there's nothing like a hot shower, even in the desert. Only my tent was so equipped," said Bob. "I also spotted a heavy electrical cable on the ground a short distance from our tent, and by getting a few items from the city of Benghazi's bombed-out buildings, I also had an electric light inside the tent. Believe it or not, not having a light in the tent was a big deal. All my early learning of mechanical skills paid off.

"Of course, the squadron needed an area to relax," Bob continued.

What officer would be caught drinking scotch in the open in the desert?

So, what happened? Bob decided early on that his group was desperate for a club.

Bob said, "We had nothing, not even a tree, just scorpions and big spiders, some natives with camels who we called Wogs, lots of dust, sand and wind that began at eleven a.m. So, I asked our intelligence officer, who was a good guy, if he could round up a truck, a cement mixer, and two-by-fours that could be used for framing. The motor pool guys gave me a wink. A couple of days later, here they come with one GI truck, four guys to assist my officer in stealing the things I needed to build an officers' club. In the truck, they had an old Italian cement mixer, cement, and wood. The guys at the motor pool got the mixer to work; the water truck guys gave me the water; and a few of the guys in the squadron built the forms. We used the desert's sand with what little cement we had—at least it was a floor."

It didn't take long for Bob's "officers' club" floor to start to turn to powder. But other pieces of the club began to take shape, and soon, it was flourishing.

"The walls were palm fronds," Bob said, "but the top was from an old English officer's tent, which was large enough to cover an area about twelve feet by twelve feet. The sides allowed the air to pass through but held out some of the blowing sand. The top shaded the area, so at least we were able to get out of the sun. Without a doubt, it was the most popular place in the desert. Even the scorpions thought so. However, now, we needed a bar."

Bob and two of the crew drove into Benghazi and found an old bombed-out house. "As it turned out," he said, "it was the summer home of Benito Mussolini, for when he visited Benghazi. All we needed were chairs, so we helped ourselves to a few and left."

Bob's officers' club stood for a long time as the favorite hangout. "We had most everything," Bob said, "but not a drop of beer. Plenty of Coca-Cola, which we took on missions. Sometimes the outside temperature [up in the air] was minus-fifty, so we kept Cokes in the tail of the plane."

⸺ ⸺

Between June and July, Bob Sternfels flew fifteen missions as a command pilot. The reality of death flew with him on every mission. On July 13, Bob saw the most horrific thing he had seen since flying combat missions—that is up, until the raid on Ploiești:

> *We were returning from Catalonian, Italy, and I watched two B-24s get hit; they just exploded at the same time, and their fuselages were covered in flames. Both started to turn left and headed straight down to the Mediterranean Sea. The pilot from the number-two position wanted to cross under the number-three element. As soon as he got under, he pulled back a little too much on the control*

wheel. His nose slammed into the belly of number one, and both of them slipped down, out of control. Both went down smoking and in flames. We lost twenty men right there.

━━━━

Landing after that mission, the crew collectively decided to name their B-24—not at Bob's suggestion, or that of any other crewmen. This was a communal decision that would bond men and bomber, a glue. Their B-24 would be "she" or "her," and whatever name they chose that would hold them together, that they would remember for the rest of their lives.

Almost as soon as they had arrived in Benina, it had become tediously apparent that the Germans weren't the crew's only opponent. The sand was a force majeure; it was everywhere, and would have a wearying, pernicious effect, not only on the men, but on the performance and efficacy of their complicated aircraft: sand in their water, sand in their food, sand in their underwear, sand in their bedding, sand in every niche and crevice of their B-24 from bow to stern.

Like men and their cars, the crew loved their aircraft and babied her with tender, loving care. What devotion they applied at home fiddling with cars to make them their own, they applied to their B-24—to her skin, her mechanicals, her spirit. They used a variety of paintbrushes to dust the sand from the delicate instruments and controls, devices their lives depended upon. The enlisted men used brooms to sweep her innards. The mechanics who maintained the engines, fuel systems, and other sensitive controls applied constant, meticulous attention to rid their aircraft of the omnipresent grit, a never-ending challenge that, once completed, would have to begin all over again.

Thus, the nuisance of the sand and its persistent intrusion generated the name for their B-24—*The Sandman*. It was their bomber, and it had to bear an apropos signature that would eventually be historically significant (little did they know at the time). They would take that name with them to the end of their lives, never forgetting her name or the day they named her. They painted her name in tall, prideful, five-foot-tall, bubble-style red letters outlined in white on both sides of her blunt desert-pink nose. It had a lot of pop, and everyone who gazed at it loved it.

Above the words, they added a five-foot-tall caricature of Walt Disney's classic Donald Duck, in mid-stride, his big webbed feet on a brown splotch of "sand," and slung over Donald's shoulder, a large, cloud-white duffel bag of sand, a la Santa Claus. The bag's bottom has a slash, and three red bombs are caught spilling out. Donald looks annoyed, aggressive; his beak is tightly clenched. After each mission, a smaller caricature of Donald would be added below the lettering. When the picture was taken with Bob and crew against *The Sandman*'s lettering, there were twenty-one little Donalds painted below her name—twenty-one missions flown. Twenty-one missions the boys survived.

When the paint dried on the lettering, the crew checked out the artwork and felt a swell of pride and fondness for an airplane that would, for the duration of all their lives, have a profound and solemn significance. *The Sandman* would occupy their dreams, be the epicenter of their nightmares, be glued to the pages of careworn scrapbooks of mind and heart, and held closer and deeper in memory until age took them to the end of their lives. Oh, no, *The Sandman* would never abandon them. Her sand would never run out. Never be swept away. Would be indelible. She would touch their lives with horror, with affection. Prompt feelings of love and scorn. Be cursed and praised.

And for all of them, she would be a heartfelt landmark of this singular and true notion: that the time with her was the most monumental of their lives, and together with her they were one and strong and indissoluble, or so they prudently believed when they flew with her.

The Sandman would vanish one day, yes, her bony metal and her oily blood and ugly pink paint would dissolve and leave her boys, never to bear or protect them again. But she would always be their dear and beautiful *Sandman*. If she was crushed and scattered by the forces of physics, ravaged and holed by the bullets of a resolute enemy, damned by age and rust and neglect, she would continue to be theirs, and no one—no force from then till eternity's fall—would ever take her specter from them.

She was theirs, and they were inseparable.

Among them, *The Sandman* would live forever.

CHAPTER 9

The Defense Did Not Rest

Everybody wants to get to heaven, but nobody wants to die.
—Joe Louis,
Heavyweight Boxing Champion of the World

In February 1942, *Reichsmarschall* Hermann Göring appointed Alfred Gerstenberg *Kommandierender General und Befehlshaber der Deutschen Luftwaffe*—Commanding General and Commander of German Luftwaffe in Romania. Gerstenberg bore the vast responsibility for the security and wholeness of the refineries around Ploiești, his highest priority—not only at the hour of his appointment, but for the duration of his military career, which would conclude at the end of the war in Bucharest. Up to the day of his appointment by old friend Göring, Gerstenberg studied, revised, and fine-tuned the defensive landscape. He had been at this since his arrival in Bucharest in 1938—ostensibly as Germany's "air attaché." And since the fizzled HALPRO mission in 1942—which gave away America's future bombing intentions—Gerstenberg had had thirteen months to devise, plan, prepare, and "gird his loins" for what he surely knew would be another, stronger, attack on the refineries, and he continued his unrelenting efforts to perfect Ploiești's defenses. When the Americans arrived in their "moving van" bombers, as the Protector referred to them, he would be ready.

His first action after his elevation: flushing out and ousting known spies throughout Romania and initiating harsh efforts to block all forms of espionage within its borders. At that time, he ordered any member of the Luftwaffe who was "noodling" with local women—which he approved of, with a wink—to report the details of such "conjoining." Collated, these contacts would yield bits and pieces of valuable intelligence and add to the mosaic of *das große Ganze*—"the big picture." This directive allowed his troops to fraternize openly, kept their morale up, and sifted information from a variety of sources that could be useful. The German forces were happy to comply, because they knew if they didn't, trains left every day from Ploieşti to the Russian front, and could take them from their comfortable Romanian tour to the horrors of combat and flying bullets on the Eastern front.

The Protector had learned—and grew to appreciate—the art of secrecy while overseeing the secret flying school at Lipetsk, established in 1926. In hindsight, American army intelligence should have initiated a "Gerstenberg desk" on the day Göring appointed him chief of staff at the DLV, in 1933. By that time, Gerstenberg had already gained plenty of organizational experience, discipline, and know-how. The DLV—the German Air Sports Association—had been established by the Nazi Party that year to unify a system to train German citizen-pilots to fly military aircraft for the soon-to-be-formed Luftwaffe. Gerstenberg's chief-of-staff role furthered the basics of secrecy, deception, and the fine art of sleight-of-hand tactics, lessons that he carried with him throughout the balance of his career, especially useful to his position in Romania. In 1933, Hitler and the Nazis had just assumed power in Germany, and it would not have taken a military strategist to determine that the Führer would start building a new, formidable armed force again, despite the strictures of the Treaty of Versailles.

Unlike other famous German general officers, like Erwin Rommel, the Protector had no "publicity," no "brand."

Military theorist and field marshal Erwin Rommel was a Hitler favorite, a larger-than-life figure both in Germany and among the Allies. (He appeared on the cover of *Time* magazine on July 13, 1942.) In October 1938, Hitler requested that Rommel take command of his elite *Führerbegleitbataillon* (escort battalion), a highly honored position because of its proximity to the Führer.

Even though Gerstenberg held a high-level, highly visible position, the Allies did not feel compelled to initiate a dossier anywhere near the scope of the intelligence they assembled on the renowned Rommel.

In essence, the outposts of Gerstenberg's mind went unexplored outside the Luftwaffe, either as a skilled officer or tactician. When World War I started, he had begun his military service riding horses in the cavalry, a lackluster career path. He later switched to the air force, at a time when "modern" motorized vehicles were developing rapidly. But Gerstenberg had "friends in high places"—namely, Göring—and that facilitated his career.

The American airmen would be shocked at the sight of the air defenses the Protector had designed when they first spotted them, just minutes before their Liberators hit their initial checkpoints. This exposed two crucial points: Gerstenberg's tactical genius and the Americans' lack of sufficient intelligence on what was a most potent defense. Because of this insufficient US intelligence gathering, the biggest surprise for Bob Sternfels and his crew would be the number of guns and their prolific placement before reaching the targets, as well as the caliber and capability of those guns.

Overall, Gerstenberg's zeal, tactical skill, and enthusiasm made Ploiești *Festung Ploiești*—Fortress Ploiești. An unconquerable city.

Ploiești is situated between two valleys cut by the Prahova and Teleajen Rivers, about 40 miles north of Bucharest. (From the air, the silhouettes of Ploiești and Targoviste can appear similar, one of the factors that caused fatal confusion on the day of the mission.) Gerstenberg placed daunting 88mm and 20mm flak guns just under the ridgelines along the higher portions of these valleys, thus diminishing the guns' telltale silhouettes against the sky.

Flierabwehr Kanone is German for "airplane defense cannon," abbreviated as flak, and often referred to as AAA (or "triple-A"), or "ack-ack." One of the most successful guns of World War II, the 88 had been responsible for destroying hundreds of American aircraft—mostly B-17s and B-24s—over Europe. The shell fired at an ear-busting 2,600 feet per second—about 1,700 mph—and up to an effective altitude of 26,000 feet. Gerstenberg also populated *Festung Ploiești* with 105mm flak guns that could rocket to a height of nearly 42,000 feet, traveling at a blistering

2,800 feet per second. Both guns were devastatingly accurate, revered, and much feared, particularly by the aircrews getting shot at.

Hermann Göring supplied the Protector with a total of 237 new 88s and 105s that greeted the arrival of the B-24s. The American airmen had no accurate idea of the placement or approximate numbers of these guns and erroneously presumed, according to the faulty intelligence they were given, that they only need be concerned with 100 Romanian guns operated by less-experienced Romanian troops—not Luftwaffe—a paltry amount in comparison. This much firepower—more guns than populated the city of Berlin—was impressive, hard to imagine, and unprecedented. In essence, it said that the Nazis had more apprehension about protecting Ploiești's refineries than anxiety over the protection and safety of the people in their nation's capital.

The flak guns, in their various calibers, had been mounted in distinctive flak towers and machine-gun pits. Some were hidden in church steeples, rooftops, and water towers, even in haystacks that would peel open like artichokes—any area or structure that would present a clear line of fire to the incoming bombers. And it seemed wherever the Americans looked they saw muzzle flashes from 2- and 3.7cm guns the day they arrived—all of it a hailstorm of unprecedented power, accompanied by shots from anyone on the ground who had handheld weapons.

To add to the defense, Gerstenberg provided another unthinkable horror, a bit of military razzle-dazzle for the Americans to confront, something no one had seen before, an indication of the Germans' genius for weaponry: a flak train, or "Q-Train." This "weapon"—and it was a daunting one—was an armored train, a massive steel caterpillar bristling with a variety of flak guns mounted on top of flat railcars protected by thick armor plating.

The Germans knew the route the Americans would be flying—there was only one pathway into Ploiești, flying from North Africa, a safe assumption by Gerstenberg; and spies around the Benghazi airfields notified the *Abteilung Nachrichtenbeschaffung* (Division I, Secret Intelligence) when the Americans took off. The intelligence division told Gerstenberg that a large force of B-24s had taken off, and so they set up the flak train to greet them along their route. The train rolled onto a railroad spur that led straight from Floresti into Ploieşti. Floresti was the final IP (initial point, or checkpoint) where the B-24s would turn right and follow the railroad tracks to Ploieşti.

Two American bomber formations—Bob Sternfels's 98th Bombardment Group (aka, the Pyramidiers, or Desert Rats), flying to the left of the spur at an altitude of 50 feet, and the 44th Bombardment Group (the Flying Eight-Balls), flying on the right of the tracks, same height— were separated below by the railway spur that connected Travesti behind the bombers with Ploieşti ahead of them. Both formations were cutting through the Romanian air at 160 mph.

The spur dividing the two formations was not a surprise; air force navigators flying the mission had been told by intelligence briefings to "use the spur as a reference point directly into Ploieşti." It had been chosen as a visual reference for the formations' navigators to follow to the target ("Take the A Train, boys" was the mnemonic trigger, referring to a famous 1939 Duke Ellington hit song; or, alternatively, follow the "Chattanooga Choo Choo.")

Call it anything you want, but devastating it would be.

"Seventy-five percent of the aircraft lost in the 98th Bomb Group were shot down by that damned Q-Train!" said Bob Sternfels. This means that out of forty aircraft flying parallel to the spur, twenty-five were either damaged or destroyed. "You only have to do the numbers to determine how many men—ten guys in each bird—were killed or wounded at that point. And that was *before* we hit the target! And," added Bob, "we were flying so low and slow, we could count the railroad ties. The Germans were firing at sitting ducks."

And there was more.

Another horrific shock was waiting in the basket of German surprises: Gerstenberg employed barrage balloons, tethered to trucks with electric winches. At the end of the cable on the ground, the Germans attached an explosive device the size of a gallon of paint, with an impact fuse. If a B-24 caught the 1-inch-thick cable on a wing or propeller, the explosive device would be yanked up to the aircraft, make contact, and explode with absolutely deadly results. Or, the cable would slice a wing or decimate a spinning propeller. The balloons were deployed when an attack was imminent.

After the attack, reconnaissance photos revealed twenty-three balloons—again, that was *after* the attack, something that should have been seen before.

Many have discounted the belief that there were spies at Benghazi's airfields, observing everything the American airmen did: what days, times, and directions they flew; the number of aircraft they had; the types of bombs they loaded; the number of men. The airfield had no perimeter fence; it was an amorphous, ill-defined area out in a desert, and anyone could come and go without being challenged.

Bob Sternfels was there for some time and has analyzed events. His version concludes that the Germans knew much more than the USAAF realized at the time. Their Luftwaffe had occupied Benina until the flooding situation had become untenable, abandoning the area for a base about 250 miles away.

"But," Bob said, "they left some spies behind. One day this guy on a camel stopped a short distance from *The Sandman*. Calmly, I walked toward him. He had what looked like a towel over his head. And as I got closer to him, he turned and gave the camel a gentle kick and they left. But I got a good look at his face. I thought, 'Libyans don't have blue eyes and blond hair.' That was not the first or last time I saw this. More of them came from time to time, and all of them had that Caucasian look. In reviewing the actual events, the facts, not notions, not the words authors have invented, the conclusion was that the Germans knew of our plans days in advance of our strike against Ploieşti. And that's why they kicked our ass the day we arrived."

In a June 12, 2006, e-mail to this author, Bob wrote: "When I coined the phrase 'spies in Benghazi' in a previous e-mail to you, this was based on the reception given us as we turned at the IP heading to our assigned target, which was the Dutch refinery called Astra Romania—we knew it as target number 44. The barrage of gunfire was astounding, unbelievable. Never saw anything like it before or after my fifty missions. My assigned position in the formation was third plane in from the deadly Q-Train, the flak train on my right. Greeting our planes was the most intense barrage of machine-gun and antiaircraft fire that anyone can imagine. With that kind of reception, the Germans knew we were coming."

One of the most effective weapons, according to the pilots who flew the strike, were smoke generators. That day, smoke, in its simplicity, fogged up the ground, obscured designated targets, and caused confusion. Often this resulted in bombardiers guessing when to drop their bombs, and many were off target.

For air defense, the Germans had four *Gruppen* of 120 nimble Me 109 Messerschmitt fighters, and an additional two hundred Italian Macchi C.200s strategically nestled on airfields covering the likely routes the American boys would take to and from the refineries.

Efficient, effective, and deadly.

That's why they called him the Protector.

— —

Like Gerstenberg, Smart stood out in his own way.

US Army Air Force officer, Col. Jacob Edward Smart, age thirty-nine, devised, concocted, and formulated some of the most sensitive military plans in American military history and, like Gerstenberg, received scant recognition for his efforts. He wasn't only working on the Ploiești strike. He and his support staff at the new Pentagon in Washington, DC, were also designing enormously intricate and elaborate plans for the most secret of military secrets: The invasion of Europe (Normandy) by Allied forces, and the defeat of Nazi Germany and the tyranny it had wrought.

But right now, on his desk, Smart was finalizing the nuts and bolts, the final draft, for the radical and perilous low-level bombing mission to Ploiești. The basic bolt in Smart's plan held that the mission would need to destroy 40 percent of the oil and refineries at Ploiești if it were to be deemed a success. One of the briefing officers told the airmen that "if 75 percent of you failed to return, the mission would still be profitable"—a statement that made 100 percent of them feel less than confident in the group's leadership.

Adding his observation, Lt. Anthony W. Flesch, *The Sandman*'s navigator, said, "The thing I remember was Kane [Colonel Kane, the 98th's commander] saying that 'if we knock the target out and none of us gets back, it'll [still] be a success.' That was a joy to hear."

— —

Gerstenberg and Smart were equals in multiple ways: Both had lengthy tenures in the military; both had talented, resourceful staffs devoted to their vision, and the means to carry through; and both possessed tactical minds for devising elaborate military strategies.

But that's where the equivalents dropped off a cliff. Variances in detail started to take over, favoring one man over the other.

The Germans had started gathering pertinent intelligence when the Casablanca Conference convened; they knew that the august group of military minds standing behind Roosevelt and Churchill at the Anfa Hotel in Casablanca intended not only to defeat the Axis powers, but to obliterate them, specifically their chief nemesis, Nazi Germany. Also, German intelligence knew that Jacob Smart was General Hap Arnold's aide; they had a copy of the historic photograph taken on the lawn showing flanks of bemedaled participants of the highest ranks and stature—it had been seen all over the world. Since the day the photo had appeared, they had been building a dossier on Jacob Smart, and as each day wore on, the folder grew thicker, heavier, and more penetrating. They never took their eyes off Smart.

Conversely, the Americans were remiss in gathering intelligence on Alfred Gerstenberg.

The Germans had another advantage on their side: The Tidal Wave strike force did not know that a coded message had been sent from the 9th Air Force to the 8th Air Force Command, alerting them that Tidal Wave had taken off from the Benghazi airfields.

Bob Sternfels recalled that the message had been intercepted, and decoded by German intelligence:

They knew a significant mission was under way, but not the destination. That information came three hours later from German radar installations in Sicily and along the Adriatic. Since the aircraft were slowly climbing as their fuel burned off and the mission profile did not call for low-level flight at this time, they were picked up by luminescent screens. Now the Germans knew in which direction they were heading. They were going not to their favorite targets in Italy, but to either Greece, Yugoslavia, Bulgaria, or Romania. All they [the Germans] had to do was wait for the next radar contact.

Gerstenberg's forces, well-designed and in place, had only to wait in the bushes, poised for the Americans to arrive. Meanwhile, the Luftwaffe's guns were in place; the Germans most certainly had spies in and around Bucharest; several fighter squadrons had been on standby, prepared to shoot down the Liberators; and there were diverse surprises copiously placed here and there.

And what did Smart's plan have?

No room for error.

Smart had to mount a force of heavy bombers designed to drop bombs, ideally, from 12,000 to 25,000 feet—not speeding at 200 mph, like a fighter plane, less than 100 feet above the ground. His plan was a multifaceted, intricate, lacework of details that had to mesh accurately and on time, or else it would crumble. Lest it be forgotten: If all went precisely as Smart planned, the attack would have had better results than initially designed.

And whose side was God on?

Gerstenberg would undoubtedly say his. And Smart would, of course, answer, "Mine."

The belt buckles the Germans wore on their uniforms bore an inscription embossed in a semicircle on the square, flat-gray metal: *Gott mit uns.* "God with us."

And American currency law clearly states that all US currency has to bear four words: In God We Trust.

Everybody was praying to God—*Favor our side.*

But God does not answer all prayers.

The devil too often does; oh, yes.

On August 1, 1943, the difference between Gerstenberg's battle plan and Smart's battle plan was that the devil would outbalance God on the field of combat.

On this day, the devil's details would favor one over the other—that of the Protector.

CHAPTER 10

Spies

When sorrows come, they come not single spies, but in battalions.
—WILLIAM SHAKESPEARE

ROBERT STERNFELS PONDERED AFTER THE WAR: "NOW THE QUESTION is: How could the Germans know where to place the [flak] train at exactly the right time, going in the right direction, on the right track, when nine rail tracks were heading to Ploiești's refineries? Was it luck? Or, did they have prior knowledge of our plans?"

He continued: "For years I have wondered how the Germans [could] have known where we would turn at Floresti [to] follow the rail spur, and what target we would hit. I have been accumulating every bit of information I could about the possibility of spies in our area [the airfield]."

In addition to firsthand knowledge picked up at his airfield outside Benghazi, where he saw things with his own eyes, Bob learned from many American airmen that "there were spies among us in Benghazi." And there was not much they could do about it, except maybe maybe try to shoo them away.

In retrospect, the Americans—particularly senior-grade officers—made no effort to secure the bases where the B-24s were parked, where the airmen slept, ate, and met in tents, as they might on a camping trip. And maybe this is why they would not accept the fact of spies; if they had, maybe they would have asked why their security was practically nonexistent in and around the bases.

Bob's "camping area," the airfield, was without protection as we know it today. The only deterrents to fend off intruders were the copious scorpions and spiders. And they were neutral. There was no perimeter fence, no main gate, no ID required, no guards with rifles, and no ferocious dogs. And many "Wogs" wandered around the area all the time. (*Wog* was a pejorative term the Americans picked up from the Brits to describe the Libyans. This offensive ethnic slur was used in Australian and British English, and is considered derogatory today. But out in the desert in 1943, among a group of mostly twenty-year-old American airmen who hadn't yet heard the term "politically incorrect," it was part of common parlance. According to Webster's, *Wog* is "used as an insulting and contemptuous term for a dark-skinned foreigner, and especially for one from the Middle East or the Far East.")

"Our briefings," Bob said, "were mostly in the open, as we did not have buildings or huge tents for meetings before a mission. So, anyone who wanted to hear could stand behind those that were seated on the bomb crates we sat on and learn what the plans were for the mission. They could even stand outside the tent flaps and listen without much effort. Many of the nomad Wogs with their camels were always present, as they had eggs to sell or exchange for Lucky Strike cigarettes."

That time in the desert was situated in a completely different mindset. Security as we know it today had a low priority.

It is hard to imagine the Ploiești mission—the airfields filled with B-24 Liberators parked there in the Libyan desert, prop wash blowing sand, the thunder of engines, landing, taking off—without wondering what they were doing there, stirring up much curiosity. What was their purpose, their mission?

"It's hard to believe that the Germans did not know of our Ploiești plans," Bob said. "The Americans imported three bomb groups from England to support the two bomb groups we had in Benghazi. Do you have any idea what kind of a ruckus three bomb groups landing at airfields can cause? You can't hide that. And German planes flew overhead a few times a week; surely, they were taking pictures of our buildup of B-24s. They must've said, 'What the hell is so damned important, to have such a huge concentration of B-24s in North Africa? What is their target?'"

Not hard to answer.

All they had to do was ask *Generalleutnant* Alfred Gerstenberg.

He knew.

After Bob Sternfels returned to the States after the war, he began researching the subject of spies in and around Benghazi.

One theory proposed that after the Germans left North Africa, they left behind some personnel who hid in caves at night around the bases. "During the day, those Germans observed airfields nearest the Mediterranean and reported what they saw via shortwave radio," Bob said.

He went on to recount another story: "Spies or insurgents were dropped in the hills behind our base one night before the Ploiești [low-level] training started in July 1943. We were alerted immediately and ordered not to leave our tents. We were told to put our .45s under our pillows. The next day [German paratroopers] were dropped, and a few were able to infiltrate the perimeter where the B-24s were being repaired." (One of those planes was Aircraft Number 4240991, named *Kate Smith* after the famous singer, radio performer, and actress. Smith donated $250,000 of her own money for the B-24. The *Kate Smith* participated in the Ploiești raid and had a sad end over the target.)

Most of the German paratroopers were rounded up. "But," Bob said, "we didn't know how many escaped into the hills."

Bob shared other accounts he had heard after the war related to spies around the Americans' airfields:

A group of American fliers were on a quail hunt and stumbled across a wooden door over at the side of a hill. Behind it was a large opening. They entered and saw what was a large room, an area equipped with sleeping and cooking items. There were many indications there that the Germans used this area prior to the Ploiești mission, and that they were part of the paratroops that had arrived.

And then there was another piece of evidence from Jim Buchanan, whose uncle was a co-pilot on a 98th BG B-24 on the Ploiești mission. The uncle, Bill Buchanan, told me that a group of four or five American airmen came across a camouflaged bunker dug into the earth some distance from the airfield, but within sight of it. They approached the bunker with some care and had drawn their sidearms. After lifting the top—the roof of the bunker—they discovered a small room with a cot and evidence of recent habitation. They felt it was a hideout [from which] to spy on the operations.

The physical configuration of American air bases made it easy to "spy" on daily activities. The island of Crete, 250 miles away from the air bases, had Junkers JU-190s, German transport planes also used for high-altitude aerial photography. During daylight hours, Bob could hear American "antiaircraft guns trying to hit them; they never did; I guess they were too high." Bob soon stopped wondering why the Germans never tried to bomb the Americans' bases: "If they bombed us—and they assumed correctly—we'd decimate their Crete Island base and the JU-190s. And they needed those aircraft, and they needed Crete."

"The rumor mill was also alive before the mission," said Bob. "Word reached us that a couple of airmen who were on R&R in Cairo were asked by a British officer, 'When will you boys be bombing Ploieşti?' This seems plausible: The British were in Cairo before our buildup of B-24s in June and July 1943, and they had their noses into everything that came along. A mouse could not move around without the Brits knowing what it was doing."

For whatever reason, the spy theory has not been accepted by many who have studied this battle. It is not a long-shot theory, but, rather, one based on undeniable facts. The lack of any security around the American bases, coupled with the Germans' ingenuity, military brilliance, and desire to secure intelligence would have given these spies easy access to vital information to pass along to their higher command, to digest and act upon.

As masters of all matters military, the Germans had a sophisticated ability to carry out complex military operations, and their efforts proved beneficial to themselves—vital, actually. Easy access to the bases, no visible security whatsoever, made such an undertaking an easy matter—an imperative in a time of unbounded warfare. With binoculars and short-wave radios, they were in the spy business. Their efforts, unabated until the day the American boys left, bore much fruit. The spies—both German and Libyan—at the Benghazi bases were, by contemporary definition, "field agents." The Germans can be seen as *agent provocateurs*, "aiding and abetting" selected Libyans atop their camels to gather information on the Americans and their big flying machines.

When Bob and the other fliers made the right turn at the third IP, Floresti, to follow the railroad spur to Ploiești and were welcomed by the Germans' flak train, that information was provided by those agents around the air bases. It was devastating. The 98th Bomb Group alone lost 40 percent of its crews and aircraft as a result of gunfire from the flak train before hitting Ploiești, the main target.

The spies at Benghazi added to *Generalleutnant* Gerstenberg's success at Ploiești and effectively and masterfully blunted one of the most historic airstrikes in history. It also provided the Americans with a massively deadly, destructive surprise on August 1.

All of them, Germans and Libyans alike, set Tidal Wave whirling on its head.

To think there were no spies at Benghazi and that they had no effect on the outcome of the battle at Ploiești would be a careless conclusion.

CHAPTER 11

Smart Descends

Any plan imperfectly executed is better than no plan perfectly executed.
—SCOTT SORRELL, ATTORNEY

BETWEEN JUNE AND JULY 1943, LT. ROBERT STERNFELS FLEW TEN MIS-
sions as command pilot of *The Sandman*.

The start of one of those missions was more memorable than others.

"I'll never forget this one day in particular," Bob said. "It was July 15,
1943, a Thursday, two weeks before Ploieşti. My crew and I were preparing for a bombing run from Benghazi to Foggia, Italy. We were in the
process of checking out everything: electric gloves, ammo, flight suits,
K-rations, flight plan. Suddenly, off on the horizon, I see a big cloud of
dust behind a vehicle I couldn't make out. Soon it got close enough, and
I could see it was a staff car—a 1941 Ford painted olive-green with a
big white star on the back door. And it was headed straight for us, fast. I
thought, 'Oh, shit, what the hell did we do last night.' I thought maybe it
was a 'disciplinary visit.'"

The closer the staff car came, the more threatening it appeared.
Menacing now, with smoky sand and dust spewing from the rear end. A
whirling dervish spinning toward them. On the front fender, a standard
displaying an eagle, the insignia of a full US Army Air Force colonel, or,
as they say in the air force, "A full-bird colonel," one grade below a one-
star general.

The driver braked in front of *The Sandman*'s nose.

"He locked up the brakes so hard the tires lost their grip," Bob recalled, "and the damned thing skidded the last ten feet. I thought for sure he was going to bust the nose and wreck our airplane."

The driver's door swung open and he jumped out, opened the rear door, and stood at attention, straight as rebar.

"Now," said Bob, "I could see the guy in the back stepping out; he was a colonel in the United States Army Air Force. He walked toward us, and we all snapped to attention and gave him the best salute he ever got."

He stopped in front of Bob, returned his salute, and said, *sotto voce*, "Lieutenant, I'd like to fly with you today."

"It was as simple as that: no hello, my name is so-and-so. Perfunctory."

It was hard for Bob to believe that a colonel standing in front of him was asking *him* permission to fly aboard *The Sandman* on a bombing run. Furthermore, it was odd that the colonel did not introduce himself, did not reveal his name. But, after thinking about it, Bob surmised it was not a request—it was an *order*.

"Yes, sir," Bob said, wondering if there was any other possible answer, like "Do you have a ticket, sir?" Or, "We're serving steaks and cold beers; does that sound okay, Colonel?"

Then he thought about asking the colonel what his name was and if he had any B-24 flying experience, but realized both questions might not be good form, so he wisely skipped the interrogatories.

Instead, he asked, "Would you like to fly the plane today, Colonel?"

In the military, if you do not know someone's name, addressing them with their rank is acceptable.

Bob was glad the colonel said no.

He did look familiar, and as they started to board *The Sandman*, a lightbulb went off in Bob's head.

The colonel that was squeezing his way into *The Sandman* was none other than Col. Jacob E. Smart—yes, *that* Colonel Smart . . . the one at the corner of the picture taken on the lawn at the Anfa Hotel in Casablanca. He was here, in Benghazi, for a short period of time, presented as a VIP, his purpose unknown.

This started Bob thinking: *What the hell is a full colonel doing here, wanting to fly on my bird?*

He would later learn that on this particular day, the mysterious colonel was going on his first combat mission in World War II, with Lt. Robert W. Sternfels. At the time, Bob didn't know much about Smart—that he'd planned Tidal Wave—he just recognized his face from a picture published in the *New York Times*. Bob recalled: "I'm sure Smart knew I would say, 'Yes, sir, you can fly with us'—what else?—because Smart's driver did not wait for a signal; he jumped back into the staff car, put his foot to the accelerator, and sped away from the group as fast as he'd arrived."

Later, Bob understood why the driver drove away so fast.

The VIP in the backseat wanted to wait until the very last moment before he boarded *The Sandman*. If his name and desire to fly a combat mission got out before he wished, it would have spread rumors all over the air bases, and possibly blown his cover; then everyone (including the spies) would have wondered what *another* full colonel was doing there at Benina.

Silently, the crew began climbing aboard *The Sandman*.

Before takeoff, after starting the engines, the B-24's gauges had to be checked prior to applying full power, and it took several minutes—standard operating procedure.

Bob instructed his flight engineer, Staff Sgt. William W. Stout, from Manson, Washington, who was also the top turret gunner, to stand between him and co-pilot, 2nd Lt. Barney Jackson, raised in Salesville, Texas, and check the engine gauges during the run-up. But Staff Sergeant Stout could not move into position in the cramped cockpit. He was blocked.

Colonel Smart was standing where Stout should be, between the seated Bob and Lieutenant Jackson.

"Smart decided that that was where he wanted to stand," said Bob. "I said, 'Colonel, please move. Sergeant Stout has duties to do on takeoff and landing, and he has to stand where you are.' I felt it strange that any experienced pilot of a B-24 would not know this. Stout had to use all eyes on the gauges to alert the pilot of any malfunctions—and the ideal location is between the pilot and co-pilot."

Recalling this, Bob shook his head and continued: "And this was only the beginning of Smart's lack of experience with the B-24."

The B-24 start-up is a bit intricate. It involves focus and attention as the pilot and co-pilot flip switches, check gauges, and confirm the status of a variety of systems. After a few minutes, Jackson flipped the start switch and fired up the Number 3 engine, the first in the start-up procedure because it is the only engine with a hydraulic pump.

"It was a normal takeoff," said Bob. "We were climbing to altitude, and suddenly I was startled to see, in my peripheral vision, a hand adjusting my engine mixture controls!"

Without asking, Colonel Smart was adjusting the controls that Bob had set! This was a duty assigned to the co-pilot. Colonel Smart was overstepping his bounds.

"I immediately placed the controls back to *my* settings. It soon became an annoying problem because thirty seconds later, he did it again without saying anything, and I had to readjust them again."

A few minutes passed, and Colonel Smart once again changed the mixture controls.

"But this time," said Bob, "I removed my oxygen mask, turned, looked him straight in the eye, and in my most authoritative voice, said: *Colonel! Please do not touch the controls!*"

Quickly, the colonel backed away.

Bob mused about what Smart's intentions might have been as he fiddled with the mixture controls. Was it a deliberate act, so he could tell everyone, "I flew the plane on a combat mission on July 15?"

Bob Sternfels's pilot's logbook for that July 15, 1943, bombing mission reads, in his handwriting, with an ink pen: LITTLE ACK ACK— HAD COLONEL SMART ONBOARD—FOUR HOLES.

The "four holes" would have allowed Smart to say, legitimately, that the holes were acquired on a dangerous "combat" mission."

Years later, after the war, Bob continued to wonder why Colonel Smart thought he needed to help Bob with the mixture controls. Fifty-two years later, he got an answer, albeit, not entirely satisfying.

"In 1995, my wife, Nancy, and I were on a recreational vehicle trip in my motor home around the country," Bob recalled. "We drove to Ridgeland, North Carolina, where Smart was born and raised, and paid him a visit. He was delighted to see me and to reminisce about the 'old days.'

He had had an outstanding career, had risen to the rank of four-star general, and was living quietly in the same house where he was born, eighty-six years earlier. It was a pleasant time, not only because we shared Tidal Wave. He was a four-star officer who was [recorded] in the history books—General Smart was central to planning D-Day, the invasion of Europe. And, flying with me that day was memorable for us both—historic for us both. It was his first combat mission in World War II.

"Toward the end of our visit, I had to ask him the big question about that day in July, when he was driven out to my plane, but then I realized he'd probably never recall the details about changing the mixture controls; too many years had passed. He was eighty-six at the time of my visit, and frail. So, I put the question another way: 'General, when you got to Benghazi that July, how many hours did you have flying the B-24?' Smart responded immediately: 'I was just checked out on the B-24 about a week before I flew with you.'"

Bob's trusty lightbulb glowed again.

After the visit with Smart, he reflected on Smart's comments.

"When you are checking out in a new plane, you do takeoffs and landings, keeping the runway in sight the whole time. Also, *there is no need to adjust the mixture controls!* So, I suppose he was trying to get a feel for them or trying to show me he knew what he was doing."

Bob paused . . . "And to think he was the man who planned the low-level Ploiești mission using B-24s."

So, on July 15, 1943, Colonel Jacob "Jake" Smart arrived in arid Benghazi, that epic threshold, entering 1st Lt. Robert Sternfels's life. He flew his first combat mission, with the skills he had honed and devotion to his country; and with a warrior's worn-out satchel, heavy with schemes, hopes, and fears, he would mark a milestone in history.

The Smart Plan would be under way the following day.

CHAPTER 12

Secrets

There is something about a closet that makes a skeleton terribly restless.
—JOHN BARRYMORE JR.,
AMERICAN FILM ACTOR

ON JULY 25, 1943, TEN DAYS AFTER HIS FIRST COMBAT MISSION WITH
Bob Sternfels, Col. Jacob Smart presented the Smart Plan to Brig. Gen.
Uzal G. Ent, the 9th US Air Force's IX Bomber Command chief of staff
at his Benghazi headquarters, the "green hut." This was Ent's "headquarters" building, a lightweight prefabricated structure of corrugated galvanized steel having a semicircular cross-section and painted olive green.

Born on March 30, 1900, in Northumberland, Pennsylvania, Uzal
Girard Ent graduated from the US Military Academy, served in the
US infantry from 1917 to 1919, and received his US Air Service commission. On May 30, 1928, while co-piloting a hydrogen-filled balloon
in the National Balloon Race—Ent was a licensed balloonist in the
army air service—misfortune struck when a hellacious bolt of lightning
enflamed his balloon over Youngstown, Pennsylvania, instantly killing
the pilot and setting the hydrogen aflame. Down it went, a massive flaming apostrophe. Instead of parachuting out, Ent held on to the blazing
mass, attempted to rescue the pilot, not knowing he had been killed,
and manhandled the inferno down to the ground. For this action, Ent
received the first of two Distinguished Flying Crosses. In 1951 the air
force opened an air base near Colorado Springs, Colorado, and named it
Ent Air Force Base. It was closed in 1976, and became the site of the US
Olympic Training Center.

Smart's Tidal Wave presentation to Ent that historic day in Benghazi was top secret. The meeting was limited to eight officers and was heavily guarded—a red flag for the "spies" in an environment where guards standing with weapons drawn was an incongruity that said, *Hey, there must be something secret going on there!*

The meeting was not *tabula rasa*. The attendees would have had strong opinions about what they would hear. Nevertheless, all were polite and civil and respectful of military protocols.

Before the meeting kicked off, Smart knew he would get some pushback from Ent (albeit, mild), who, at that point, had not been persuaded that Smart's low-level attack would be propitious. Ent, forty-three, was "old school" Air Force, seeing traditional high-altitude bombing as the way to pulverize the Ploiești refineries. Smart, however, was more inclined toward modern aviation methodologies and contemporary strategies. The thirty-nine-year-old was well prepared to counter with his controversial low-level "stunt," as some snipingly framed it. At the meeting's end, Ent concurred with Smart's low-level option as having the best chance of immediate success. (Later, in his official order for the mission, General Brereton noted that the targets "*may be destroyed by either high- or low-level attacks* [emphasis added]." He did not mention which he preferred, and appeared to be riding the pony down the middle of the track.)

Both Ent and Brereton knew that Smart had already presented the plan and received approval from Smart's superior, Gen. Henry "Hap" Arnold, commanding general of the Army Air Forces, in Washington, DC, as well as Gen. Dwight D. Eisenhower, President Roosevelt, and Prime Minister Winston Churchill. Undoubtedly these approvals predisposed both Ent and Brereton toward agreement—particularly Brereton, who had narrowly escaped a severe career nosedive involving his failing, contentious marriage and faltering military career. He was now making a solid comeback, having divorced his wife and righted his military profession. Thus, both Brereton and Ent had positioned themselves, politically and tactically, for any post-mission criticism. Should the mission fail, or partially succeed, both could say, "I told you so." Their bases were skillfully covered, both being gifted in the Machiavellian skills necessary in US Army Air Force office politics.

In essence, Smart, Ent, and Brereton were following orders handed down from the president of the United States to Hap Arnold, and from Arnold to Smart, a fact they would wisely not contend. Smart's meeting with Ent ended with firm handshakes and satisfied smiles.

Before the meeting with Ent in Benghazi, Smart had conferred with Maj. Gen. Lewis H. Brereton, 9th US Air Force commanding general, at his Cairo, Egypt, headquarters. Brereton's 9th US Air Force would have overall responsibility for Tidal Wave; in fact, Brereton had been looking forward to flying the mission aboard the lead ship as mission commander, which would undoubtedly springboard his career to a much-sought-after higher level.

But a signal containing an order from Hap Arnold hit some like a lightning bolt at the eleventh hour.

Brereton was supposed to fly aboard Keith K. Compton's B-24, the *Teggie Ann*, but Arnold forbid him to fly the mission, saying he was too important to be lost. General Ent, who was initially meant to fly aboard *Hail Columbia*, Colonel Kane's ship, would instead take Brereton's place as mission commander on the *Teggie Ann*, making him responsible for the five elements of the strike force. Ent was more than happy to comply.

Brereton wrote his own draft of Hap Arnold's order and gave it to Maj. Gerald K. Geerlings from the 8th Air Force, the architect and artist who had designed the oblique maps, customized drawings of the refineries, photographs, and so on, to deliver to Colonel Smart and Colonel Timberlake. Geerlings's responsibility had been to gather sufficient material necessary to brief the crews, but dependable resources were drying up. One of the best sources for this material was in London, England, at the Admiralty Library. But Geerlings could not just walk in, particularly in the uniform of a US Army Air Force officer, and then walk out with what he needed. Instead, he ditched his uniform, posed as a civilian, and took a bogus job as an air raid fire warden working the night shift at the library. Ingenious and simple. For two weeks, Geerlings was involved in the "exciting" game of subterfuge and espionage, and soon acquired the necessary information from the Admiralty Library—maps, photos of Ploiești, the oil refinery layouts—and then left, a surreptitious apparition.

Geerlings took the note Brereton gave him—it denied permission to fly the mission to Col. Edward "Ted" Timberlake, the tactical planning officer for Tidal Wave. Timberlake could have been a double for Spencer Tracy, the movie star, but sadly lacked the acting skills to hide his heart-broken reaction that day. According to Geerlings, when he handed Timberlake the order, "Timberlake's face became grim, and he cursed softly but vehemently. There were tears in Timberlake's eyes, and he said, 'God, my men will think I'm chicken.'"

Geerlings then handed the message to a stunned Colonel Smart, who was also meant to fly with the 93rd Bomb Group (BG). Smart, too, had been denied permission to fly the mission; he knew too many Allied secrets.

In two signals, Arnold, Brereton, and Smart, three vital mission participants, had been denied the chance to fly one of the most perilous missions in military aviation history. All were deeply hurt. All saw career opportunities contract in a flash. Uzal Ent was now in the enviable position to burnish and promote his own military career to a high degree—if he survived—and on his way toward more stars on his shoulders. (Sadly, an unfortunate event would impact General Ent's life after Tidal Wave; fate would not allow his imaginings to flourish.)

When the mission ended, history would note that not one of the original planners of Operation Tidal Wave—Brereton, Smart, and Timberlake—flew the attack on Ploiești that day.

On July 19, 1943, the five groups were ordered to fly a bombing mission to Rome, Italy. Many of the crewmen were fervidly opposed to it, particularly the Catholic boys. They objected to bombing or damaging Vatican City, which had buildings throughout Rome's city limits. So, a decision had been made: If you were Catholic, and you did not want to go on the mission, you could stand down.

The mission was a success. While the main targets in and around Rome were decimated, Vatican Palace had been spared. Everybody was happy, particularly the Catholic boys.

When the bombers returned to Benghazi, they were met with an unexpected and unusual surprise: an announcement that the five bomb groups had been ordered to stand down. They would not fly combat missions for an undisclosed period. The decision spun the rumor mill with dizzying speed and initiated a flood of suspicions that something "big" was imminent, or, as the airmen put it, something "super-duper." Soon, speculation abounded from the realistic to the fantastical: The groups were going to skip-bomb submarine pens in Hamburg and Bremen, Germany; more exciting, they would bomb Hitler himself; or, attack the *Tirpitz*, the German dreadnought battleship, the pride of Germany. The rumors were underscored when the Norden bombsight was removed from the Liberators flying the mission. The top-secret Norden was a high-altitude bombsight, and crews would go to extremes to destroy it if they had crash-landed. Since there would be no high-altitude bombing during Tidal Wave, the device was removed. It was replaced by a gunsight, the type used on attack planes that bombed at lower altitudes.

That same day, July 20, the five group commanders, along with key staff members, were summoned to General Ent's Command HQ—the "green hut." Before they walked into the oppressive heat in the small space, they were sworn to a secret oath. Then the Tidal Wave mission was laid bare.

The tropical air inside the hut was not the only factor that caused the heat to rise.

Several of the attendees at the meeting stated their doubts—in varying degrees of intensity—about the viability of the plan and its potential success. Their main concern? Skimming on-the-deck in a tight wingtip-to-wingtip formation typically flown at much higher altitudes was, to some, "totally insane," "nuts," and "just plain stupid." They had not been trained for such low-level flying; this was a grave situation. It was, many vocalized, an unconvincing undertaking. After dropping practice bombs from 150 feet in a rehearsal, a debriefing officer said, "This ain't the way we learned it back in the States." However, many were looking forward to the challenge and the excitement it would provide; it was a break from the usual high-altitude missions they had been flying.

Toward the end of the meeting, they were told, forcibly and without hesitation, that the mission was going to be done at low level, "come hell or high water."

Four days later, July 24, officers who were set to fly the mission were told that the "super-duper" mission was a low-level bombing attack on the refineries around the Romanian city of Ploieşti. (Two days before this, the lead navigator for the 98th BG had guessed correctly, writing in his diary that the target was Ploieşti; the pilot of the 98th's *Northern Star* B-24 had recorded the same thoughts in his journal.)

This briefing was the debut of a special film that would present the details of Tidal Wave. It began, of course, with a beautiful shot of a nude woman that provoked a deluge of catcalls, whistles, hoots, and applause.

On July 25, aircrews were given the details regarding the target. The end of "tent conjecture" had finally arrived.

Major General Brereton issued orders, clearly stating the main objective:

- To destroy installations in the Ploieşti area, which will deny to the enemy the petroleum products produced and distilled from the Rumonian [*sic*] oil fields.

Brereton then presented specific points regarding the targets:

- The objective consists of 9 principal refineries [eventually only seven warranted attacking] consisting of 27 vital installations, which, if destroyed, will stop refining processes and, depending on the degree of destruction, will keep the refineries *out of operation for a prolonged period, probably for the duration* [emphasis added]. The objective is a suitable target for heavy bombardment and may be *destroyed by either high- or low-level attacks* [emphasis added; here, Brereton appears to be "covering his bases" again in the event the low-level attack was not successful].

Regarding Ploieşti's defenses:

- The targets consist of pre-war installations, the compositions and arrangements of which are generally known. Information concerning additions, camouflage, and defense is meagre [*sic*]. Every effort to secure new information is being exerted without sacrifice to the surprise to be attained in the initial attacks. It is expected that the number of AA [antiaircraft] weapons, balloons, and fighter aircraft will be known prior to launching the attack. Present information is extensive but possibly not recent. The target can be made inoperative by one group mission against each of the nine refineries by high-level attacks and by lesser units in low-level attacks [here again, Brereton seems to be pulling his punches]. Neutralization can be maintained for the period necessary to complete destruction to the degree that restoration is impossible.

Brereton's orders did not mention the conspicuous vulnerabilities in Smart's plan of attack, but most of the crew saw the obvious: (1) The B-24 had been designed as a high-altitude bomber (a fact all crewmen knew). As such, it was ill suited to the Smart Plan's extreme low-level attack requirement. The B-24, not a fighter plane, was not nimble (below 100 feet), and thus, down-on-the-deck was "absolutely nuts"; (2) Because of its slow speed and bulky size, the "pregnant cow" (another sarcastic *nom de guerre* for the B-24 Liberator) would be vulnerable to being shot down. Many B-24s in Bob Sternfels's group were shot to pieces; crashed even before reaching their designated targets; or limped away, mauled; and (3) Although custom-fitted for the long flight with Tokyo fuel tanks that extended the round-trip mission to any other "safe port," the flight would be extremely taxing on the crews and the aircraft.

Despite these objections and apprehensions, Operation Tidal Wave was under way, and the air bases began to hum with enthusiastic preparations.

CHAPTER 13

The Courage

Courage is being scared to death but saddling up anyway.

—JOHN WAYNE

THE BOMB GROUPS WERE NOW FOCUSED ON PREPARING THE B-24S FOR "The Battle of Ploieşti," as some call it, a battle none had seen before, none could have imagined, and none would see at any other time, any other place. The attack, after a breeze cleared the malefic scent of battle smoke, would take its unique place in history, never to be duplicated— exclusive and deadly, its results, baneful and searing. After all, this is the "super-duper" one, and the boys know it.

The American boys went to work, assiduously, wholeheartedly, and with American muscle and eagerness applied to the vital tasks that were theirs alone: mounting, modifying, calibrating, loading, hoping that their toil would keep their birds whole enough to return to the scorpions and rats and spiders and bleached airfields they loathed, but where all were safe.

Shirtless and sweating, some wished their planes would be condemned, deemed incapable of joining the mission, and that they could stay there with them, earthbound by some real or concocted affliction, and the crews would stay, too, in safety, unwounded, whole and earthbound and forever young.

But a secret endures as a secret until it lands on the blistering sand, and then it reveals a truth, things impossible to suppress. Many of these planes, with unforgettable names of girlfriends, mothers, naked women, and war cries drawn on their rounded noses, will leave their caretakers' caring hands, never to be taken care of again. And that is the harsh truth of it. This will come to pass. The world will continue spinning, after all; this they know. The boys who fly in these cherished ships who do not return will not be diminished by time. Like the sting of the sun's daily radiance, the heat of loss will modulate, but throughout their lives, it will never leave their hearts entirely.

And that is the way it will be as they continue their mechanical work on this historic day of preparation for the Battle of Ploieşti.

The airfields they worked at were former Italian air force bases until the Luftwaffe chased them away, spread out on the flat coastal plain around Benghazi. Semi-desert and sand-blown open-air furnaces, the work to prepare the bombers in this dreadfulness was done in temperatures that spiked at a miserable 125 degrees, and this without the refuge of air-conditioning. In this climate, aircraft paint seared and faded, thus creating "pink bombers." One rumor said a couple of cooks pounded some dough into loaves, shoved them into a compartment in *The Sandman*, waited hopefully, and out came two tasty loaves of bread (without real butter to spread on their warm surfaces).

And nowhere could the crews work without "pharaoh's flies" pursuing them, seeking accidental food drops, and threatening all with God-knows-what diseases. The Pharaoh fly has the distinction of looking like a yellow bumblebee and large bulbous housefly. Some of the boys said they were so big they actually had to get permission to take off from the control tower. Instead of carrying firearms, airmen carried flyswatters neatly holstered in their web belts; but armed or not, they are outgunned and outmanned by the wily flies, as well as the crafty desert mice and kangaroo rats that hold secret intentions better than the secrets kept at headquarters.

And the food: unappealing, despite the best efforts of the cooks under such primitive conditions. Always on the menu: the wearisome-ness of powdered eggs and Spam, and more powdered eggs and Spam, a food product introduced in 1937, and ascending in popularity all over the world (just not in Libya). If Spam and powdered eggs did not satiate culinary tastes, there were other easy choices: dried cabbage and reconstituted nonfat dry milk. Beans were served occasionally, applauded and considered a "treat."

And the maintenance boys were always exposed to the sun, which prompted dehydration, ulcers, fatigue, sunburn, sunstroke, heat prostration, and blindness. And some other ailments no doctor had diagnosed. There were no sanitary facilities. No showers. Toilet paper was scarce, and dropping trousers in the cold desert air and hot blowing sand was common—for officers and enlisted men alike. "The word *primitive*," Bob Sternfels said, "does not begin to describe the living conditions on the desert!" Equally awful were the bouts of uncontrollable dysentery, which took a few men offline and would prevent some from flying to Ploieşti, but the American spirit surmounted what the least of these cares were. Aircrews still had to go out and face gunfire and return fire and drop bombs, and pilots still had to outmaneuver cannon shells, cable lines, treetops, and smokestacks: a far greater menace than the food, the flies, the aboriginal creatures, the pervasive heat. Yes, it was possible to die by disease, dysentery (aka "desert two-step," and "Karachi Krud"), sunstroke—also, death or wounding by explosion, cannon fire, or sudden impact against the ground.

And so, the maintenance guys worked and worked without an eye on the clock, and after time managed the challenges and did what had to be done for their country—and themselves. This was an integral, vital aspect of the great, ubiquitous American spirit, of working as one, of positive effort, and taking pride in work done.

To increase the fuel range, they fit each B-24 with rubberized Tokyo fuel tanks. The tanks were initially designed to be installed in B-17s to extend their range. In early 1943, through redesigning, some Tokyo tanks were reshaped to fit the B-24; they were self-sealing, and consisted of eighteen removable containers, called cells. These fit inside the wings of the bomber, nine to each side of the fuselage, at the wing roots. The word "Tokyo," an unashamed exaggeration, implied that a B-17 fitted with them had enough fuel to fly round-trip to Tokyo, Japan, from any point on the US map. In reality, this aeronautical feat could not be done from any point in the United States.

The Tokyo tanks added 1,080 US gallons of fuel to the 1,700 US gallons already carried in the six regular wing tanks, and the 820 US gallons held in an auxiliary tank mounted in the bomb bay, for a combined total of 3,600 US gallons. The tanks were temperamental: There were no definitive means to measure the remaining fuel, no fuel gauge in the cockpit. After they were drained, or nearly drained, residue vapor buildup made them explosive hazards in combat, which took down quite a few B-24s. And adding more fuel to the B-24's weight diminished the bomb loads they could carry. Armorers installed .50 caliber machine guns in the nose of the first-wave aircraft of the groups. This added weight. On top of that, ammunition for the machine guns added more weight. The armorers provided incendiary clusters to the waist gunners, who would spill them out through their side windows onto flammable targets.

The armorers also loaded a variety of bombs and incendiaries aboard all Liberators. Not all B-24s carried the same bomb load. The bombs ranged from 500 to 1,000 pounds, and were filled with Tritonal, a mixture of 80 percent TNT and 20 percent aluminum, which improved the total heat output of the TNT. They packed a wallop. The total bomb loads added 3,812 pounds to 4,480 pounds on each ship. Delay fuses were set at sixty minutes for the first wave of B-24s, and forty-five seconds for the second wave, to allow following aircraft to clear the target. Because of confusion over the refineries, this did not work as planned. Several aircraft were damaged or blown apart by "friendly bomb fire."

The ground crews, maintenance workers, cooks, armorers, and administrative staff never got the credit they deserved. Those who benefited from their labors, however—particularly the aircrews that depended on them and their unending, round-the-clock work—knew that it took courage to endure at the airfields as well as in the clouds.

At this point in the operation, there was a total of 193 B-24 Liberators standing, waiting, almost ready to fly the mission. The number Colonel Smart initially required was two hundred, but mechanical ailments took the number down. Between takeoff at Benghazi and the end of the attack, this number would be critically diminished.

Officially, the 98th Bomb Group (H) was listed as the Pyramidiers. The name signified their association with the pyramids of Egypt; it was innocuous, as appealing as the dried cabbage they frequently ate. So when the group arrived in Libya—they came via Egypt—the airmen in the group referred to themselves as the Desert Rats, much more suited to a warriors' self-image.

The commander of the 98th BG was a legend, then and now.

John Riley "Killer" Kane, thirty-six, a colonel in the army air force, had a talent for driving a B-24 better than most. Killer was not a nickname applied for his flying acumen or leadership—it was influenced by a character in a 1930s comic strip, *Buck Rogers*. During his cadet days in the army air force, Kane became close friends with a fellow cadet named Rogers, and the duo became known as Killer Kane and Buck Rogers.

Bob Sternfels liked Kane a lot, respected him. The men below Killer felt the same. The men above him, the "brass," did not like him, but did respect his flying skills and most of his leadership qualities. By the time Tidal Wave came and went, Kane's qualities and personality had turned into controversy and contention, particularly between Kane and Col. K. K. Compton, Kane's nemesis. Kane was not a team player—something the brass typically does not appreciate. Kane bucked Bomber Command, and that did nothing to promote his career in the army air force. Kane was his own man, and in the end, he would suffer for it.

When Kane heard the details of Tidal Wave, he said, "What armchair idiot warrior in Washington dreamed up this idea?!" This rude comment did not ingratiate him with Colonel Smart, Colonel Compton, or Brigadier General Ent. Oh, no. And there were many more who felt the same. Recalled Norm Whalen, who flew as Kane's navigator in Europe, "He was a controversial figure, and he told the higher-ups what he thought. Colonel Kane was very direct and outspoken. He expressed himself without holding back on what he felt." According to Jacob Smart:

Colonel Kane's behavior might have been predictable. He was a courageous able bomber pilot, a stern, intense, and unforgiving commander, a firm believer in the righteousness of his own values and his judgments and highly skeptical of those of others. Kane opposed the low-level attack intellectually and vocally. . . . He doubted that the B-24s would have [sufficient] fuel to fly to Ploiești and return to base despite the demonstration that they could do so, with fuel to spare. He believed that the prescribed speed as flown by Compton's group consumed excessive fuel. He thus flew at lower power settings, which resulted in an unplanned separation between the first two and the last three groups. Kane felt a deep responsibility for the care and well-being of the young men in his group. He regarded them as lambs that would be led to the slaughter. He steeled himself to lead them to Hell and back home—if he could!

As of July 1943, Col. John Kane had flown forty-three missions, far more than the thirty that typically sent a pilot home after duty in the Middle East. He was determined to lead the Desert Rats into their most dangerous mission yet. Many of the men had thirty missions, but as the plans became evident, Kane announced: "All available crews will go on the mission regardless of completion of their combat tours." He received no complaints from his men. Their courage and devotion and trust would prompt them to follow John Kane.

In a 2002 interview, Norm Whalen added a similar note of devotion: "I'd go back up with him tomorrow morning if he was still around and asked me."

In his youth, Kane, tall, barrel-chested, and brash, was an excellent boxer. He resembled Clark Gable, a major movie star of the era. Like Gable, Kane wore a mustache, not favored by the brass at that time. He had a soft-sided nature, and a fatherly relationship with his men, his boys, whom he nurtured. This inclination toward caring for people had led him to Baylor University, where he enrolled in medical school, to become a doctor.

"But I couldn't stand the stink and the smells related to medicine," Kane said, "so I dropped out." After graduating from Baylor in 1928, Kane joined the US Army Air Corps, as it was known then, and earned his pilot's wings.

CHAPTER 14

"Hit Them for Six!"

Bob Sternfels asked, "How low can we go?"
He was told, "As low as you want, Bob—just don't hit a camel."
—Lt. Robert W. Sternfels

On July 22, B-24s not under the hands of the maintenance boys started rehearsing for the low-level attack on Ploieşti.

Most of the aircrews found this exciting or hard work, or both; it required a new and unfamiliar concentration on the part of the pilots—wholly dissimilar to flying at high altitudes and turning on the Sperry autopilot. This form of flying demanded an "all eyes on," "all hands on" approach the pilots had been disallowed from employing since their first days in flying school, as it presented a lethal potential: One wrong tap of the control column at 50 feet and 200 mph, and you got a disagreeable amount of B-24 windscreen and the Libyan desert in your face.

Initially, the rehearsals started with three-ship formations, to get the pilots familiar with the new type of flying. As the rehearsals progressed over the next couple of days, the B-24s got down lower and lower to the desert, until they were flying at the prescribed 50 feet, "on the deck," at 200 mph.

To the south of the air bases, the 835th engineers constructed a mock "Ploieşti" on the vast desert floor—a nearly full-scale representation, excluding actual building and smokestack heights, showing the oil refineries' outline on the sand. At first it was a problem, because at 200 mph and 50 feet, the pilots could not see the "target" until they were on top of it. This problem was partially solved after the engineers scoured the bases for materials that gave "Ploieşti" an approximate vertical silhouette—of course, this was not exact, but it was the best they could do. The engineers scrounged steel girders, empty oil drums, and other usable items left by the Italian and German air forces. With their ingenuity, they were able to construct a massive outline of the refineries on the desert floor, and now the pilots could see this virtual Ploieşti thirty seconds before they arrived.

As their rehearsals continued, Bob Sternfels asked "How low can we go?" He was told, "As low as you want, Bob—just don't hit a camel."

Flying in formation at 50 feet, one B-24 moved to avoid a collision. The pilot pressed the nose down a little too low and slammed and skimmed the belly along the flat desert. When the plane was parked and inspected for damage, there wasn't a millimeter of paint left on the belly; it was pure shiny aluminum. The rumor was this happened to several other B-24s.

"Formation flying at just fifty feet," Bob said, "and at two hundred miles per hour or more over the flat desert and sand dunes of Libya, and in close formation, yet. This was absurd, but exhilarating nonetheless. The true height of the many structures and two-hundred-foot-high smoke-stacks of the refineries could not be simulated. Next, the approach to the actual targets would be over the plains, rivers, and forests of Romania, not the flat sand of the Libyan desert. My experiences of the 'training—hedge hopping over the desert'—was learning how to keep away from other planes. *That* was the hard part."

Bob voiced other significant and valid criticisms: "These were not full-length practice missions. There was only one [practice mission] with a few aircraft of the full 2,700-mile mission with a full bomb and fuel load. It was conducted to establish the fact that the aircraft could fly that distance and return with reserve fuel. That was accomplished, and proved the technical aspect of the range and bomb load. But it was done without regard to several significant factors: It was not done flying in close formation. In that case, the lead aircraft must set the pace, and all the other aircraft flying 'wing' must continuously adjust and readjust their throttles and re-trim their aircraft, and constantly weave about through 'prop wash,' or turbulence of the airstream from a preceding aircraft, while avoiding a midair collision."

A group of experienced British antiaircraft gunners observed one of the low-level rehearsals. After witnessing the event, they wrote a top-secret memo to General Brereton, saying, among other things: "We could have easily shot down all the B-24s."

Brereton made sure the memo got no further than the safe in his office.

— ~ —

The last briefing assembles en masse in a Quonset hut—a corrugated cathedral with fluted gray walls, a corrugated arched ceiling, sweat-soaked air, and creaky wooden folding chairs, the faithful impatiently waiting for anointment by the vicars of the High Command, perhaps a spritz of holy water.

Details and revelations will be a blessing. The congregants will listen to words of inspiration, caution, and support that for some of the faithful will undoubtedly portend death and grief, surely. Among them, many feel a sense of peril: *This one will surely kill me, this damned fucking mission.* Others, unreasonably assured of their safety, nonchalant, without knowing why they think they will survive: *The other poor bastard, the one tapping his foot next to me—he's gonna die, but not me.*

Most will feel anointed and blessed as much as possible, and will be suitable opposition for cracking the devil's spear. Some will carry their scapulars and crosses and furry rabbit's feet, or lockets with pictures, or relics of saints, or photographs of family, of girlfriends, whatever juju they trust. Whatever amulet they think has the power to repulse German bullets and cannon fire. At least the moment has arrived—*Thank you, God, for this*—when they will finally know *all* the details of what the "super-duper" mission means to each of them.

Then the presentations begin.

The boys digest each parcel, link one with the other, until, combined, they evolve into the Smart Plan—designed by that same Col. Jacob Smart that Bob Sternfels took up in *The Sandman* on his first combat mission, the guy who had about an hour's time flying the B-24, the lynchpin of the mission.

This is starting to turn into a mighty big deal.

It's a *Holy cow!* moment.

As the briefing moves on, mixed feelings wash through the audience, especially the 50-foot, 200 mph facet.

Oh, boy, that's a doozy!

A film is introduced.

It begins with the holiest of holies, and for many, the best part of what they are about to view: a woman most beautiful, and wonderfully naked, all those secret luscious areas visible up there on the large screen, albeit, for only a few stimulating seconds, here in the land of deadly warfare. The young woman brings the boys up onto their feet. Hats bounce off the cathedral ceiling. The boys whistle and applaud and growl and moan their boundless delight and deepest yearning.

Amazing, the priests murmur to each other, how naked flesh and lovely breasts can trump the terror of potential death. Amazing what a pair of rosy nipples can do to calm young men's anxieties.

Then the young woman disappears, as young women often do in the romantic lives of young men. The audience groans and yells their displeasure.

Reality resumes.

Then the president of the United States appears, where the young woman had been a moment ago.

Wow!

President Roosevelt!

Here for us!

Yes, Roosevelt is here—for them.

He appears too soon, causing the lovely nakedness to fade—*With all due respect, Mr. President, we could have stared at her a bit longer, sir.*

Suddenly, the president's presence gives the boys pause: It could only mean something big, something dangerous and deadly, right around the corner. You cannot fool the troops, old, young, wise, naive; no—it has never been done, never will be done in any man's army. They have noses like bloodhounds and pick up the scent of danger in the air. They know omens when they smell them, these American boys.

Roosevelt, his eyes stern, his mien officious, faintly grave. So appropriately Waspy.

His presence gets the boys' attention. They are glued to the moment. They simmer down. After their hats flop on the floor, after the erotic electricity fizzles, the president begins, with his singsong delivery; but this time he is not talking to millions of Americans on the radio, or giving a Fireside Chat, or speaking from his wheelchair at his desk in the White House.

The president of the United States is talking to *them*, the flyboys of the US Army Air Force.

And suddenly they are one . . . the audience and the president. Roosevelt has become one of the aircrews, *sans* uniform. The president, the boys sense by his demeanor, is *a true leader . . . our* leader. And his leadership at this moment emboldens them. He is a pair of spurs on the muscled flanks of a great warrior stallion, and the boys are proud to have him up there in the saddle, leading the charge.

Roosevelt's narration of the film makes them feel good, appreciated:

Okay, you know what the deal is. You know you can't see this film too often. You know you must memorize every detail of this plan. Success depends on how well you do before you do it. Study your target folders. Know which target is yours and how you must hit it. . . . Germany needs Romania's oil desperately. Mechanized war struggles and bogs down without oil. Romania's oil provides the fuel for the whole German fleet, for half of the German air force in Russia, for one-third the German army. You knock out Romania's refineries, and you take out the fuel for ninety percent of the whole Italian army and air force. You may knock Italy right out of the war. You may screw up Hitler's plans for his offensive against Russia. The job of knocking out the refineries in Romania is the biggest job of the war. We believe that the last days of the Fascists have asked for it, and they are going to get it. The job of knocking out the German refineries is the biggest job of them all. It's your job! Okay, let's hit it!

The boys have never heard anything like this. This is special, and confers significance and responsibility on their mission—even though some of the boys don't want to be words on a page of history, but rather, on a porch in their hometown with their family and a pretty friend.

Roosevelt's presence and words anoint them, Christians, Catholics, Jews. There are no favorites. Everyone has an equal opportunity to get killed.

There is meditative silence for several seconds.

Then the baritone voice of WOR Radio personality Tex McCrary narrates the remainder of the film. McCrary, a captain in the army air force, had been popular on the radio, along with his wife and radio partner, Jinx Falkenburg. The narration covers the purpose of the mission and other details that help them understand what they are about to embark on. It is all-inclusive, an excellent overview of Tidal Wave.

Someone mumbles, "Ploiești? I never heard of the place."

"It doesn't matter; you're going to see it from the air."

"Where the hell's Romania?"

The remainder of the briefing includes elaborate scale models of the refineries, meticulous, detailed information provided by former British and American employees, and dutifully re-created and constructed maps and schematics by Major Geerlings—many of which he got from his stealthy activities at the Admiralty Library in London.

"So," Sternfels said, at this point, "the targets and individual refineries were known. But what about the routes to the target? What was known about that? This is information that usually comes from high-altitude photoreconnaissance."

In Washington, DC, the idea of photoreconnaissance had been presented to Smart, suggesting to him the use of the capable British de Havilland Mosquito, a twin-engined, nimble fighter-bomber, made almost entirely of wood ("The Wooden Wolf"). The role of the Mosquito had evolved into many purposes. The Mosquito PR Mk I, a highly respected, photoreconnaissance version, was well suited for capturing detailed photographs of the Ploiești refineries, and could have provided invaluable defensive information. Powered by two Merlin 21s, the PR Mk had a maximum speed of 382 mph, a cruise speed of 255 mph, a ceiling of 35,000 feet, and a range of 2,180 nautical miles. It was nicknamed the Wooden Wolf, or, more aptly, the "Mossie," as the Brits would anoint it.

On January 30, 1943, the tenth anniversary of the Nazis' seizure of power, two Mosquito squadrons knocked out the central Berlin broadcasting station, while "the fat one," *Reichsmarschall* Hermann Göring, was on the microphone, speaking, knocking him off the air. A second attack in the afternoon inconvenienced another speech, this one by Joseph Goebbels, the propaganda minister.

Göring was furious:

In 1940 I could at least fly as far as Glasgow in most of my aircraft, but not now! It makes me furious when I see the Mosquito. I turn green and yellow with envy. The British, who can afford aluminum better than we can, knock together a beautiful wooden aircraft that every piano factory over there is building, and they give it a speed which they have now increased yet again. What do you make of that? There is nothing the British do not have. They have the geniuses, and we have the nincompoops. After the war is over I'm going to buy a British radio set—then at least I'll own something that has always worked.

After one last practice mission, General Brereton and General Ent, the high priests, make the rounds of the five groups to impart their blessings. They have no holy water, but they are accompanied by two historically significant aviation figures:

Eddie Rickenbacker, America's most successful fighter ace in World War I. A Medal of Honor recipient, an American hero of the first rank, credited with twenty-six aerial kills and immensely admired by all, the boys rejoice in his presence here, as if a movie star has descended among them. Rickenbacker is also a race-car driver, automotive designer, a government consultant in military matters, and a pioneer in air transportation, in fact, the longtime head of Eastern Air Lines.

Also there to lend his support is British Air Marshal Sir Arthur Tedder, 1st Baron Tedder, a living legend. A fighter pilot and squadron commander in the Royal Flying Corps in World War I, he went on to serve as a senior officer in the Royal Air Force. At the end of Tedder's lively British pep talk, jingling with cheeriness and enthusiasm, he shouts something so typically British that a tidal wave of goose bumps percolates through the gathering.

Hit them for six! he shouts, an exclusively British term referring to a hit in cricket equivalent to a grand slam in American baseball.

In this context, Tedder means *Kick the shit out of them!*

When the boys hear this imperative, they leap to their feet, repaying Tedder's British fire with American thunder and vim heard 'round the world.

HIT THEM FOR SIX!

HIT THEM FOR SIX!

HIT THEM FOR SIX!

And that was that.

The briefings had ended.

There was not enough time left to digest their fear.

CHAPTER 15

Everything Will Change

In Color
That was my tail gunner ol' Johnny McGee
He was a high school teacher from New Orleans
And he had my back, right through the day we left
Yeah, a picture's worth a thousand words
But you can't see what those shades of gray keep covered
You should've seen it in color
(Should've seen it in color)
—SONGWRITERS: JAMEY JOHNSON, LEE MILLER,
LEE THOMAS MILLER, JAMES OTTO

SATURDAY, JULY 31, 1943
NOTHING STAYS THE SAME.

Bob Sternfels and *The Sandman*'s crew know that nothing in their lives will remain unchanged after tomorrow's sunrise. When they landed at Benina with the 98th Bomb Group, their hope and sanguinity would take them only so far. In Benina, the runway is only so long, and cannot lift them from their dread. The runway ends where the runway ends. A storm that seems unending wanes, another front opens. This is a hard notion for them to take. Today's gold bright sun will turn coy, descend and wait patiently, then glow boldly and brighten tomorrow's dawn, altered by new radiance, new hope, challenging them to survive the heat of the fresh day.

The boys' trepidation will intensify when they strap *The Sandman* on and continue from takeoff until Ploiești's hostile silhouette resolves on the horizon, unyielding in its beckoning—until gunsmoke commences and chaos ensues. Tonight, foreboding will change to chilling fear. And before today's lunch, after tonight's what's-it-called dessert, after day dawns tomorrow, after takeoff, every understanding that they had about themselves—about each other, about war, everything felt in heart and mind from the day of birth till now—will pale and feel peculiar and ill-tempered.

The change will not take long. It will start for most when their heads hit pillows tonight, then endure uncomfortably till morning's stars vanish. Even in their youth, they were sure of certain things: All life ends, death arrives, emboldened by more death. Air will bloody and blemish unblemished fields. Buddies will vanish. Hope will fade. Sorrow will descend, then go. But never forever. Maybe *The Sandman*'s boys are too young to know, but even tomorrow's grief will arc after tomorrow's mission. It will come and go, an arrow, up, up, then down, down with simplicity, pure, but indiscernibly different with its colorful feathers stained, tail up in the soil, no longer imperious from bowstring to sky, but impotent until the next flight, and then a new arc will begin again.

Yes, the boys know that nothing stays the same—especially life's serenities. Some ponder this with quiet fright while holding their breath. Ice cream cones melt. Pretty girls next door grow plump. Boys go paunchy and bald. The first kiss never endures. Hopes fade. Nothing is static. The drumroll of gunfire will wail then subside and ululate again. If the boys hold dreadful thoughts, these thoughts will explode and multiply into a tumult of rudimentary questions: Will I live? Will I die? Will I come back whole? Will I see Mom and Dad again?

There's nothing quite like thunder in the distance.

But tomorrow the boys do not want its din.

Everything will change.

Nothing stays the same.

Because it never has and never will.

———

This weekend, back home, Americans had their Zenith radios on, and for many there were hushed tears when they heard the lachrymose lyrics to an apropos song lyric: *You'll never know just how much I miss you,* went the popular song heard almost everywhere: *You went away, and my heart went with you / I speak your name in my every prayer.* How much they loved that song; it reminded them of longing for someone they might never see again. The lyrics were heard in diners while they enjoyed a simple breakfast. Diners were popular gathering spots to meet friends and trade news, rumors, hopes, and sadness; they were the crux of "social media" of the war years, that and backyard fences and church dinners. This safe environment, as opposed to the war-filled skies over Germany.

Americans bore no fear that German hellfire would fall on their heads, or German fighters would tear up their railroad yards. This year, 1943, approximately 108,000 American boys would be killed—and there were still eight months remaining. Breakfast was a small price to pay for news, rumors, chitchat, and friendship. The average breakfast at an American diner cost $1.30, and that included bacon, eggs, and coffee. Of course, Bob Sternfels's breakfast at the Benina airfield outside Benghazi was gratis. Those people in the diners back home were paying for it— *Thank you, too, Uncle Sam,* and, please, not to worry about a two-dime tip.

Bob and the rest of the airmen at Benghazi were told not to miss the special breakfast Sunday morning, because the cooks were slogging about, conjuring a treat not seen in mess kits there for a long time: "real eggs, real bacon." Bob was delighted. But then, just for a second, he pondered what real eggs and real bacon *actually* meant.

"It didn't take long to figure it out. I knew then for sure," he said. "There was a better-than-average chance a lot of us were not coming back to the wonderful Benghazi desert. It was a condemned man's last meal—that's how a lot of guys looked at it." It was a dreadful notion, one that Bob allowed, but just for the time it took to wipe his plate clean with a slice of toast (alas, without real butter).

The brass were not thinking when they ordered eggs and bacon, or when they had steaks flown down for dinner Saturday night. Of course, they meant well, and probably paid no mind to the potential reaction among their men. And so, the two "special" meals had the opposite result: a double-whammy effect on everyone.

And there was more . . .

To add to the confusion of the mismatch of emotions, today was also payday, the last day of the month. Everyone lined up, as was the military practice. They were handed their pay, had to sign for it, then turned away from the paymaster table and thought: *What the hell am I going to do with this today?* Some stuffed the greenbacks into envelopes to send home, others paid debts, and some just sat down and gambled it away. Others would take it with them on the mission and possibly use it to try and pay their way to freedom if they got captured.

They appreciated the pay they received; they were better paid than their civilian counterparts. Base pay for a private first class with less than three years' service was $54 per month. A second lieutenant got $150. Colonels Compton, Kane, and Smart received $333.33. Brigadier generals earned $500 a month. These were all base-pay figures, and there were extras for combat duty laid on top of overseas duty, and so on. Almost all of it was money in their pockets, to keep, spend, send home, or piss away, because no one had to pay for meals or hospital care or other sundries.

But for all the men, tonight was a time to ruminate, to wonder about their lives—if they would live or not. No matter; all knew that by tomorrow night, nothing would be the same again.

Everything would change.

There was no better time to reflect than after the clock struck midnight—especially on the eve of a historic combat mission that would, realistically, kill many of them.

———

Colonel Kane had been relentless all day with details and last-minute ideas. And worrying about his flock of young men, always uppermost in his mind.

Colonel Kane, the ex-boxer, the barrel-chested, tall, mustached, go-against-the-grain, superlative B-24 pilot, devoted leader of men, took a long walk in the desert this evening. He made more than a few steps through the blackness, then stopped and pondered the gravity of the mission. Kane, more than most men at Benghazi, knew what war could bring, and how it would change a man's heart, his entire life.

Later, Kane penned an entry in his diary, recording his feelings:

There was a quietness, quite unlike the usual buzz. Some crews were quietly giving away their belongings. I sat on my perch, an old engine, and stared a long time at the stars. In my short lifetime, the stars have stayed in their places as they have for countless lifetimes before mine. They would remain unaffected; whether we died in the near future or years later from senility, [it] mattered not in the great scheme of things. Yet the manner of our dying could have far-reaching effects. I have a young son I may never see again, yet I shall be content if I feel that his freedom is assured and he is never forced to be humbled in spirit and body before another man who proclaims himself master.

Colonel Kane's thoughts came from the mind of an experienced air force colonel, a bomber pilot who, like others—officers, noncommissioned officers, and nonmilitary types back home—had reservations about the Tidal Wave strategies designed by Col. Jacob Smart. A lot of this thinking came from Kane's instincts, years of experience, and lessons learned the hard way. Kane had verbally voiced his concerns about Tidal Wave in front of Colonel Smart in an indelicate manner—adding to the list of things that diminished his chances for advancement.

Smart, unlike Kane, had never flown a combat mission until the day Bob Sternfels had taken him up in *The Sandman* and had had to admonish him (*"Colonel, please do not touch the controls!"*). Smart did not fly *The Sandman* that day, two weeks away from the Ploieşti raid; he mainly stood between Bob and his co-pilot and fiddled with the mixtures for reasons unknown, annoying Bob. When Smart was boarding *The Sandman* he had told Sternfels he'd been "checked out on the B-24 a week ago"—long after he'd begun to plan Tidal Wave. Meaning, that was the first time Smart had flown the B-24 (he'd done several touch-and-go landings on the runway, not coming to a stop, a basic procedure taught to student pilots in the early stages of learning to fly).

Kane, however, was an experienced flight leader and had many combat missions to his credit by the time he came to Benghazi. Much of his thought process was based on years of experience and flying some of the most dangerous missions of the war over Europe. Ploieşti, to him, was "just plain nuts!" Kane felt uneasy because he was sure the Americans did not know everything that needed to be known about the raid. His concerns were valid, as he knew more about flying a B-24 on a bombing mission in tight formation than Smart. He knew the shortcomings, strengths, and weaknesses of the airplane—and they didn't match up well with the Smart Plan.

Unknown to the Allies was the fact that the Germans had placed a new signals interception battalion (*Signalabfangbataillon*) in Athens, Greece. Their first achievement was cracking the code of Allies in North Africa—communications between the 8th and 9th Air Forces. As soon as they did, they knew that elements from the five groups from the 8th and 9th were planning to bomb the Vatican on July 19—although they bombed Rome, the Vatican itself was untouched. Further, the *Signalabfangbataillon* was getting detailed information from the spies Rommel left behind when he exited Africa. If the *Signalabfangbataillon* could not intercept future target information, at least they knew what time the Allies were taking off from the Benghazi airfields and would have a good idea how many Liberators were taking off.

For Gerstenberg and his gunners, all the rest would fall into place.

CHAPTER 16

Fortune's Wheel

By your patience, Ancient Pistol, Fortune is painted blind, with a muffler afore her eyes, to signify to you that Fortune is blind; and she is painted also with a wheel to signify to you, which is the moral of it, that she is turning and inconstant, and mutability and variation.
                                                        —WILLIAM SHAKESPEARE

SUNDAY MORNING, AUGUST 1, 1943

Ploieşti wakes to a Sunday routine.
The Americans picked this date for Tidal Wave for two reasons: First, most of Ploieşti's citizens, including the refinery workers, were not working, and their absence would reduce civilian casualties; and second, the uniformed German and Romanian troops who manned the weaponry would be less inclined to be alert. Further, the Allies had cracked the German meteorological code, which was changed on the first of each month. July 31 was the last day data could be obtained until the Americans broke the code for the following month.

Among the thousands of uniformed German and Romanian troops and administrative workers in Romania on this day, two German Luftwaffe officers would be historically prominent in the tactics of Black Sunday: *Generalleutnant* Alfred Gerstenberg, the Protector; and *Oberst* (Colonel) Bernhard Woldenga, Fighter Controller of *Jagdfliegerführer Rumänien* (Fighter Command—Romania), whose fighter aircraft— including both state-of-the-art Messerschmitts and substandard Romanian fighters, the antique IAR 80—would take on the B-24s.

Gerstenberg's and Woldenga's whereabouts on this historic day answer a question that has endured since August 1, 1943: Could spies have penetrated American intelligence folders and obtained the exact date, time, and targets the Americans intended to launch Tidal Wave?

The short answer is, no.

Why?

If they had known the Americans would be attacking that day, why were they away from their commands?

One of the most prominent facts: On August 1, 1943, Gerstenberg and Woldenga were not at their posts. Gerstenberg was relaxing in a mountain resort above Ploieşti. *Oberst* Woldenga was inspecting Luftwaffe fighter squadrons at bases around the Black Sea. If there were spies at any time before this, in the Benghazi airfields or at Brereton's vault-tight Cairo headquarters, who knew that today was the day the Allies would be dropping in on Ploieşti, they would have certainly notified Gerstenberg with the utmost speed. He would not have been lounging in the sun on the side of a mountain resort, or inspecting troops. If spies had informed Gerstenberg and Woldenga of the Smart Plan, both would have been derelict in their duties, and, without question, put up against a wall and executed. So, this notion is absurd.

What the Germans had access to on August 1, as they had many days prior, were the clock times, the number of B-24s taking off from the Benghazi airfields, and the general direction of their flights. When Erwin Rommel vacated North Africa, three radiomen were left behind; they set up camp in a gulley, or wadi, near one of the American airfields, and established a small, efficient spying operation. Well equipped, the radiomen provided local weather information to the Athens station and reported the number of B-24s that took off. They could not determine targets, and could only broadcast the initial takeoff clock times and general compass headings—knowing the bombers would change their flight paths once out over the Mediterranean Sea.

When the Smart Plan was drawn up, it purposefully avoided an obvious "beeline" route to the target (or, as "the crow flies," from the Benghazi airfields direct to Ploieşti). This would have been tactically imprudent—a giveaway regarding the forces' target intention. Besides, most of the time the Americans took off, they were heading to almost the same targets, in Italy and Austria.

To delude the enemy, the five groups, once assembled and away from their Benghazi airfields, would fly a northerly heading at an altitude of 2,000 to 3,000 feet, at 195 mph. Then, when north of the enemy-held island of Corfu, their first IP, they would climb to 10,000 feet and head northeasterly above the Pindus Mountains and across Albania, Yugoslavia, Greece, and Bulgaria. Once over the mountains and passing over the historic Danube River, the force would lower down to an altitude of 100 feet. At this flight level, German radar would not detect them—the bombers would be flying below the radar's capacity. This devious, somewhat cunning, nondirect flight plan would add about 300 to 500 miles to the round-trip mission and would forestall German awareness of their presence for as long as possible. According to Smart and his planning staff, this route would not give away Ploieşti as the target until much later in the flight.

While flying over the Mediterranean—a three-hour flight—German or Italian naval vessels could have spotted the group and reported their altitude and direction. Still, they would have no clear notion of the target. But now, the Germans' ears perked up. At this time, Woldenga, probably back at his command post, was holding back his pack of German and Romanian fighter boys because he had no clear idea what the bombers' target would be. Sometime between departing Benghazi and reaching Corfu, the Germans had their first indication, albeit still unclear, that the bombers were flying toward a target in Romania. At Corfu, the American attackers had made a change in the heading, because they had no other viable choice, changing to a northeasterly compass heading. Could Bucharest be the target?

Strict radio silence had been ordered for the bombers before takeoff. This had both a positive and a negative effect: positive, because the Germans would not pick up any detailed American radio chatter until the last moment before they approached Ploieşti; negative, because several crewmen saw Colonel Compton's 376th Bomb Group scribing a fatal turn but would not break radio silence until it was too late to warn him of his error. (K. K.'s radio, like all the others', was turned off).

Back in Benghazi, the German radio operators in the wadi reported the clock time the B-24s started warming up their Pratt & Whitneys. Around dawn on August 1, 1943, they unknowingly announced the start of one of the most historical days of World War II, telling the Athens station that a considerable number of B-24s had fired up their engines. It was the most significant force they had ever seen taking off.

Because the operation was under the command of General Brereton's IX Bomber Command, one of its groups, the 376th—with mission commander General Ent aboard, and Colonel Compton flying—Compton's *Teggie Ann* was selected to lead the mission. The 376th would be followed by the 93rd, the 98th (Bob Sternfels's group), and the 44th. To mollify the 98th, led by Colonel Kane, the 98th was assigned to knock out the most essential target: the Astra Romania Refinery, at one time owned by the Dutch Shell Oil Company, the largest refinery in Ploieşti.

One hour had been designated for assembling the five groups after takeoff from Benghazi airfields. The German radiomen sat there, cramped in their tight wadi amid an unusual silence, wondering what the target would be on this day, because that's all they could do at this point.

Bob Sternfels recalled:

Unknown to the strike force a coded message from 9th Air Force to 8th Air Force Command, that Operation Tidal Wave had taken off, was intercepted and decoded by German Intelligence. They knew that a significant mission was under way, but not the destination. That information came three hours later from German installations in Sicily, and along the Adriatic. Since the aircraft were slowly climbing as their fuel burned off, and the mission profile did not call for low-level flight at this time, they were picked up by luminescent [radar] screens. Now the Germans knew which direction they were heading. They were going not to their favorite targets in Italy, but to either Greece, Yugoslavia, Bulgaria, or Romania. All they had to do was wait for the next radar contacts.

The intercepted and decrypted message from the 9th Air Force to the 8th, that Tidal Wave was under way, went from one high-frequency radio set to another with the speed of a malevolent spear. The signal sped, sleek and resolute, with strength and gravitas—and pending calamity for the aircrews of Tidal Wave. The American force had no notion of the message's transmission, nor its import. If they had, their apprehension would have turned to dread.

~⌒~

6:00 A.M., AUGUST 1, 1943

Cometh battle, cometh, let us join limbs . . .
The Benina airfield is painted sternly with silhouettes of B-24s, causing a storm of swirling dust, a commotion of pulsing exhaust notes cracking, snapping the desert air, angrily announcing a historic start at a clock time that must be abided by, at all costs. At airfields dotted 40 miles along the Libyan hump, 179 Liberators prepare to depart.

Now desert rats, spiders, and scorpions are crouched on the sideline of battle, bemused by the uproar, watching as these horrid machines agitate their dull sandy surface. Massive billows of sand and exhaust smoke roil across the cold, sleepy desert. These creatures own this desert, and patience, too; that is how they have survived. For centuries occurrences have descended here and then gone. But the desert tenants have never seen such a cacophony as this, not at this magnitude. And they wait, withdrawn, as the wonder before them brings their varied species together, as one vital, living part of their desert. Life among them comes to a halt until this dissonance settles. The world and the universe come to a halt. There is no room on the planet for anything but this. This tilting of their home, this land they stand on, this planet, has the right-of-way. Everything succumbs to the thunder, the vitality, of 1,200-horsepower engines flailing the atmosphere with their furious roar, big machines rocking impatiently, trembling on their rubber heels, anxious to grab the air and get away from here. Figure it: 179 airplanes, four engines apiece—a total of 716 1,200-horsepower engines.

Earlier this morning, Lt. Bob Sternfels and the crew strapped on *The Sandman* for a scheduled 7:00 a.m. takeoff. They checked for sufficient ammunition, intercom connections, maps, water, K-rations, helmets.

Some of them have paperbacks for the long flight when they are merely passengers on a passenger plane, their machine guns flaccid, silent.

Bob thinks about the flak jackets he and his crew don't have.

In a photo before takeoff, K. K. Compton and the *Teggie Ann*'s co-pilot, Capt. Ralph "Red" Thompson, are smiling as they fit a flak jacket onto a grinning General Ent. Only one hundred sets of flak jackets were sent down from Britain, and not a one has been issued to anyone in Bob's crew.

Bob starts *The Sandman*'s engines.

For them, the mission has commenced.

It's part of an intricate procedure that he and co-pilot 2nd Lt. Barney Jackson from Salesville, Texas, share. Their fingers flip, turn, tap switches, buttons, and levers. David Polaschek, the bombardier, stands between them and watches their hands move, double-checking their checklist.

The Sandman coughs, which they all do, then sounds eager—this means healthy, according to Bob's seat-of-the-pants instinct. First, Number 3, which has the generators and hydraulic pump to aid the start-up of the other engines and systems. Number 4 is next. Then Number 1, and last, Number 2. This is the standard procedure. All the instruments are "in the green," or within normal ranges.

One of the aircraft has fouled plugs (whether intentional or not). In starting an engine, a fouled plug problem can be deliberately caused by idling the engine for an extended period. Later, it was discovered the plug was broken, not fouled. "It could be," Bob said, "that the pilot did not like the mission and thought this might be a way out; who knows?"

Now, 179 B-24s are waiting for their takeoffs at two-minute intervals. The whole process is tediously slow. Each bomber has to wait until the dust of the other bomber has settled—not only for the sake of visibility, but to prevent dust from entering the engines' intakes, fouling fuel lines and scoring cylinders.

Kickapoo, piloted by 1st Lt. Robert Nespor, twenty-one, from Oklahoma, rolls down the runway at Lete airfield, miles from where Bob has just shoved the throttles forward, where *The Sandman* has taken its turn down the runway, leaving the spiders and scorpions and rats with one less dreadful machine to contemplate.

Great Council of War: The Casablanca Conference at the Anfa Hotel, Casablanca, Morocco, January 14–24, 1943. Seated: President Roosevelt, Prime Minister Churchill. Front row standing left to right: General Arnold, Admiral King, General Marshall, Admiral Pound, Air Chief Marshal Porter, General Brooke, Field Marshall Dill, and Admiral Mountbatten. Extreme right looking down the line to his right: Colonel Jacob "Jake" E. Smart, Tidal Wave's chief planner. An assemblage of the dramatis personae of the world's most astute Allied military planners. The world had never seen such an illustrious gathering, and it signaled the intent of the Allies to end world tyranny. Bettman/Getty Images

Col. Jacob "Jake" Edward Smart, thirty-nine, left, conferring with then Lt. Gen. Hap Arnold. At the Casablanca conference, Arnold ordered Smart to "get this done," and Smart set out planning the Ploieşti raid. Smart completed his Air Force career as a four-star general, working for the Rand Corporation after retiring from the Air Force. Arnold earned five stars and retired as General of the Army and General of the Air Force, an extraordinary feat unmatched before or after.

Commander of Operation Tidal Wave, Maj. Gen. Lewis Hyde Brereton, Commanding General, Ninth US Air Force. A man with a troubled past. Denied permission by General Arnold to fly and lead the attack on Ploieşti; he knew too many Allied secrets. Arnold's decision devastated Brereton.

Col. John Riley "Killer" Kane, commander of the 98th Bomb Group. One of the central, controversial figures during Tidal Wave and its infamous "wrong turn." Six-feet tall, barrel-chested, a former medical student and boxer at Baylor University, Killer was rough around the edges, loved by his men, and disliked but respected by his superiors. Immediately after the mission, Killer and Colonel Compton almost came to blows and had to be separated. Compton asked Smart if he intended to court-martial Kane for the manner he flew the mission.

The youngest full colonel in the USAAF, "K. K." Compton clashed with Killer Kane. These differences, particularly in flying styles, would lead to the mission's controversial "wrong turn." Here K. K., from a tony Washington, DC, family, is wearing a non-regulation high-quality officer's grade shirt. In hand, an expensive Parker Duofold fountain pen to address a USAAF envelope. All outgoing mail was opened and censored before wending its way to the addressee. Michael Ochs Archives/Getty Images

On the right, Col. Leon Johnson, one of five Medal of Honor recipients (three post-humously), awarded for his actions during the raid. Commander of the 44th Bomb Group, Johnson flew as copilot on the Ploieşti raid aboard *Suzy Q*. He led White V force to the target. On his left ring finger is his class ring from West Point. The dog here is unidentified. However, another mascot, Rusty, a cocker spaniel, flew the Ploieşti mission aboard *Avenger*. When Rusty heard loud explosions, he crawled under the pilot's seat and put his paws over his ears. He survived the mission and retired as a four-star general. MICHAEL OCHS ARCHIVES/GETTY IMAGES

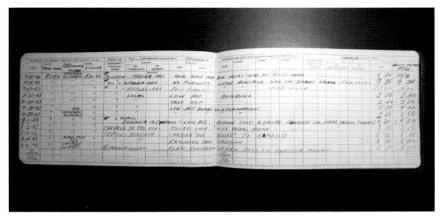

Robert W. Sternfels's pilot's logbook from 1943 still in superb condition today despite flying with him for fifty missions. Most notable entries: "7.15.43: Col. Smart aboard. Four holes." This was Smart's first combat mission. And the historic Tidal Wave entry: "8.1.43: Ploiesti to Romania to Cyprus: Lost 6 ships. Followed Colonel Kane across Turkey." This entry is referring to the raid on Ploieşti and Sternfels's flying cover for Killer Kane to Cyprus after the mission. Sternfels's 98th BG lost many more than six ships that day. He found out the exact number over the next few days.

Privacy? This is it. The distance between here and the nearest tent was all the privacy a man had. This was especially uncomfortable at night when the temperature would drop to 40 degrees. MICHAEL OCHS ARCHIVES/GETTY IMAGES

Bob Sternfels, left, and his copilot, Barney Jackson, in front of *The Sandman*'s nose. Jackson liked wearing cowboy boots when he flew.

One of the last pictures taken of *Wongo Wongo*. After takeoff, the ship lost an engine. The bomb load was salvoed over the Mediterranean. Approaching the airfield, the right wing tip hit a cement light pole, and the *Wongo Wongo* cartwheeled and exploded. Eight of the men aboard were killed.

The *Brewery Wagon* with the ship's line crew. Note the handwritten inscription made the day the photo was taken in the lower white margin: 7/29/43. Over the target, pilot Lt. Palm's leg was severed by a 20mm round, which he only discovered when he could not apply pressure to the rudder pedal. The ship was the first to crash onto Romanian soil, and the survivors were taken prisoners.

The crew of *Exterminator* suiting up prior to a mission over Germany. Note the variety of flight equipment. Subsequently assigned to Benghazi, it flew on the Ploieşti raid piloted by Capain Hugh R. Roper, pulling on a boot. Badly damaged by flak, the *Exterminator* suffered a mid-air collision in a cloud bank on the return to Benghazi. All eleven on board were killed, including an extra pilot flying the mission as an observer. TIME LIFE PICTURES/GETTY IMAGES

The totemic image of Black Sunday: Bob Sternfels flying *The Sandman*, clearing the smokestacks by several feet. "I was certain I was going to die at that moment," he said. Two seconds earlier, Sternfels saw the silver glitter of a steel cable tethered to an explosive charge on the ground. He kicked hard left rudder, and the cable was sliced by a propeller on the number three engine.

Seconds after slicing the cable and narrowly missing the smokestacks, Sternfels has *The Sandman* flying straight and level. From here, he headed away from the maelstrom and flew to Cyprus alongside Killer Kane's damaged ship providing cover. The next day, they returned to their base in Benghazi.

Left to right: General Brereton and General Ent having a happy-chat-moment at Benghazi after the Ploieşti mission. Note the cigarette jutting from Brereton's lips. Smoking was not allowed this close to aircraft, but R.H.I.P (Rank Has Its Privileges). Brereton seems oblivious to the three disappearing in a massive ball of fire. Ent was the Mission Commander and flew aboard *Teggie Ann*, Compton's B-24. While Brereton and Ent seem engaged in their light chat, Lieutenant Colonel Keith "K. K." Compton seems exhausted and duly pensive, perhaps thinking of the "wrong turn" he made a few hours earlier. The hole in the fuselage next to K. K.'s head is undoubtedly the result of a shrapnel hit or a 20 mm bullet.

Debriefing. Left to right: Anthony W. Flesch, navigator; Bob Sternfels, pilot; Barney Jackson, co-pilot; and David A. Polaschek, bombardier.

Taken after the attack. Left to right standing: Major Robert W. Sternfels, pilot; Barney Jackson, co-pilot; Tony Flesch, navigator; Dave Polaschek, bombardier; Bill Stout, flight engineer. Kneeling: Frank Just, radio operator; and the gunners: Harry Rifkin, N. Petri, Merle Bolen, and Raymond Stewart. To Sternfels's right shoulder note the slash mark on the fuselage made by the tethered cable that almost killed the crew over the target.

Killer Kane's severely damaged *Hail Columbia* crawled back to Cyprus on three engines and extensive battle damage. The berm at the end of the runway was a traditional feature of British runways and prevented the ship from overshooting. From here, Kane flew aboard *The Sandman* back to Benghazi via Palestine, where Bob saw the totemic image of his ship for the first time on the front page of the *Stars & Stripes* newspaper. The image was immediately sent throughout the world and appeared in countless publications.

Bob Sternfels about to shake hands with Maj. Gen. Jimmy Doolittle. Bob's commanding officer, Killer Kane, is about to hand Doolittle the Silver Star to present to Sternfels for a mission he flew to Italy. Bob was impressed: "I got a big kiss and a hug from Doolittle's wife!"

Some of the remains of *The Sandman* on display at the Commemorative Air Force Museum in Mesa, AZ. Visible is a piece of tire, a piece of the manifold from one of the engines, and a part of the aircraft's Fowler flap.

EXHAUST HEADER

RECOVERED FROM
TE OF THE SANDMAN

SECTION OF FOWLER FLAP

Nancy Barker and Bob Sternfels. They met on a blind date in Vineland, NJ. Bob vowed he would marry Nancy within a month; he did. They were wed in Trinity Episcopal right on schedule.

Consolidated Aircraft's heavy bomber, the B-24 Liberator, over the mountains of Southern California. The German's called it a "flying moving van." American aircrews said it was the plane the B-17 was shipped in. They made fun of her. Until they flew her in combat. MUSEUM OF FLIGHT FOUNDATION/ GETTY IMAGES

Bob Sternfels at his Laguna Woods, CA, residence. Circa 2006. Bob passed away on January 24, 2018. He was 97.

Nespor has three hundred combat hours. His regular crew had been placed in other bombers. He was given *Kickapoo* to fly today, and then he would be finished with flying.

This is the moment where the mission starts going rotten.

———

At Lete airfield, *Kickapoo* does not want to leave the desert floor. The air ahead—bright sky, pink sun slatting through wispy clouds—does not beckon the ship. Instead, the innards of the Pratt & Whitney Number 4 engine are not in harmony.

Something is wrong.

Lieutenant Nespor takes *Kickapoo* down the runway, hits 130 mph, and pulls back on the control column, expecting a typical rollout and climb. Instead, *Kickapoo* refuses. She has an unusual temperament today. Maybe she knows what's up ahead—*That Ploiești place, yeah, this might be better, right here, right now—get it over with.*

The Number 4 engine quits whooping and coughing and the propeller flutters, tries to reengage, then jolts to a stop.

Nespor and his co-pilot now have a large, stationary pile of American-made metal on their hands, forcing them through a litany of situational choices. Nespor has to make up his mind quickly and select one that might work.

Kickapoo obeys a law of physics: The bomber does not have sufficient air flowing over its wings to keep it where Nespor wants it, and she starts to tip toward the ground, toward her conclusion. A small flash of gray smoke blips out from the dead engine, scribing the aircraft's sickening descent.

Of course, Nespor realized days ago that he would have his hands full with this mission—that taking off when the ship is configured this way—the bomb load, the extra fuel, the ammunition—would be about as close to suicide as he'd ever want to get.

He opts for returning to the desert and begins drawing a wide half-circle, careful not to dip the wing too far and stall the ship. He can see the runway there, off the left wingtip. He's as close to being in control of the ship as he can get it in this situation.

Kickapoo has 3,100 gallons of aviation gasoline, a 4,300-pound bomb load, plus ammunition for its .50 caliber guns, thermite sticks, and ten humans on board. It's a miracle the ship was able to lumber off the ground in the first place.

Before Nespor flattens the turn, he pulls the emergency bomb release toggle on the pilot's pedestal and salvos 4,300-pounds of trouble, which falls into the Med. Then *Kickapoo* lifts up from the lightened load, and Nespor and his co-pilot, Lt. John Riley, imagine for a moment that they might have squared away the problem. They trim the ship, bring the landing gear up, idle the mixture control, shut off the boost pumps, feather the prop on the dead engine, and pull up the landing gear. They can't do much more but fly the bird the way they were taught to do, under these conditions.

They have *Kickapoo* lined up for a short, straight-in approach at Lete airfield, where they took off from, coming in low over the desert sand.

Too heavy, too fast.

A few hundred yards from touchdown, *Kickapoo*'s right wingtip catches a light stanchion, a brute made of ferroconcrete. Six feet of wingtip slashes off like a cracker and *Kickapoo* slides right, then noses down, then noses up, then cartwheels for two horrible seconds, desert sand, scrub, and bomber parts thrashing the air.

Nespor and the rest of the crew have no time to assess what—

The impact scoops a hole 10 feet deep and 45 feet wide. The largest intact section is the tailplane.

The forward portion of the nose slams—Plexiglas, metal spars, electric wiring—dead center into the hole.

The explosion shudders the air, shock waves roll out, then come rolling back. A ball of orange and red fire hides what remains. The pyre burns with vicious intensity.

In the 45-foot-wide hole, shreds of the fuselage and engine chunks and insulation rest, burning.

One of the tires severed from the strut is visible.

Then a couple of thousand pounds of .50 caliber ammunition and thermite explosive lights off with the remainder of unburnt aviation fuel and brightens the sky like a Fourth of July gone irrational. Sand 300 yards away is charred devilish black.

There is the stench of burnt flesh, and hot carbon and hot metal tinkles like delicate cymbals.

Out of the roasting tangle, wonders emerge: Two airmen have escaped, both badly burned.

The navigator, 2nd Lt. Russell Polivka, and one of the gunners, Sgt. Eugene Garner, stagger from the burning wreck, clothing aflame. For the next eighteen months, Polivka would be hospitalized, enduring multiple operations before eventually recovering from his burns. Sgt. Garner would also undergo multiple operations before he passed away, in November of 2005.

"Yeah, that wasn't a good start," said Lt. Barney Jackson, co-pilot of *The Sandman*. "I remember we were circling after liftoff and were turning north. That was my side. I saw him go in on the approach. He hit short and from there just splattered."

At this hour, not everyone flying in the vicinity sees the crash, the flames, the smoke. In unison, those who do think: *This is one hell of a way to start a mission.*

Now there are 178 aircraft going to Ploiești, flying toward fortune's wheel.

Circling over the Mediterranean, Bob is in a holding pattern, waiting to collate with the other aircraft. Years later, he would recall:

> *The mission plan was to form a line of five groups, each in succession, led by the 376th Bomb Group under the command of Colonel K. K. Compton. The overall mission commander, General Ent, flew with Compton. They were followed by the other four groups, but it is not clear how this very large number of aircraft was to be gathered and assembled in a single massive formation.*

To this, Bob's co-pilot added: "I'm sure there was [a plan], but I couldn't say for sure there was anything in mission briefing about assembly. We didn't do it, except for our own group."

It takes the groups an hour to form up in some semblance of a group and begin the flight to Ploieşti, to fly first toward Corfu.

Uneventfully, the groups fly for three hours over the Mediterranean until landfall appears ahead: Cape Asprókavos, a portion of the Nazi-held island of Corfu—the first checkpoint, and a pivotal one. It is here, approaching Corfu, that the group is meant to make a 90-degree turn, take a northeasterly heading, and fly over the Continent.

Here, a bit of mystery stands amid the pending battle.

Misfortune slams again.

～

This is the portion of Tidal Wave where speculation, ignorance, doubt, and confusion intertwine and leave behind a beclouded, inaccurate picture of exactly what misfortune occurred next. It is the first of several misunderstood, confusing situations that not even the passage of history can clarify or purge. Even some who flew the mission can only add to the misinformation of it all.

The lead group—the Liberandos, the 376th BG—is led by Colonel Compton, and comprises two sections, "A" and "B"—a total of twenty-six B-24s. There are three B-24s in the lead group of "A." One, *Teggie Ann*, flown by Compton, is in the lead, or the "point of the spear," where it should be. Below and off to Compton's right wing, *Wongo Wongo*, is piloted by 1st Lt. Brian W. Flavelle.

Suddenly, *Wongo Wongo* begins to "stagger," drunk somehow, "dipping down and nosing up," according to Maj. Norman C. Appold, pilot of *G.I. Ginnie*. ("*Wongo Wongo* stood straight up on its tail. Then it slid over on her back, then, slowly gaining speed, planed straight down into the sea.")

Just before the dive, the ship barely misses crashing into another B-24. As the aircraft dives down, "three objects flew out or off [the fuselage]."

When it hits the water, the aircraft explodes, and a plume of black smoke rises 1,000 feet. The whole incident takes just thirty seconds. First Lieutenant Iovine, the pilot of *Desert Lily*, breaks formation—which he's been forbidden to do—and circles the pyre on the water, searching for survivors, but he's sure there are none. Because he has a full bomb and fuel load, Iovine heads back to North Africa, too far away from the formation to catch up.

The mission is cut down to 176 B-24s.

Then, at 8:40 a.m., *Scarlett O'Hara* has to abort the 98th's formation when one of the crewmen has an acute attack of dysentery. They turn and head back to Africa, and at 500 feet pass over the spot where *Wongo Wongo* went in. They see a Mae West, an oxygen bottle, a can, and an oil slick.

Now 175 B-24s fly on toward the target.

A few minutes later, *Big Time Operator*, also of the 98th, has mechanical trouble: Her Number 3 supercharger fails, and fuel pressure falls on the Number 2 engine. The aircraft turns, heads back to Africa. Like *Scarlett O'Hara*, she does a double-check pass over *Wongo Wongo's* sea grave to check for survivors. They spot an oxygen bottle, a deflated life raft, and what appears to be a white object, presumed to be an opened parachute.

Now, there are 174 bombers.

Some think the mission is "snake-bitten."

Tidal Wave is enduring misfortune after misfortune, and not a shot has been issued.

⟋ ⟍

There were two controversial issues to this aspect of the mission that lived for years. The first: *Wongo Wongo's* navigator, Lt. Robert F. Wilson, who, according to inaccurate, misinformed sources and reports, was supposedly the lead navigator for the mission to Ploieşti; and second: Harold Wicklund, K. K. Compton's navigator in the *Teggie Ann*, the lead ship, and the officially designated lead navigator.

According to a statement given to Bob Sternfels many years ago, in the first and only interview he ever gave, Compton shed light on this "who was the official navigator" controversy: "The Mission Lead Navigator was Captain Harold Wicklund," said Compton. "He was also the Group Navigator for the 376th Bomb Group, and he flew aboard [my ship], the *Teggie Ann*."

There is a lot more on this matter, and others, with Colonel Compton later on.

The mission was now down to 174 bombers. And once they turned toward the Continent, that number would go lower and lower.

And the group still had to confront the German flak train.

CHAPTER 17

Crumble and Crackle

No battle plan survives first contact with the enemy.
—HELMUTH KARL BERNHARD GRAF VON MOLTKE,
CHIEF OF THE GERMAN GENERAL STAFF

"NO ONE TOLD US ABOUT THE DAMNED FLAK TRAIN," SAID BOB STERNFELS.

This oversight will have catastrophic results for Bob Sternfels's Group, the Pyramidiers (the 98th BG, aka, the Desert Rats), led by Killer Kane; and the Flying Eight-Balls (the 44th BG), led by Leon W. Johnson, who, four months after Ploieşti, would be awarded the Congressional Medal of Honor in England for his actions at Ploieşti: "By his gallant courage, brilliant leadership and superior flying skills, Colonel Johnson so led his formation as to destroy totally the important refining plants and installations which were the object of his mission." Johnson was one of two Medal of Honor winners who survived Ploieşti; the other three Medals were awarded posthumously.

Five Bomb Groups at Benghazi were now ready to initiate the attack on Ploieşti: the 43rd, 44th, 93rd, 98th, and the 376th. Moments after the Groups began taking off from airfields and started to form up over the Med, the newly installed German signals interception battalion in Athens, Greece, caught multiple blips on their luminescent screens, noted the takeoff times, and relayed the information throughout Gerstenberg's command. Greece was on the way to Romania and had to be flown over. It was not far from Corfu or Albania, and they also had to be flown over. The Germans had placed their new radar in the perfect spot. Since the mission force took an hour to take off and form up, the Athens radar station had ample time to track the bombers departing from Benghazi and flying toward the Continent.

By mid-morning, Gerstenberg's staff felt confident that the American force was over the Mediterranean at 3,000 feet, and heading their way.

Gerstenberg would be ready.

The flight over the Mediterranean took three uneventful hours. To pass the time, many crewmen read paperback novels, ate rations, daydreamed, napped, or yakked a bit on the intercom.

At 8:55 a.m. local time, at 10,000 feet, Colonel Compton and his Group, the 376th BG, passed over the northeasterly coastline of the island of Corfu, the first checkpoint. Compton wagged *Teggie Ann's* wings—the signal—and the Group followed him, heading in a northeasterly direction over Greece, Albania, Yugoslavia, and Bulgaria.

The 376th aimed for the first checkpoint in Romania, where the situation would soon turn into a grim swamp of irretrievable chaos.

A spotter noted the large Group and reported the sighting to German intelligence.

Minutes later, once the force had straightened out, another spotter ID'd the formation and relayed the sighting.

At *Oberst* Woldenga's command post, activity went from passive to frenetic. The certainty of the target, still unclear, seemed to be either Bucharest or Ploieşti—or, more problematic, both. Woldenga had to hold back his fighters until he was confident of the Americans' target; Gerstenberg concurred. However, the first stages of the alert—from the new Athens radar station in Greece, and the two visual sightings—went out, and preparations began for a counterattack at the most propitious moment.

As the Groups approached Albania's coastline, the aircrews were flying with several liabilities, albeit unknown to them.

First and foremost, they were spotted by German radar at the newly installed Athens station. Up to this point, detection should not have surprised the Americans. How Colonel Smart and his staff could have assumed the attack force, with over 170 B-24s, could not have been spotted is hard to comprehend. The only "surprise" at that moment was the date and time they took off, and the fact that the Germans had no notion of the target(s). Flying below 100 feet provided the attack force a masking ability, and allowed them to fly undetected by German radar when "down on the deck." But when the Groups ascended after leaving Corfu, they confronted an unexpected mother-of-all clouds: German radar picked up a speckled mass of blips on their screens about to confront this massive cloud that varied between 10,000 and 15,000 feet.

Something big was up.

A clearer picture of the target was coming into view.

The second liability: Months earlier, tests in the United States were conducted to determine what percentage of the bombs the B-24s were carrying would explode—in other words, would the bombs work? Conventional thinking assumes the bomb load you have will explode after hitting the ground. Not so. These were the same type of general-purpose bombs the B-24s would soon be dropping on the refineries, that they held in their bellies right now, that the crews were counting on to destroy the refineries and neutralize the defenses.

The results were dismal.

Fifty percent of the tested 1,000-pound general-purpose bombs did not explode, and 25 percent of the 500-pounders failed to detonate— wholly unacceptable statistics. Of course, aircrews had no notion of this at the time, because the test was top secret; plus, it would have been devastating to morale. (After the stench of battle dissipated around Ploieşti, the Germans went about the refineries, de-arming and hoisting away unexploded American bombs.)

Third: According to "Field Order No. 58—Bomb Loading Annex," each aircraft was ordered to carry a minimum of two boxes of British-type incendiaries; today, incendiaries are outlawed for use on military targets with a concentration of civilians. The incendiaries on board contained thickened triethylaluminium, a napalm-like substance that ignites on contact with air. If at all possible, the waist gunners were meant to throw the incendiaries out of their windows to start fires and increase mayhem and havoc at the refineries. The negative side of this was they were aboard aircraft loaded with aviation gas and were getting shot at. A stray bullet or bit of shrapnel, and the incendiaries would go off and melt through the fuselage or cause a massive explosion from the fuel. On paper, this must have seemed like a good idea. In fact, some of the incendiaries were hit, detonated, ignited, and burned. As a result, some of the B-24s were unable to put out the onboard fire, exploded and crashed.

A fourth liability was the extra fuel tank installed in the bomb bays of the B-24s, and the abundant fuel loads in the wings and newly installed Tokyo tanks. This massive amount of 100 percent aviation gasoline was highly susceptible to exploding and, collectively, amounted to hundreds of thousands of pounds of fuel. When the bomb-bay doors were open, this extra fuel tank—which displaced bombs—was fully exposed to gunfire and shrapnel.

The Germans were working latitudes and longitudes and azimuth now: They knew a mass of B-24s had left Benghazi. Now, that information was being refined through German radar stations in Sicily and the Adriatic coast. Strengthening these radar hits, ground observers were posting reports along the route the B-24s were flying.

At this point, the Americans spotted four obsolete Czech-built Avia B-534s designed and built in the mid-1930s, more aerial antiques, with a meek 600-horsepower engine—no match for the B-24's firepower. They also spotted some German-built, Bulgarian-piloted Me 109s. The B-534s were bi-wing aircraft—the Americans thought they were trainers—and they were not within striking distance. The B-534s gave up the chase and scooted away, along with Me 109s, like a group of disappointed houseflies.

At 9:00 a.m. Bob Sternfels and the 98th BG passed from the Adriatic Sea to Albania. Ahead, mountain peaks rising to 9,000 feet were visible in the pilots' windscreens.

Sternfels's entire crew, the Desert Rats, found the lush topography and rolling hills a pleasant change from the arid desert. To provide a safety margin, the Group climbed to 11,000 feet to hump the mountains. These peaks, plus a thick shelf of cumulonimbus clouds, presented a challenge. To go around the clouds would take too much time; to go through them in a tight formation was dangerous. To get above them, 17,000 feet, would consume too much fuel.

At this point, the first tactical errors were committed.

Michael Hill, in his book *Black Sunday: Ploesti*, explains:

We should recall the previous debate between Colonel Compton and Kane. Compton felt the normal cruise power should be used for the sea leg, then added power to get over the mountains. This should keep the formation tighter so that they would all be together for the charge to the target. Kane, on the other hand, wanted to save power all the way, then power up for the run in and out of the target. Both were sound tactics provided that everyone stayed together *[emphasis added]. Staying together was already becoming a major problem.*

Two colonels, at odds with each other, and two types of flying, was an insufferable concoction.

Now was not the time to argue the finer points of either procedure, or getting everyone to agree on whether or not to go above, through, or around the clouds ahead. Coordinating now was out of the question. Muddling the matter further was the strict radio silence that had been ordered—an enemy of the Groups right now—particularly at this point on the map, where the Germans were undoubtedly trying to pick up radio signals.

To go through the clouds, a maneuver called frontal penetration, meant the entire Group would initiate a circling pattern before reaching the clouds. Once circled like a bunch of Conestoga wagons, the lead section would peel off from the circle and fly through the clouds. The procedure is repeated until each section flies through the other side of the clouds. Once the lead section is through, it starts flying in a circle again—consuming time and fuel—which gives the next section time to catch up. Once they are all caught up, the sections straighten and resume formation flying again. This was not thought of, not planned for. This is a risky procedure. The thickness of the clouds is unknown, and where it stops being a cloud, only angels know. It is also hazardous because, at times, pilots cannot see their wingtips. You are driving down the freeway at night in thick fog with cars all around. You dare not move out of your lane.

This frontal penetration maneuver was not Compton's choice.

He took the 376th high, skimming the tops like a knife sliding over a muffin top, thinking it would save fuel and time. In a year 2000 interview with Bob Sternfels, Colonel Compton (then a retired lieutenant general) asserted that he did not climb higher than 9,000 feet, in order "to conserve fuel."

In the meantime, because of the radio silence order, none of the mission commanders could communicate with each other to coordinate a unifying strategy, or collate a clear picture of the situation.

This was the first major error of the mission.

Unlike Compton, Kane decided on frontal penetration, taking the 44th and the 389th through the thick clouds, but staying at a flight level of 10,000 feet. At the same time, Kane stubbornly refused to adjust his airspeed to to match Compton's.

Meanwhile, two serious issues complicated matters here: delusion and radio silence.

The Americans still believed they had not been detected by the Germans—lack of tactical judgment, hampered further by poor initial planning—and the radio silence, once again their enemy, led to a lack of mission coordination. Things were about to devolve into chaos.

The Smart Plan had started to crumble and crackle like an overbaked cookie.

Two experienced officers, Kane and Compton, were flying large groups of airplanes. They did not like each other, which can never be good in any organization with serious goals (in this case, targets). Each had their own styles, their own methods of flying B-24s, but at the same time, both were excellent pilots. Kane was old-school army air force: beefy, gruff, and unpolished, perhaps why he was not "fawned over" by the brass. Compton was new-school—young, slender, and handsome, the kind of polished officer the air force had started to look for before the war began to represent the vanguard of a bright future, the new US Air Force.

These different representations would affect both men's careers, and lives—and, at this juncture of the mission, the lives of many crewmen as well, who were following them into an increasingly deadly situation.

Now, once again, misfortune struck.

No battle plan survives first contact with the enemy!

Compton's Group had picked up a tailwind, increasing ground speed, and further distancing them by about 60 miles from Kane's Group, and the others. This would mean Compton would arrive at the target more than twenty minutes ahead of everyone else.

This was not good. This, in and of itself, wrecked the Smart Plan. This would cause endemic chaos over the target, with aircraft flying in and out of various directions. And now, there was no way around this situation, no fallback plan. The closer the Groups got to Ploiești, the more the chaos would increase.

At this point, the five Groups were spreading out into one unbroken column. At odds on how to use power on this mission, Kane and Compton were using opposing power-setting philosophies. Compton expected his airspeed—higher than the others—to be matched by all Groups, in order for the formation to stay with him. This was not happening. In fact, before the mission, this had only been assumed; it had not been laid down in stone.

Compton was taking advantage of the Davis Wing design, which provided a lower drag coefficient and allowed for higher airspeed and lower fuel consumption. He believed Kane and the others would follow his lead, but they did not. Kane stubbornly and predictably refused to use the same power settings as Compton. Perhaps this was a result of old-school Kane versus new-school Compton. This situation should have been ironed out before the mission began, but it was obviously not on the agenda.

Killer Kane, leading the 98th in *Hail Columbia*, has lost contact with the 376th and the 93rd.

Now, Kane, piloting *Hail Columbia*, asks his tail gunner for an update on what he sees behind them.

Sgt. William Leo, Kane's tail gunner, tells Kane, "There are two Groups back here, sir—the 44th and 389th."

As a result of the different power settings and airspeeds, Kane, flying lead at his own selected airspeed, causes the 44th and 389th to back up into a "traffic jam" behind him; they are trapped, and have no choice but to follow Colonel Kane.

Killer Kane has caused this unexpected separation of the Groups. A dogged and iron-willed individual, his responsibility during this phase of the flight was simply to keep pace with Colonel Compton, who is now out of sight. Kane did not do that.

Compton, meanwhile, has no idea that his climb to a higher altitude has been detected by the German *Würzburg* beaming from Athens, Greece.

The different paths through the clouds, the power settings, the Davis Wing, and the tailwind—*and* Killer Kane—infuriate Compton.

(After the mission, when Compton lands at Benghazi at nightfall, he will rush to Colonel Smart and ask if he will court-martial Killer Kane.)

Gerstenberg is now sure of the route the Americans are following; he has been well-informed by spotters and reliable radar sightings. He still is not sure of the target: Ploieşti or Bucharest? Or both? But why would the Americans fly 1,200 miles and bomb Bucharest, he wonders, a city with no strategic value? (He's a bit surprised, too, that the Americans are "working" on a Sunday, traditionally a day of rest in the United States.)

Nevertheless, here come the Americans, in their bulbous moving vans.

No, the American force is not going to bomb Bucharest *and* Ploieşti.

Ploieşti is the target of this attack. They had tried ineffectively once before, in June 1942 (HALPRO), and there is an excellent chance this time that they have no idea how extensive and deadly the Luftwaffe defenses will be. These defenses will disrupt the Smart Plan. (The surprise Smart had sought from the beginning was ruined the moment the Groups went wheels-up from Benghazi.)

The phones in Gerstenberg's control center jingle like Christmas bells with incoming calls announcing updates.

Hört dich, hört dich, die Amerikaner kommen! (Hear ye, hear ye, the Americans are coming!)

Then a signal shoots out from Gerstenberg's command radios to the commander of a *Flak-Zug*, a German flak train, located at Campina.

The train is idling, puffing a copious column of thick steam. It sits on a railroad spur not too far from Campina, pointing arrow-like with ill intent toward those oil refineries, the huffing, puffing engine ready to propel down the track at a moment's notice.

The engineer is ordered to fire up the train as fast as it will go. It will reach 100 mph just as the Americans' B-24s arrive overhead. Perfect German timing.

Another important point: The railroad spur, pointed out to the navigators during briefings, was relatively new; there were other, older rails nearby, and visual differences between them will lead to additional confusion.

Right this way, gentlemen!

This spur is an important landmark, a 10-mile arrow pointing perfectly straight, directly into Ploieşti.

No battle plan survives first contact with the enemy!

Gestenberg's *ein falle*—his trap—is starting to mesh together rather nicely.

Cocked like a gun.

CHAPTER 18

Flak-Zug

If you lay with a scorpion, don't be surprised when it finally stings you.
—DaShanne Stokes,
SOCIOLOGIST, AUTHOR, PUNDIT

THE GERMAN *FLAK-ZUG* WAITING TO LURCH WAS A BEHEMOTH, TWENTY-three cars long, a clever invention of the Russian army that the Germans amended to a higher level of lethality, as only they could. Gerstenberg looked to it to shock the American forces coming his way—a "weapons system" that with its sheer firepower would decrease their numbers, ruin them, make them impotent before they had even arrived at the outer boundary of Ploieşti's first defensive ring of flak.

As soon as Gerstenberg received word of the spotters' first sightings, around Corfu and Albania, he had the *Flak-Zug* standing at attention, sitting on the spur, a fuming heavyweight, anxious, a massive iron caterpillar with deadly forceps, waiting to easily snag a few tasty bugs for lunch.

The Germans had used flak trains like this one since the beginning of World War II, with mixed results. Highly effective because of their mobility and kill power, they were somewhat limited due to their position on railroad tracks. Nonetheless, the *Flak-Zug's* inflicted severe damage to tanks, troops, and aircraft, especially the notably slower heavy bombers, such as the "moving vans" of the Ploieşti mission.

The disadvantage: Since they had to be ready to roll at a moment's notice, they, too, were enormous targets, favorites of American and British fighter pilots, who loved to shoot up the locomotives. Hit the engine, and that was the end of the line—for the train, and the rail it was on. The bonus: a massive heap of railroad cars blocking the rails. And if the fighter pilots got lucky and hit an ammunition or gasoline cache in one of the cars, a gigantic explosion usually lit off, blowing the entire assemblage off the tracks and sending up a large, cerise-colored ball of fire, smoke, and train parts.

A *flak train* is exactly what the term implies: a specific number of railroad cars, usually modified flatbeds, that bear a variety of antiaircraft weapons used primarily to shoot down military aircraft. The guns aboard the flatbeds ranged in caliber from 20mm to 88mm, as well as machine guns of varying calibers. The train was self-sustaining, consisting of a steam locomotive—usually situated in the middle of the train; flat armored cars shaped like bread boxes, with guns and armored panels for protection; and a command car with a comprehensive communications system, including phones and radios.

Gerstenberg's *Flak-Zug* had an armored tender behind the locomotive and an identical auxiliary tender in front, to increase range. Next came utility wagons, each with some accommodation for the crew and armed Wehrmacht troops, and a kitchen or medical car. Some carried a 7.2cm (2.83-inch) or 10cm (3.93-inch) howitzer, neatly housed in a ten-sided revolving turret. Articulating armor plates allowed the crew to move between the wagons under cover of armored plating. It was an enviable duty for the troops aboard, because they were able to ride around the countryside, sleeping and eating in comfort, unlike their comrades in the field.

While Gerstenberg's troops were expecting the attack force, what they did not expect was two Groups, one on either side of the *Flak-Zug*. The hunting would be even more natural. A bonus.

Never again would such a formation of aircraft encounter a flak train with such firepower, producing such startlingly horrific results. Nowhere in any history book, lecture, white paper, or nightmare would there be an encounter of such significant elements—forty B-24s of Kane's 98th BG on the left; thirty-six B-24s of Lt. Col. Leon Johnson's 44th Eight-Balls on the right; and a heavily armored, rolling monster gun system chugging right down the middle.

The Americans had figured they would be shot at by flak guns, brought down by machine-gun fire, picked apart by fighters, and ensnared in balloon cables—but they had never imagined being decimated by a flak train with such massive firepower, about to start down the tracks and initiate unparalleled mayhem. Building now to a crescendo, a gunfight the likes of which is seen only in Western movies, both Groups firing at the train, and the train firing back at both Groups. One Group would have provided ample targets for the train, but here they have an unlimited choice—B-24s on the left of them, B-24s on the right.

The battle was one of historic magnitude. Few had ever seen anything like it, and no one will ever experience its like again.

When the train's commander received the flash message from the Protector's headquarters regarding the incoming Americans—that they were flying at almost dirt-level height—the gunners on the flatcars lunged for their 88mm shells and adjusted the proximity fuses on the tips, which were usually set for the high altitudes bombers frequently flew. To their delight, the flak troops had been told the bulky bombers would not be flying higher than 200 feet.

Like shooting ducks at a pond on a beautiful day.

And the ducks had no idea.

—◆—

The 98th and 44th BGs are down so low—50 feet—that some aircraft snag branches with their belly antennas and big, bright yellow sunflowers dance in their bomb bays.

Bob Sternfels's navigator, 2nd Lt. Anthony Flesch, announces the first IP, Pitesti.

(According to Bob, "Anthony Flesch was a CPA before joining the air force, the best navigator in my squadron. He was a replacement during one of the training periods—the best replacement that one could ask for—and took his job seriously. I realized that early in training. One night on a cross-country training flight, around two or three in the morning, we had to feather one engine [shut it down]. I called him on the intercom and said, '*Where in the hell are we, and what is the nearest military airfield?*' In less than two minutes, Flesch said, '*Roswell, New Mexico, is straight ahead!*' Now you've heard the story of the little men from outer space landing at Roswell. The true story is, that was me who landed there, in the middle of the night! And, thank you, Anthony Flesch.")

After they pass over Pitesti, Flesch gets on the intercom again. *"We've got the next IP coming up, a town called Targoviste. Then we continue on to Floresti. There, we hang a right and pick up the railroad tracks, and follow the tracks straight into Ploiești."*

The plan had seemed simple on paper: One Group, the 389th, with thirty aircraft, would fly from the first IP, Pitesti, split away, and head for Campina, and bomb the refineries there. Compton's 376th and the 98th would fly almost parallel to each other, then turn right at the railroad tracks at Floresti. Once over the tracks, they would fly straight into Ploiești—like a "tidal wave."

That was the plan.

As such, it would fizzle.

During one of the briefings, the navigators had been told to "use the spur as a reference point directly into Ploiești." It had been chosen as a visual reference for the formation's navigators to follow to the target. ("Take the A Train, boys," was the mnemonic refrain, referring to a popular 1939 Duke Ellington hit song; others referred to it as the "Chattanooga Choo Choo" line.)

In *Hail Columbia*, the flagship of the 98th BG, with Killer Kane leading, Kane hears Norm Whalen, his navigator, observe on the intercom: *"Rolling countryside. People walking around. Farming country, cows and horses in the fields. Looks like people going to church or a Sunday outing. It's a beautiful day out there."*

Kane knows what Whalen is talking about; he sees the topography, and casually agrees.

They leave Pitesti, pass over Targoviste, the next IP, and are on the lookout for the last IP—Floresti.

Then, a couple of minutes later, Whalen presses the intercom button. *"That's Floresti straight head, the next IP. Now, we pick up the railroad spur and hang a right; it'll lead us straight into Ploiești. No tickets required, Colonel."*

Occasionally, there are people on the ground waving at the bomber boys, and the bomber boys wave back, as they would at a stateside air show—*Have a nice day!*—making the attendees feel welcome.

At Floresti, the final IP, Bob sees Killer Kane's ship banking right, and the rest of the Group following. He gets lined up neatly, and the Group jabs down to less than 100 feet, ground speed 160 mph.

And at that moment, with dreadful suddenness, the flak train below erupts.

Seventeen flatbed railroad cars, open on the top, thickly armored on the sides and ends, starts spitting fire and clouds of blue gunsmoke at the Pyramidiers and the Flying Eight-Balls. Racing along at 100 mph, a belligerent black armadillo prickling with weaponry, firing an assortment of flak guns and smaller-caliber weapons with stunning accuracy. The train, "coincidentally," is heading toward Ploieşti with just enough speed to keep up for a while, causing extensive damage to both formations, just before they reach the refineries.

The flak train had used the takeoff time from North Africa to figure out exactly when to be at this spot, right as the two groups arrive, hiding camouflaged under a nest of tall trees until spotters tell them where the Liberators are.

Less than a minute after the turn, Bob's tail gunner, John Tramley Weston, shouts into the intercom: *"Holy shit!"*

From the sound of Weston's voice, Bob knows he's just seen something terrible.

———

The *Flak-Zug* spits into the open like a malevolent snake from under a rock—perfect timing. It seems unstoppable, a plunger of such weight and magnitude that no might in the world can contain its brutal power.

The spur it rolls on splits two parallel Groups: the Pyramidiers on the left, the Eight-Balls on the right—both flying at 60 feet above the ground, 160 mph, and separated from each other by about 100 yards. The two Groups of B-24s and the train are neatly lined up, heading in the same direction—toward Ploieşti—and the track runs arrow-straight for about 10 miles. If the Germans had designed this on paper, it could not have been better.

The air is a massive bubble of drumfire with every cannon, rifle, and machine-gun blast. Tracer rounds from the aircraft and the train criss-cross like a fiery cat's cradle. The train is followed by a massive cape of gunsmoke, blackish-white.

At the moment Weston issues his exclamation, he sees the steam, gauzy white against the black-green trees. He understands enough about steam locomotives to know that the beast down there is running at top speed and the son of a bitch is shooting at him.

Now he sees muzzle flashes and puffy clouds of gunsmoke.

Tony Flesch estimates the train is running around 100 mph—not fast enough to keep up with the B-24s flying in Bob's formation, but enough to bring down a few of the moving vans with its firepower.

"What?" asks Bob, responding to Weston's shout.

"A train—it's shooting at us? Can I return fire?"

"Hell, yes!" yells Bob.

Earlier Bob had given orders to the gunners to hold their fire until he said it was okay.

Now, he is too busy flying to take a look at the train.

"You guys shoot, I'll fly," says Bob.

Everyone on *The Sandman* hears the jarring, jagged burst of Weston's twin .50 caliber machine guns trying to target the flak train.

Raymond E. Stewart, twenty-two, the ball turret gunner on the plane's belly, is 5-foot-5. He couldn't be much taller because then he wouldn't fit into the turret. He is now on his back, his knees in his chest firing the twin .50 caliber guns. He's got the best deflection, firing in long bursts, the rounds sparking off the armor and kicking up clouds of brown dirt.

All the guns on the train are lit up with muzzle flashes and puffs of blue gunsmoke. They're shooting at everything: the 98th and the 44th. They can't miss, and they are unrelenting. The fields of fire interlace. They do not need to pause and aim. They shoot up in the general direc-tion of the formations and hit B-24s; they shoot, they score. It's a B-24 shooting gallery. B-24s flame up, roll over, and explode when they hit the ground. Some catch fire, but keep flying. The air is blotched with clouds of gunsmoke and flak bursts and flaming engines and parts made in America and other fragments whirling off the train made in Germany.

Gerstenberg has put together a daunting defense so far.

Weston finds this surreal. He has never fired his guns this long, at anything like this; the barrels are approaching red-hot heat, and the hot .50 caliber shell casings are pinging and panging on the walls of gun positions in *The Sandman*.

John Tramley Weston has a teenage boy's cute face and looks like he's fifteen years old. He is actually twenty-two, from Skowhegan, Maine, a town you can't get lost in, where there is nothing louder than the bird-like squeaks of squirrels munching on tasty chestnuts.

He is 5-foot-5, weighs 120 pounds, has an appealing smile, and fits snugly in the cramped tail gunner's station. He's coordinated enough to disable the *Flak-Zug*. The kind of young man you want back there, trying to kill a flak train. Coming from the calm and silence of Skowhegan, Weston grew accustomed to being alone and flying backward in the rear of *The Sandman*.

This is a turning point in Weston's life. None of his friends back home have fired twin fifties—maybe .22s. And certainly no one he knows has ever fired a machine gun at a moving train that's trying to kill him. If he gets through this, he will have some story to tell.

He drops these thoughts and fires again and again.

Now, right waist gunner Harry Rifkin has his M2 .50 caliber Browning machine guns deflected as far as they will allow, the muzzles protruding from the open window. *The Sandman* is in a three-plane formation, Section "E." The train seems about 100 yards off *The Sandman's* right wingtip. Beyond that, about 50 feet away, are two other B-24s. Rifkin has to be careful so his gunfire won't hit them. His tracer rounds pock the dirt and draw a path of bullet holes to one of the railroad cars. The powerful rounds explode or spark off the armor. As he fires, hot empty brass shell casings litter the floor.

The train's gunners have an easy time hitting their targets. It's simple shooting today. Better than shooting ducks, because these explode and crash. Every gun on the train is firing. The 88mm gunners show their athletic abilities, tossing spent 88mm shell cases into the air with their gloved hands. Trees and bushes on either side of the speeding train are butchered, splattered, splintered, and fall. Bright orange muzzle flashes precede puffs of blue-and-white smoke. There are so many guns firing that every few seconds, the side of the train is obscured by skeins of gun-smoke and sprays of dirt and gravel. The leaves bow to the sound's shock waves from the cacophony of drumfire. One 88mm shell catches a B-24 in the bomb-bay area and ignites the spare gasoline tank, and the aircraft explodes into a sphere of fire and aircraft parts. Less than three seconds later, it smashes into the ground and explodes again.

No one survives.

Now, a few pilots are salvoing their spare tanks from the bomb bays, fearful of having them hit—*"Kick that bastard out of here!"*

Someone on the intercom asks Bob to tilt *The Sandman*, right wing down, for better deflection.

The Sandman's turret gunner, William W. Stout, deflects his twin .50s to aim downward, and starts kicking the train with halting bursts. His head is up into the glass-enclosed turret so he has a panoramic view of the battle. The air is streaming with black smoke from burning B-24s and crisscrossing tracers. One B-24 is going down in flames. Two crewmen jump, but they are too low. The 'chutes don't open. The aircraft vanishes into the ground, aflame, concentric shock waves rippling away through trees and grass from the point of impact.

The flak train starts to fall behind, but all the guns on the flatcars are still sending up hundreds of tracers and bullets, a malicious fusillade of steel, almost none of it missing their targets.

Another B-24 on fire attempts to pull up to gain altitude so crewmen can jump. The aircraft stalls, flips, noses up, falls over, then crashes.

Stout is stunned when an 88 explodes over his head and lights the sky with a brilliance he's never seen. It sounds like a stick of dynamite blew up inside his skull.

Now, the B-24s are bobbing around, fighting prop wash, trying to maintain order. The air is a rat's nest, a plague of smoky white tracers. The sounds of this battle are immeasurable: aircraft engines, flak, machine-gun fire, exploding flak shells. And *The Sandman's* airframe rattling and shaking from machine-gun fire. Bullet holes appear in the wings and fuselage, and when they hit they sound like silver dollars falling onto a steel tabletop.

This is Dante's Inferno, and the bombers are flying through nine concentric circles of hell, wondering where the last circle ends. Some bombers trail spirals of fire but continue to Ploieşti. Flames melt spars and wing roots and they tumble out of the sky. The bombers maintain their purpose, determined, flying 160 mph and 60 feet over Hades' surface.

Spent shell casings from the bombers flicker into the airstreams—brass rain, it is, hitting and tearing the leading edges, the propellers, and jamming the air intakes on the engine cowlings. A few bounce off the windscreens of one B-24 and shatter the glass, leaving spidery lines.

Off Killer Kane's left wing, *Hadley's Harem* bucks up from a powerful direct hit. In the aircraft's glass-enclosed nose, shell fragments kill the bombardier, Lt. Leon Storms. Bleeding from shrapnel fragments, Lt. Harold Tabacoff screams from the decimated nose: *"They got me too!"*

Russ Page heeds the command of Hadley, the pilot, and salvos the bomb load. Then he hustles down to the nose, clutching a first-aid kit. He's met with a horrible vision. The kit is for naught. The compartment is spattered with sheared metal and glass fragments and burnt wiring; the crewmen's blood and flesh are mingled with the debris. There is nothing he can do to help the dying Tabacoff. His chest is cut to pieces. ("I never want to see anything like that ever again," Page said.)

Finally, the gunners from the 44th and 98th slam the locomotive with a burst of concentrated firepower, and the colossus shatters. It leaps from the track, a massive wounded cow. A second later, it slams down on the rails, leans left, shatters, falls off the rails, plowing dirt and railroad tracks—flatcars, guns, troops, a mess of wreckage—and finally dies.

—⟡—

Severe damage has been inflicted on the 98th and the 44th.

The *Flak-Zug* was wholly unexpected. It knew the precise time the B-24s would fly over the rail line; they had ample preparation time, plenty of speed, an array of numerous weapons to bring down or damage many B-24s. The train caused unexpected mayhem. The flak train's participation in the battle was more devasting than the actual bombing of the refineries, Bob thought.

Many of the bombers were damaged or brought down by "friendly fire." No one can say whose guns might have shot down planes, but they were sure it happened. It was inevitable. No plane goes through the gauntlet without harm from bullets or flak.

Bob Sternfels said, "Twenty out of the fifty-seven B-24s in the two Groups were shot down by that damned flak train before reaching their targets!"

The mission had decayed, in a most deadly fashion.

The Smart Plan . . . the entire plan . . . pieces of the plan . . . the scribbled notes . . . cryptic handwriting . . . the phone calls and conferences . . . names on doors . . . signs in Pentagon hallways . . . arguments heard, laughter suppressed, prayers . . . the misspellings . . . the typewritten memos . . . good coffee, bad coffee . . . Rorschach coffee stains . . . top-secret stamps . . . the red ink, the blue ink . . . pencils and Waterman fountains pens . . . paper clips and bond paper and staples . . . cigar butts and crushed cigarettes, congested ashtrays . . . the hand drawings . . . the maps . . . defenses . . . notebooks and thick binders . . . eraser refuse . . . the futility and optimism and eye rolls . . . the yawns . . . conference rooms . . . the doodles. . . . the opining . . . the odds . . . false notions . . . diminished imperatives . . . handshakes . . . friendships formed . . . the endured nightmares . . . colonels, generals, politicians . . . men-at-arms . . . the crews . . . the marriages moribund . . . the families distraught . . . the ammunition . . . the bomb loads . . . the estimates . . . range to/from . . . flight times . . . fuel consumption . . . fuel reserves . . . it was good . . . it was bad . . . it was holy . . . but not holy . . . anointed . . . unanointed . . . praised . . . denigrated . . . cherished . . . cast aside . . . almost forgotten . . . revived . . . revered.

It had been the Smart Plan: acute, sharp, richly detailed with certainty and finicky precision.

And now the damned Plan was out of focus. Fading.

And now the Plan did not matter. The young men, the older ones; the boys, the colonels and privates and generals and sergeants—they are cruelly surprised. The Plan didn't work for them. It wasn't theirs. Now it belonged to no one.

But they had been the ones flying toward those 200-foot-high smokestacks, those oil fields. Rosary beads flew with them, and scapulars given to them by mothers and priests, and the tiny feet of furry rabbits and other talismans and murmured prayers that were meant to prevent all this shit. But now their magic was gone. No more juju. The signs of the cross and mumbled prayers matched the clatter and the hammer of bullets banging the airframes, tightening up their asses. No rosary beads, no scapulars, no rabbits's feet to fend off their fate now.

Luck will out. Chance. The odds. Today you will die. Today you won't. Today you will dine with scorpions and rats and spiders and spit sand from your soup spoon. Tonight? Who knows?

It was behind them, the Plan. They left it in the halls of that new Pentagon . . . in the 9th Air Force headquarters in Cairo, Egypt, General Brereton's perch. The clarity of it lounges back there in Washington, in Smart's brain, the five-sided cement castle of power and pronouncements. But here it is unfocused and futile. All of it is pallid and pasty now. Shot to hell like half the Liberators that dueled that bastard *Flak-Zug*, that Caterpillar of Death, just moments ago. No longer fresh and crisp in their minds and all zipped up with certainty, the Plan is now as bloodless as a Virgin Mary—great name: no gin, no punch. A *virgin* Mary. Impotent. Long ago gone.

The target, Ploieşti, sat ahead, dim in the suffused light against a graying horizon of oily smoke, a grimace of pain and horror on her oily face.

Many feel the sting of inevitability.

No more feeding pigeons in the square or stealing a kiss in street cafes or listening to vespers holding hands, and soon wintertime will come and summer will never be seen again. Many lives will be once upon a time, they know.

Now, another surprise awaits them, not signed off on in the Plan: A drizzle hits their windscreens like little rivers mixed with a sheen of black brownish oil. The smoky odor of burning oil fills cockpits and fuselages. *The Sandman*'s waist gunners' faces are covered with a black smoke and soot. A damned omen. And some will never have anything else to see beyond that target. Because now they know.

The plan has twisted into a sham, and they have been deluded.

The only thing that matters now is the skin on their bomber and the skin on their bones. And they are unsure of both.

The bombing of the oil fields will begin shortly.

But oh no, not before another spin of fortune's wheel.

Go ahead, Ancient Pistol, give the wheel another turn!

Let us see what fortune your hand lands on.

CHAPTER 19

"Wrong Turn! Wrong Turn!"

When you hear hoofbeats, think horses, not zebras.
—THEODORE WOODWARD, MD, MEDICAL RESEARCHER
(A MEDICAL APHORISM, A LA OCCAM'S RAZOR)

K. K. COMPTON'S 376TH BOMB GROUP PASSES PITESTI, THE FIRST IP, and flies toward Targoviste, their second IP. From there they will fly straight, about ten minutes, to Foresti, then turn right at the railroad tracks that will take them in to Ploieşti.

All is well so far.

Teggie Ann's navigator, Capt. Harold Wicklund, considered one of the best, most experienced navigators in the group, is on the maps, squeezed into the glass-enclosed nose, looking to identify Targoviste, and, later, Floresti, where the group is to make a right turn and follow the railroad tracks where the *Flak-Zug* has just been disemboweled a short time ago, and then make a dash for Ploieşti.

It is not so easy for Wicklund or K. K. Compton to identify landmarks because *Teggie Ann* is 200 feet above the dirt and flying along at 160 mph; the topography is blurred.

Wicklund looks out the nose and spots a small group of reasonably prominent, large buildings. Among them supposedly is *Manastirea Dealului* (Monastery on the Hill), a Romanian military academy. Before the launch of the strike force, the briefing officer had told them, "If you pass anywhere near Targoviste, you cannot fail to see *Manastirea Dealului*, as it is the only building of this size on a hilltop within a radius of many miles."

At this point, Wicklund is busy doing time and distance calculations for their ETA at Targoviste. He recalls the briefing officer's presentation, tries to match it to the distortion speeding underneath them. He spots something he thinks is familiar, then, shit, it's gone. He remembers that the briefing had continued: "You will be flying over the last foothills of the mountains so that to your left you will see the rolling, gradually rising country, whilst on your right hand, the hills die away into the vast plain within a distance of 2 or 3 miles. The hills you will be flying over are mostly rather thickly wooded, with only a few small straggling villages. At 16 miles from Targoviste, the hills beneath you recede rather suddenly into an open valley about fifteen miles wide."

Wicklund's view of what he sees on the ground seems to match the briefing, which described the topography that spread between Targoviste and Pitesti.

(In his year 2000 interview with Bob Sternfels, General Compton described the problematic situation they now faced:

> As we approached the first IP, I was flying very low, about 200 feet, and very fast over unfamiliar territory. Captain Wicklund was doing the navigating using his dead reckoning time and distance calculations for his ETA from the Danube River to the third IP, at Floresti. I had my charts and special prepared visual aids spread out on my lap and was following the terrain as best I could, while Red Thompson, my co-pilot, was busy flying the airplane. By that time, the nose compartment was pretty hot, and that glassed-in nose was also very crowded, with two men, the bombardier and navigator, and the two machine guns, along with ammunition boxes, flak vests, helmets, and their parachutes and briefcases. They barely had enough space to turn around, and Wicklund had to have his charts and calculations out on his small navigator's table. It had to be very cramped and distracting down there.)

Up top, K. K. has maps on his lap, spread over the controls and on the cockpit's floor—a bit unusual, as maps are typically the paraphernalia of the navigator, but Compton wants to be sure they hit the IPs on schedule, so is following the topography and matching it to the charts. It's not that he doesn't trust Wicklund; he just wants to be sure.

General Ent is not saying much, just observing; he has no hand in navigating or issuing orders at this point. K. K. somehow "thinks" he sees Floresti:

All of a sudden, this village [Targoviste] with the right landmarks appeared ahead that looked just like Floresti. At our speed, I had to make a quick and firm decision, so I turned to the briefed run heading. Wicklund may also have been somewhat uncertain, as he did not correct me. I lead my Group on the course I thought would take us to the target. Wicklund has recently assumed all the blame for the wrong turn. That is just not totally correct. It was also my decision, my mistake, and was my responsibility.

So *Teggie Ann* slips into a lazy right turn, and the whole 376th Group starts following behind like birds flying off a telephone wire. To add to the confusion, both K. K. and Wicklund see railroad tracks that lead into Ploieşti; however, these tracks are not the new, shinny tracks the other groups would follow, where the *Flak-Zug* had been wrecked; these are old railroad tracks.

Years later, Wicklund would remain firm in his belief that the wrong turn was his error, and his alone:

I gave Colonel Compton the wrong time to turn to the target. It was a wrong ETA and the error was mine. I did not correct him during the turn. I simply made a mistake.

The Group bombardier, Maj. Lynn Hester, verifies Wicklund's point:

I was on the intercom during the approach to the IPs and never heard anything spoken. Wicklund had given Compton the time of the ETA, there was a village with a railroad track going east, and Compton made his turn at that point. Nothing was said about a wrong turn.

The 376th has scribed a wide right turn—the *wrong* wide right turn—above Targoviste, believing they are over Floresti, which is some 20 miles after Targoviste.

Confusion spreads virus-like throughout the Groups.

What the hell is going on?

The 93rd Bomb Group, Ted's Traveling Circus—led by Lt. Col. Addison Baker, piloting *Hell's Wench* and following K. K.—wonders whether to continue to follow. He thinks, hopes, Compton might realize his mistake immediately, turn back, and head for Ploiești.

K. K. and Ent continue, oblivious.

Lt. John Palm, the pilot of *Brewery Wagon*, flying with the 376th, turns, following Compton's path.

Then in his headset, Palm hears navigator William Wright: *"John, why are you turning here?"*

"Beats the hell out of me, Willie. Compton says turn, so I'm turning."

Confused, Wright says, *"Well, by God, if this is the IP, I'm lost as shit!"*

Doubt punches Palm's stomach, because he trusts Wright's judgment; he's superb at navigating. *If he's lost as shit, then we're all lost as shit!*

But Palm deliberates, holds course for one or two minutes, and does not see the target. If his navigator told him the target's to the left, not straight ahead, *then for Christ's sake, it's to the left!*

Maybe Compton's lost? Could that be possible? His commanding officer? The young, rising star?

Palm shouts into the intercom, *"Willie, you must be right! Give me a course to the right place!"*

Palm has more trust in Willie, his navigator, than in K. K. Compton, his Group leader.

In less than thirty seconds John Palm has a new course, and *Brewery Wagon* is on its way to bomb Ploiești.

Palm peels off left, northwesterly, grips *Brewery Wagon* by the horns, and jerks her from her languor, from the misguided 376th's path to who-knows-where, and points her eager nose toward Ploiești.

She responds with vitality and her Pratt & Whitneys whine, an insect-like buzzing, loud, urgent. The airframe, mellow a moment ago, shimmies and creaks. Something back there in the fuselage, a buckle or cable or who-knows-what-the hell-it-is, knocking on something, causing a damned racket. All of them feel the speed change, the whole crew—the urgency in the physics of aerodynamics, the airframe's rush through the slipstream, the higher pitch of the paddles. Seat belts tighten. Machine guns are triple-checked. Their lethargy evaporates into deadly concentration, and they forget about waving to smiling people down there in the fields and on the roads, and to hell with their doses of sweet American congeniality.

"We're going to Ploiești, boys!" shouts Palm into the intercom.

"Yeah, fuck Ploiești!" shouts someone, glee straining his voice.

"Let's get this shit over with; I want Mama's sweet apple pie!"

To Ploiești they wing, a singular lethal arrow, straight from their own bow, flying with purpose, not knowing that in minutes they will be recording a few paragraphs of historical value, their action soon to be met with grievous conclusions in a peaceful wheat field, in a country none had heard of before, but would revisit endlessly.

Who now can know how they felt that day? Who now can say why Palm turned away with suddenness and urgency? Palm? Willie? Clay? The whole crew? Who the hell knows why?

Palm realizes, as does the crew, that they are disobeying an order. He could be in for a court-martial upon return—if there is a return.

From the ground, they have been spotted, their height and direction logged and reported to Gerstenberg's tactical mind. His trick bag is still brimming with an abundance of jolts and hardhanded tactics. He is, after all, the Protector.

Solitude now in a hostile sky showering the *Wagon* with cannon shells and spits of steel and firebursts the size of circus tents. It is the Fourth of July up here, without the hot dogs and tasty baked beans and children's squeals. It is mesmerizing—the explosions, the tracers, the flying chunks of steel shrapnel. The sky, deep blue, limitless, a backdrop of crisscrossing death and misdirected cannon fire. All of it implies a historical change, a sea change of unprecedented moments that will pile up in history books, and scholars and authors will thrive on long after.

Who can say why they turned when even they do not know why?

For country? For honor? Call of duty?

Maybe the boys will allow the riddle's question to linger into old age and come up fallow?

Maybe Palm turned the *Wagon* simply because . . . because he heard hoofbeats, and it was the sound of horses—not zebras.

Why?

Because . . . there are no zebras in Romania.

Simple as that.

The turn was something Palm will live comfortably with for the rest of his life.

In less than a minute, *Brewery Wagon* is 26 miles from the burning refineries and flying lower than the lush treetops, flying through bursts of 88s and cannon fire. The rattle of the aircraft's machine guns mixes with the rasp of treetops brushing against her metal belly. Hastening along, *Brewery Wagon* shudders and bounces and flutters and catches steel shards from the gun batteries that blow Swiss-cheese holes in her olive-drab skin. She is pocked and bloodied.

But the boys are lucky so far. They are still flying. Flying at this height and speed makes them a hard target to hit for the Luftwaffe and Romanian gunners. *Brewery Wagon* is the only B-24 in the area, making it a target for every antiaircraft gun, rifle, pistol, rock, and Romanian *fuck you*.

Palm is figuring maybe he should turn back—that breaking away from Compton is going to cost him. He's going to catch a rash of shit when he gets back to Africa, oh, yeah.

Now it starts raining, a drizzle.

The *Wagon's* windscreen is a delicate veil of rainwater. Palm is temporarily blinded. There are no windshield wipers on B-24s. Palm looks out through his side screen for landmarks and holds the *Wagon* true, on course, unrelenting, purposeful, while the boys in the back continue their business with their nasty guns. Brass shell casings litter the floor 6 inches deep. Sgt. William Thompson, the belly gunner, scores, hitting a flak gun hidden in a haystack. The emplacement vanishes in an explosive beige cloud of splintered cornstalks, dirt, and smoldering gun parts, twisting, looping through the cornfield, sending little shock waves across the cornstalks.

Then the rain stops, and Palm sees the smokestacks of Ploieşti, tall, stout beasts made of red brick, looming, dangerous at 200 feet. He gives a touch of right rudder to get around the stack.

There are balloons tethered to winches.

Palm, on his intercom: *"I don't give a rat's ass whose refinery or whose target that is out there; we're dropping a load on it, and getting the fuck outta here!"*

"Gotcha!" someone replies.

"Yeah!"

"Fuck this shit!"

"Kickin' some Ploieşti ass now!"

"Balls to the wall, John!"

(This is not a reference to testicles. The throttles on the console have knobs on them. When a pilot grips and pushes them to the instrument panel, he is pushing the balls on the throttles, the knobs, to the wall for full power.)

Palm has *Brewery Wagon* lined up to the right of this unknown refinery's smokestack that seems as tall as the Empire State Building and gets ready to drop his load—1,000-pounders, 500-pounders with forty-five-second-delay fuses.

Just then a stream of 20mm shells rakes the *Wagon*, rattles the bird silly like a pile of pots and pans falling off a shelf. The decibel level is painful.

Palm is over the target. Bomb-bay doors are open. He grabs the emergency bomb release cord on the pilot's pedestal and salvos the bombs, not waiting to coordinate with the bombardier.

The left inboard engine fragments, the cowling spirals in the slipstream, and a piece starts flapping on the leading edge of the wing. The prop stalls—a plume of blue and gray smoke marks the *Wagon's* flight path—and 20mm shells find the nose section.

Continuing along the fuselage, tracer rounds wound Austin Chastain, the right waist gunner; he keeps firing his .50s.

In the fusillade and hellfire, navigator Willie Wright, who just minutes ago had given Palm reliable directions to Ploieşti, is killed. Bombardier Robert Merrill is ripped apart and dies instantly.

Then—a painful surprise—something harsh bursts through the floor on Palm's side of the cockpit and severs his left leg.

A few minutes earlier, at Mizil, Romania, a Luftwaffe airfield west of Bucharest, *Hauptmann* Wilhelm Steinmann had been ordered to take to the air by his commanding officer, *Oberst* Bernhard Woldenga.

Woldenga sends his eager German and Romanian fighter boys up with an assortment of vectors he hopes will meet the moving vans heading for Ploiești and sandbag them before they get to their targets.

A bomber pilot before the war started, Steinmann knows their proclivities. He has the eye of a masterful fighter pilot, an eagle's eye, yes, and has been working toward a Knight's Cross since joining the Luftwaffe in 1936—although he has made a career-ending blunder.

On May 18, 1943, Steinmann shot down an RAF Hawker Typhoon over the English Channel. On June 1, he claimed his second victory, an RAF Spitfire—or, at least he *thought* it was a Spitfire. It was actually a Luftwaffe Bf 109G-6—and the pilot happened to be his *Gruppenkommandeur, Hauptmann* Erich Hohagen. Wounded, and forced to bail out, Hohagen was most unimpressed with Steinmann's "eagle's eye," one that could not distinguish friend from foe—although, to be fair, the silhouettes of a Bf 109 and a Spitfire *are* quite similar.

On the day he shot down his *Gruppenkommandeur, Hauptmann* Steinmann was promptly ordered to board the first train to Bucharest. He had been transferred to the backwater command of the *Jagdfliegerführe—Rumänien* (Fighter Command—Romania), arriving on June 10 with his pilot's wings between his legs and his peaked Luftwaffe hat droopy, reporting to Woldenga.

That is how Steinmann wound up here in the bright, bright light of Romania, chasing after a stricken bomber.

As he circles southwest Ploiești, Steinmann spots a lone B-24—the afflicted *Brewery Wagon*—limping through the air, smoke trailing behind her shot-up fuselage. Steinmann eager to make up for lost time in his career. He has been punished, yes, but he's up today in his warrior bird, determined to make good.

Steinmann charges his guns.

The Bf 109G-6 has two nose-mounted 7.9mm heavy machine guns, one 30mm MK 108 cannon firing through the propeller hub, and two 20mm cannons slung under the wings; this is formidable firepower. He selects his nose cannon and the cowl-mounted guns. He initiates his attack, comes over the top of the *Wagon*, and sprays the wings and engines. He overshoots the stricken B-24, performs a screaming barrel roll, and circles back in a tight loop, trailing a wisp of exhaust smoke, then comes full-on at the *Wagon*, guns blasting the nose section. Shells rip through the nose, killing bombardier William Merrill. Co-pilot Bill Love, sitting to the right of Palm, is wounded, as is the bombardier, Alexander P. "Rocky" Rockinson survives.

———

Palm's left leg bleeds severely below the knee. His leg is joined together tenuously by a strand of plantaris muscle and a slim band of bloody flesh. The flooring and foot pedals are awash in flesh, bone, and slimy red liquid.

"I lost my leg!" screams Palm.

Steinmann's not finished.

He circles back again for the kill shot, flies at the *Wagon*'s nose, the engines. He sprays the *Wagon* wingtip to wingtip, shredding it, then loops away, certain he has scored a kill.

One step closer to a Knight's Cross.

Because right now, *Brewery Wagon* is going down right here in Tartani, Romania.

Palm saying, *"We gotta get to that cornfield!"*

No one hears him; the intercom is shot.

Palm has Love working the foot pedals because he can't use his severed leg, and using the control column, he guides the *Wagon* toward that field of sky-high cornstalks.

"Keep it level!" shouts Palm.

Brewery Wagon cuts a deep, wide furrow in the cornfield. Props bend, the airframe buckles, wings scythe the agriculture, burrowing in. The nose crumples. The cockpit is crushed and twisted. Windscreen braces and cabling and flanges and tubing hand-assembled by American women shower the air.

Love had hit the fire extinguishers, so the engines do not flare up.

The air stinks of burnt rubber and smoldering fuselage parts and fresh Americn blood.

Palm grabs the windscreen sill on his side of the cockpit and tugs hard, trying to get himself out. He's stuck—his belt buckle or pants are snagged on who-knows-what, he can't figure it.

(Palm would recall years later: "With the adrenaline flowing, I was able to pull myself out halfway. My leg was still attached by muscle and flesh. I took the leg and laid it across my lap, and tried to fall backward out of the airplane. I think I was the first man out of the ship!")

Bill Thompson, the radio operator, finds himself nestled among the shattered cornstalks near the tail section, dazed, lying like a snow angel in the dirt.

Love and Sgt. Alexander "Rocky" Rockinson are behind Palm, crawling through the crumpled mass. One of them grabs Palm at the collar and yanks him to the ground, Palm holding onto his severed leg; the boot is still on his foot, tied as it was that morning.

Tail gunner Dallas Robertson is with them. Blood creases his face and has soaked his shirt. He will have to have a 20mm splinter removed from his head.

Palm, his crew, and what's left of the smoldering *Brewery Wagon*, together in a cornfield, the first Americans downed in Romania by the Luftwaffe.

All become Romanian prisoners of war.

About 60 miles southwest of Ploieşti somewhere near Corlăteşi, Lt. Milton Teltser's *Pudgy*, rests aflame in a cornfield. A pyre of black smoke indicates the crash site. A local official leads a mob of peasants to *Pudgy*'s crew and drags them off to a local saloon; he tells them they are on display. Peasants straggle in to gape at the Americans. Sergeant Bob Locky, one of *Pudgy*'s waist gunners, says, "After we settled in a guy comes up to me and says, matter-of-fact, and in perfect American English, 'How are the Detroit Tigers doing?' I almost fell off my chair."

The guy who asked the question was the saloon owner. He was a former Ford Motors employee.

CHAPTER 20

Wings of Madness

Today, I felt pass over me / a breath of wind from the wings of madness.
—CHARLES BAUDELAIRE, FRENCH POET

OVER THE REFINERIES FLY TIDAL WAVES OF B-24S, ONE BEHIND THE other, fighting through the fire and smoke, the shell fire, dropping their bombs, many aircraft falling from the sky and crashing.

Bob Sternfels is about two minutes from his target, the Astra Romana refinery, codenamed White IV. He is in the fourth wave of forty B-24s, ten aircraft in each wave, having a difficult time fighting the prop wash from multiple B-24s flying ahead of him. He expected this; he had been briefed about this. ("It's like you're in a motorboat and there are bigger boats ahead of you making multiple waves, and if you're not careful, one of those waves will capsize you. It took a lot of muscle; sometimes, you need two pilots to manhandle it.")

Flying like this in a tight formation is exceedingly dangerous—one wrong tap on the rudder pedals or a small jerk on the yoke, and you could smack the wingtip of the plane closest to you.

Over the intercom, Bob yells at his co-pilot, Barney Jackson, who likes to fly with cowboy boots—*"Full rudder, Barney! Push harder!"*

Bob flies *The Sandman* with his hands on the yoke, trying to keep her level. Barney is working the rudder pedals. White IV is about thirty seconds ahead, and *The Sandman* is 75 feet above the ground.

Bob glances down at the yoke, and reads a placard on the bottom of the wheel:

THIS CONTOL IS UPSIDE DOWN

("I read it twice before the right wing responded and came up," recalled Bob. "In the meantime, from here all the way into the target, we were getting shot at by everything they had.")

⁓

In his own handwriting, in black ink, Bob Sternfels's sortie report graphically recalls his experience after turning into the target:

First met AA at IP [Floresti]—light, scattered, and open. On our left observed flashes from long camouflaged trenches, also from towers among the wells and within the target, each manned by 3–5 men. Nearing the target they threw everything at us. MG [machine-gun] pom-pom, heavy AA—everything but monkey wrenches.

From a slight hill to the right, a battery of 88mms were shooting down *at us [emphasis added]. Turning on our run, the 98th and 44th were in pretty good formation until we hit the wall of smoke. During the run, the right waist gunner strafed a long string of boxcars on the main railroad, some of which were shooting at us. We came in over our pinpoint, threw out four boxes of incendiaries, and toggled six 500-lb. GP [general-purpose] bombs, fused 45 seconds. We're quite sure we hit within the pinpoint area, but were immediately enveloped by a huge cloud of black smoke and flames which came right into the right waist window.*

Half a second after coming out of the smoke over the target, saw one pink B-24, 300–400 ft. to our left, wheels down, not on fire, headed for a green field under control. Probably made a safe landing. A second B-24, also pink and to our left, had its wheels and flaps down. No. 1 engine was on fire, but as it landed in a field the fire went out after a short run. A moment later the ship blew up, but the crew might well have gotten clear and done so itself.

A moment later a third pink B-24, 2,300 ft. up to our left, nosed up right alongside a balloon. The engines and waist were on fire; three 'chutes opened from the waist immediately; 2 men jumped out from the nose, but their 'chutes didn't open. The ship crashed. A fourth pink B-24, about 50 ft. ahead just to our left, was burning amidships as it came out of the smoke. It broke in two and crashed.

A fifth B-24, just off our left wing, suddenly nosed into a clump of trees after slowing down behind us; we saw no fire. A few minutes later a sixth B-24 50 ft. above us, with its bomb bay on fire, hit on the right wing after doing a sudden wing-over and exploded.

The tail gunner saw three more pink B-24s, some 300 yards behind and between 5 and 7 o'clock, with their bomb bays on fire, but didn't see them crash. About ten minutes after leaving target, a pink B-24 right below and off our right wing suddenly burst into flames from nose to tail, skidded across a field into some trees along the edge of a road. The tail flew off, no one got out.

Ten minutes later still another B-24, well ahead at 1:30 o'clock, about 500 ft. up, flying well, suddenly broke into flames, did a wing-over, and crashed.

Hauptmann Steinmann, at 2,000 feet, straight and level, goes for one more kill.

He spots a target—*Satan's Hell Cats*, flying at 200 feet.

Steinmann executes a nosedive but has to throttle back and cut a sharp circle to bleed off airspeed and get behind the B-24. He charges his guns, figures he has just enough bullets for one pass.

Satan's Hell Cats' pilot is Capt. Rowland B. Houston. The left out-board engine on his bird has been deadened by flak, and smoke trails a long black tail against green cornfields and silky blue sky.

Steinmann behind, following the smoky route, but he's too high. He flips the Messerschmitt over onto her back, her eggshell-blue belly facing the sky.

Satan's Hell Cats' tail and turret gunners open fire, and tracers streak past Steinmann's canopy. At 200 yards out, he lets loose with a blast from his cannons, then has to pull away abruptly. Bullets smash into the 400-gallon Tokyo tank in the B-24's bomb bay, and the aircraft ignites into a thick ball of fire, smoke, pieces of aluminum.

Simultaneously, the gunners score, too. Their .50 caliber rounds slam into the 1,400-horsepower engine block of Steinmann's fighter. The block cracks, and hot, brownish oil rivers along the fuselage. The cowling flips loose, wiggles off. Oil, at 1,000 degrees or so, streaks the thick bulletproof windscreen, and Steinmann's flying today is *beendet* (finished).

Satan's Hell Cats slowly rolls over, shutters, then stalls as Houston tries to keep her level; he probably knows his effort is for naught. Because in the next instant, the *Cat* splatters into the cornfield and explodes into a blistering sphere of orange flames and bleak, fiery smoke.

Steinmann manages to hold on for a few seconds before making a wheels-up belly landing not far from a gun battery manned by incredulous Luftwaffe flak gunners. He jostles out of the cockpit, jogs over to the gun crew. Steinmann's out of breath, nerves, tension. He is as surprised as the gunners rushing toward him.

At that moment, a photograph is taken: Steinmann is frozen standing in a fortified trench, probably a gun emplacement manned by the Luftwaffe boys about 600 yards from the burning B-24. He's looking up at gray-haired Luftwaffe officer who is glancing down at him. This is the tableau of the moment. Steinmann has no cap, no flying mittens, and he's wearing his flight blouse with his rank insignia and the Luftwaffe version of Nazi Germany's sovereign eagle and swastika over his right breast pocket. At this second, the older Luftwaffe officer is looking down at him and has what appears to be a piece of paper the size of a driver's license in his left hand. Could he be checking Steienmann's pilot's license, his bonafides? Noting German efficiency, it's possible that the older officer wants to be certain Steinmann is on their side. Steinmann is expressionless, no giveaway signs on his face. Is he happy? Sad? Ebullient because of today's score, his good fortune? One wonders. One wonders if there is regret in his heart over his moments-ago score? One has to pause and wonder what Steinmann is thinking there. After all, this is war: He just killed ten Americans; destroyed their aircraft. But what does Steinmann *feel* at this moment? The flames from the B-24 are seeking the heavens? Both Steinmann and other officer are frozen in time by the mechanics of photography, the snap of a button, oblivious to the burning wreck in the mid-distance in the cornfield. Surely all are burning alive at that moment or died on impact. One has to wonder what is in Stenmann's mind right now, after this incredible moment in his life. The wreckage is pinned to the cornfield like a burning butterfly, multivarious colored flames and skeins of smoke, an inferno. A credit to Steinmann's airmanship. Steinmann's aircraft not far from the scorching heat of the B-24. There is a simple spiral of blue smoke snaking from one of the exhaust stacks, the shape of an apostrophe. Does he recall that the oil, the fuel, in his dead bird, was sucked out of the oil fields here in Ploieşti? Refined here. Pumped into his tanks before today's sortie? And that behind him, the pillowy cloud of smoke and flames are caused by the opposite—American gasoline and American oil extracted from American soil. Odd contrast.

What is Steinmann thinking? That he was lucky today—he survived, shot down one of the moving vans and took a step closer to a Knight's Cross?

Hauptmann Wilhelm Steinmann died in Nuremberg at the age of fifty-four. Exactly twenty-three years to the day, August 1, 1966, that he shot down *Satans Hell Cats*. He did achieve the Knight's Cross. He is credited with 44 kills in 234 missions, including seven P-47 Thunderbolts and eleven P-51 Mustang fighters; this makes him one of the highest scoring Luftwaffe pilots against those Allied type aircraft.

Perhaps he survived the war because he never looked back at the hellish blaze behind him.

———

Breaking radio silence, the navigator in the nose of Joey Uptown yells, *"We turned too soon!"*

Other voices, a chorus, jump on the airwaves....

"Wrong turn! Wrong turn!"

"Too soon—you turned too soon!"

"Where the hell are you going? This isn't Floresti—you've turned too soon!"

And then another voice replies with a sickening affirmation:

"Not here! We're turning too soon!" Mistake! Mistake! We're turning twenty miles short of Floresti!"

But K. K.'s radio is obedient; it's turned off. He and Ent hear nothing, and they still believe the Germans are not aware of their presence.

K. K. continues straight out, Targoviste diminishing behind him.

The nose compartment in *Teggie Ann* is a greenhouse of isolation; navigators have threatened to grow plants here. Wicklund crammed in a space with multiple maps and charts; one other crewman, the bombardier, is with him. They have the maps and charts spread all over. The sun cooks the nose. There are ammo boxes, machine guns, C-rations, paperbacks, a jammed ashtray, and people sweating in the insufferable heat. It is a difficult place to work—to try to be accurate.

One can only guess what might be going through the mind of Lt. Col. Addison Baker, commander of *Hell's Wench*, obediently following Compton. The way he sees it, he only has three choices: Abort the mission and circle back and head home for North Africa—but he made a promise to his boys that they were going to bomb Ploieşti, and he wants to sustain that promise. The second choice, a bit dubious, is to break away from Compton immediately and try to find Ploieşti and bomb it themselves. And the third choice: fly steady, continue toward Bucharest with Compton.

But that sounds preposterous.

Baker needs more time. If he decides to break away from Compton and fly toward Ploieşti, he can't turn too soon, because he would fly head-on into his Group.

At this point, *Hell's Wench* has been on course with Compton for about six minutes (approximately 20 miles), and Ploieşti is nowhere in sight.

In a nearby B-24, *Ready and Willing*, Capt. John Roche thinks: *We're going to Bucharest—what a hell of a waste of money.*

Finally, someone breaks radio silence again: *"Look at nine o'clock! Smoke, steam, smokestack. We're headed too far south!"*

What the Group spots on the horizon with certainty is Ploieşti, obviously under attack.

This means the whole Smart Plan is shot, in tatters.

When Baker hears this and sees it for himself, he makes the turn toward the target.

But a B-24 needs a wide circle to turn; it takes time and miles, a steady hand and cautious eyes. It takes the formation 8 miles to turn and straighten out and head toward Ploieşti.

The Germans now believe the targets are Ploieşti and Bucharest, and send two groups of planes up in the air, one toward each target. The fighters flying up around Bucharest find the sky devoid of American bombers. Gerstenberg believes this is an American tactic, a clever ploy to pull his Luftwaffe resources away from the oil fields.

———

Now, Compton has covered 40 errant miles, heading in the wrong direction.

Suddenly he and Wicklund spot the spires of the Romanian Orthodox Patriarchal Cathedral, a landmark church constructed in 1654 in Bucharest.

All aboard the *Teggie Ann* are stunned.

Compton and Ent realize the mistake. It hits them like a cruel punch to the gut.

Years later, Compton reflected on the moment he knew they had to ad-lib the Plan:

> *It was several minutes before I confirmed that we had made the wrong turn. I never heard anything on the radio, such as "Mistake, mistake!," as has been reported. That is simply because I was on the plane's intercom and not on the Command channel. We were under an imposed "radio silence" dictum, and there was no reason to be listening to the radio. I was more concerned about lining up my Group on the correct heading and at the correct altitude for the first minutes after the turn. It was when we recognized the outline of the city of Bucharest ahead of us that I realized my error.*

Compton and Ent feel the stabs of harsh realization. Cold sweat tickles their skin.

The cockpit is mournful and elegiac; they fly on, stunned, silent.

They knew it would be impossible now to properly collect the Groups, sort them out, and make a planned, coordinated attack on the targets. One of the basic precepts in the Smart Plan was through a synchronized attack that would not allow the Germans time to get their thoughts together.

Because the entire attack force is now disorganized, the Plan is shot to hell.

There is no way to untangle the mess and get it back on track.

It takes Compton six to eight minutes of pondering the mistake and the alternatives to decide how to correct their erroneous course. Now, he makes a command decision:

> *I turned to General Ent and told him we had turned too early and had missed the target. There was little choice, as we could not get back on the planned bomb run heading. I asked him for permission to bomb any other target. Ent agreed, so I then went on the Command Channel and ordered all other aircraft to "bomb targets of opportunity."*
>
> *Various accounts and books state [that] General Ent radioed that command are incorrect. That was my command on the radio, with the approval of General Ent. By that time, we had bypassed Ploieşti, so I then turned to a heading of zero degrees and began to search for my own target to hit. The aircraft behind me were in trail rather than a tight formation, so a much sharper turn could be made.*

—◆—

Lt. Col. Addison Baker, commander of the 93rd Bomb Group, has taken charge, leading the 93rd to the correct target, flying up from a southeasterly direction, passing Brazi below off their right wing, and flying toward White IV, the Astra Romana refinery that had been assigned to Sternfels.

Neither the 93rd nor the 98th know that both are now heading for head-on collisions with Compton, coming from the east.

No one is thinking about a plan at this point. They're thinking about dropping their loads on "targets of opportunity," about ack-ack, fuel loads, oil tanks, small-arms fire, balloon cables, confronting fighters as soon as they pull away from the refineries, getting home—and dying.

The 93rd BG, following K. K.'s "bomb targets of opportunity" order, selects the target previously assigned to Bob Sternfels's 98th, led by Colonel Kane. Now, two Groups are heading from opposite directions to bomb the same target.

They will bomb White IV, attempt to avoid ground fire, and avoid head-on collisions.

But it's not that simple.

Because he does not follow K. K. Compton's wrong turn, Killer Kane and the 98th BG turn at the prescribed IP, Floresti, following the new railroad tracks south to Ploiești. And because he has selected a lower power setting than K. K. and is twenty minutes behind him, going through the cloud bank, Kane, by accident, is in the lead, with the 44th trailing behind.

This confusion has the plan of attack in a state of crisis.

Kane's 98th BG and Leon Johnson in the flagship leading the 44th BG have flown in parallel on either side of the tracks, enduring the hellfire spewing from the *Flak-Zug*. Kane, in the lead, is hit multiple times but flies on; one of the engines is on the verge of quitting.

Ahead, Kane sees Ploiești in flames and rightfully assesses that the mission has gone haywire. He now assumes the duty of attack commander.

What Kane is unaware of is that Addison Baker's 93rd has gotten there first, because they broke away from Compton's errant direction. The 98th was supposed to hit White IV first, but Kane leads the Group despite the carnage ahead.

The refinery is about two minutes away. Kane and his Group cannot avoid the wall of cannon fire. They must fly through it to hit the refinery. But Kane has a choice: avoid the target because it has already been struck, or bomb it again. (Kane recalled later: "By the time we were close enough to recognize the target, we [saw that it was] on fire. At that point, it was too late to turn away. Besides, we carried that big load from Benghazi, and we were here to do what we were assigned to do.")

Lt. Col. Leon Johnson, a taciturn, solid leader, is the commanding officer of the 44th BG. He is flying in *Suzy Q*, the 44th's flagship, piloted by Maj. William H. Brandon. Like Kane, Johnson sees the target in flames and immediately assumes it has been bombed. Despite flak, antiaircraft, and 20mm fire, Johnson directs Major Brandon to continue to the target and set up the bombing run. Before they get the bomb-bay doors open, the ship is hit innumerable times, drops its ordnance, and flies through the smoke and flames.

(On November 23, 1943, at an awards ceremony in Shipdham airfield in Norfolk, Lt. Col. Leon W. Johnson received the Medal of Honor "for conspicuous gallantry in action at the risk of his life above and beyond the call duty on August 1, 1943 . . . By his gallant courage, brilliant leadership, and superior flying skill, Colonel Johnson so led his formation as to destroy totally the important refining plants and installations which were the object of his mission.")

At twelve noon, Lt. Harry Kroger, the bombardier, yells *Bombs away!* *Hail Columbia* lurches from the lightened load; she has done her job. The ship passes through the smoke and flames at 200 feet.

Kane throttles back and feathers the Number 4 engine.

It took a direct hit and is spitting oil and losing altitude.

The scene over the refineries is labyrinthian.

There are massive columns of smoke, a spiderweb of balloon cables tethered to bombs with impact fuses. A B-24's wing flies into a cable, pulls up the bomb, and it explodes. No chance for recovery. Too low.

The gunfire coming up from the ground is so intense, Addison Baker orders everyone to prepare to toggle their bombs whenever they can.

Bob Sternfels heads directly toward the Astra Romana refinery—White IV—at 100 feet, 180 mph indicated on his gauge, and on a collision course with Baker's Group. ("At that moment," Bob recalled, "my stomach tightened up, and I said to myself, this is where you are going to die.")

Ahead of *The Sandman,* two ships away, a B-24 is enveloped in a thicket of flames and smoke. Bob watches as one of the waist gunners leaps from his window at an altitude of 75 feet, knowing if he stays, he's dead.

"*Too low, too low!*" Bob screams into the windshield.

The gunner—Bob can see him reach for the D-ring to pop his chute—cartwheels through the air and splatters into the wingtip of a B-24 and tumbles down lifeless and hits the ground. The impact of his body has torn seven feet off the B-24's outer wing. She does a wing-over, seeking lift, then impacts the earth with a concussive explosion.

(Sternfels later recalled:

Fighting the prop wash was minor to what I saw in our path ahead: Directly on course was a shining steel cable silhouetted against the velvet black oil smoke from the burning refineries. What the hell do you know! Let the cable hit using the wing area, which could drag a bomb attached to the end of the cable, or bank, risking a collision with other B-24s? Almost by instinct, I banked just a little as the cable hit our Number 3 prop. When contact was made, it sounded like a thousand cannons firing all at once. The cable hit the blades of the prop, wound itself around the hub, and by the grace of God, cut the cable off, slicing into the right edge of the fuselage.)

Flying ahead of Bob, *Chug-A-Lug*'s belly camera, set to take pictures automatically, snaps a totemic photograph showing *The Sandman*'s wing tilted slightly downward moments after cutting the cable. Below are flames, thick smoke, and three chimneys Bob has just barely missed. The picture is historic. When stories and photographs of Ploieşti are printed, they include this iconic photograph.

("I wish I had a nickel for every photograph printed backward," says Bob.)

Chug-A-Lug is over the target at 3:12 p.m. and is hit six times from ground fire, wounding the navigator. Another cannon shell explodes in the top turret. The gunner, Tech. Sgt. James Van Ness, will die the next day.

Chug-A-Lug lands at 9:10 p.m.

David Polaschek in the nose compartment salvos *The Sandman*'s bombs. He turns to Tony Flesch, the navigator. ("He was as white as a sheet," Polaschek recalled. "I called Bob and told him to get the hell out of there." Waist gunner Merle Bolen remembered: "I'm standing in the waist taking pictures when suddenly the plane banks sharply. I damn near fell out of the window. I cannot believe what I am seeing. I wonder if any of us are going to make it back home. Bombs are exploding, oil tanks on fire, gasoline tanks burning and exploding all around us. We, in the back of the plane, are really covered with black soot from fires so near us.")

Chug-A-Lug's camera snaps two more shots of *The Sandman* coming off the smokestacks, straightening out. Below, the area is a mass of flames and black, oily smoke.

From his perch in the nose compartment, Polaschek has the best view of what *The Sandman* is passing through. (He recalled later: "We were flying through cornfields with our belly dragging in the corn. When we landed in Cyprus, the engine nacelles were full of cornstalks. He [Bob] was so low I was afraid that he would hit some telephone lines, so any time he came to a line I'd tell him to pull up.")

Kate Smith, the B-24 named after the popular American singer, the one she wrote a personal check for, reaches the target seriously shot up. Then, a massive blast in the bomb bay—the Tokyo tank—sets the aircraft on fire. The ship does a lazy rollover and is simultaneously hit in the wing root, then crashes.

Co-pilot Clinton Foster and gunner James Howie are the only survivors.

A few seconds before reaching the refineries, *Hell's Wench* is torn and tattered, mortally damaged by German antiaircraft guns. But Baker, unyielding, maintains formation and bombs his target.

A few moments later, "*Bombs away!*" says the bombardier in *Hell's Wench*.

Baker acknowledges the drop, feels the upturn in *Wench*'s nose. The bombardier has let loose a load with forty-five-second-delay fuses. Baker has fulfilled his promise to his boys to get them to Ploieşti.

Coming off the target with a lightened aircraft, Baker has to abruptly break formation to avoid a midair collision with crisscrossing bombers from Kane's 98th BG.

The bombs with the delayed fuses start to explode just as the 98th reaches its assigned target, just as the ships are—

The delayed fuses pop and the bombs explode.

Two B-24s ahead of *The Sandman* kick up from the concussions from "friendly bombing." Their bomb bays are open, inviting. The Tokyo tanks are exposed. Both ships shatter from the explosions, go wings up in flames, then barrel over and slam into the ground.

Baker and his Group slice through the intersecting, overlapping B-24s.

Bedlam is in the air. So close, crews recognize faces.

Baker needs sufficient altitude so his boys can jump, because if they don't, everybody is going to die here. But despite Baker's efforts, *Hell's Wench*, a shambles, has nothing left in soul or body to abide by Addison Baker's wishes.

She crashes, and everything she is and everything she had been vanishes in an explosion.

Two of the five airmen awarded the Medal of Honor posthumously were in *Hell's Wench*: the pilot, Lt. Col. Addison Baker, and co-pilot, John L. Jerstad, both killed in the crash. Jerstad did not have to fly today; he had volunteered. The other eight crewmen killed were: Alfred W. Pezzala, George J. Reuter, George P. Allen, Charles E. Bennet, John H. Carrol, Morton O. Stafford, Edgar C. Faith, and William O. Wood. Baker's body was never recovered. He was given a memorial site in Florence, Italy, at the American Cemetery and Memorial. Seven years after his aircraft was shot down, the military notified Jerstad's family that his remains had been located. He was buried at the Ardennes American Cemetery near Neupré, Belgium.

Five miles from the target, *José Carioca* takes a massive jolt in the bomb bay's Tokyo tank. *Carioca* shimmies and shutters. Flames indicate disaster. Pilot Nicholas Stampolis and co-pilot Ivan Stanfield feel the heat wave from the blast and their eardrums ring from the concussive shock wave. Smoke in the cockpit obscures their vision. A second shell hits *Carioca*, and flames spread from the cockpit to the tail gunner's station. They fly on to their assigned target, aflame for the next three minutes; it is impossible to extinguish the fire.

This is the first combat mission for Lieutenant Stampolis and Lieutenant Stanfield. They told one of the mechanics at Benghazi that they wanted to get on with it, that they wanted to notch twenty-five missions and go home. Immediately after takeoff from Benghazi, they had a leaking fuel cap, returned, and then hustled to rejoin their formation.

They arrive over the target now, toggle their bombs, then fly toward the city of Ploiești.

The fire spreads throughout their plane, burns through control cables, melts hydraulic lines and aluminum fuselage. Approaching Ploieşti, Stanfield and Stampolis see a tall building that they must surpass; they do.

But their efforts are futile.

José Carioca is not doing any more flying today. Her glowing belly crunches and slides and slams over roof chimneys and parapets in a spray of bricks, flames, and brightly hued sparks. Down below rooftops and skidding on Redului Street, wings shear off, flaps, ailerons spiral away. Flames, plane parts, smoke, trail *Carioca's* path until she slams nose-first into the Ploieşti Women's Prison with deadly finality. Political prisoners and American fliers commingle in the firestorm.

Her nose hits so hard and explodes so loud, people a mile away hear the tragedy; some make the sign of the cross. Ten crewmen are killed; five crewmen's remains will be recovered. There are sixty-one dead and eighty wounded. The fire burns for the rest of the afternoon.

<hr />

Teggie Ann is inside Gerstenberg's "inner defense ring," the "death zone," and ahead, they see the inferno set off by the 98th and 93rd BGs, billowing clouds of smoke, B-24s aflame and crashing, cannon shells bursting in the air. Near misses between bombers as they crisscross each other. The 376th Group is still intact, but the Smart Plan is in tatters.

Capt. Ralph "Red" Thompson, *Teggie Ann's* co-pilot, and two other airmen in the 376th BG are anguished. They flew the HALPRO mission and missed the target that time, and now, Tidal Wave is the second target they miss.

General Ent instructs radio operator Lawrence M. Vaughan to send a coded signal to General Brereton, who is waiting in Benghazi for the Groups' return. The code Vaughan sends out consists of two letters: "M.S.": Mission Successful. Hardly anyone in the 98th believed it.

Compton sees a "target of opportunity." He inexplicably pulls the lanyard cable on the pilot's pedestal through two stops: The first opens the bomb-bay doors; the second releases the bombs. Compton's action is so quick, the bombs crash through the bomb-bay doors and are earthbound to a pinpoint of their own choosing.

A paragraph in the technical manual on the B-24's armaments system explains the emergency bomb release handle and cable on the pilot's pedestal. The first pull allows the release of the bombs in the event the bombardier is incapacitated; the second is in the event of power loss, and the pilot has to lighten the aircraft:

The first pull [of the emergency bomb release toggle] opens the bomb bay doors. After the doors are open, a continued pull on the toggle will jettison all bombs. In a salvo release all bombs are dropped UNARMED unless the fusing unit switch is turned ON by the bombardier prior to the salvo of the bombs.

It is safe to assume that the bombs fell inert and did not explode. Maj. Lynn Hester, *Teggie Ann's* bombardier, did not know whether or not they exploded. Years later, Hester recalled:

I pulled the arming pins from all of the bombs while over the Mediterranean Sea and still have the pin and tag from one of the delayed-action bombs. I don't remember the fusing unit switch on the bombardier's panel, so I cannot verify if it was on or off. In later years I have repeatedly asked that question—about the bombs exploding—of Compton and Thompson at Group reunions, and have never been able to get an answer.

At this point, K. K. Compton feels he has completed his mission. Later, he recalled:

There was no time for me to coordinate the bombardier and myself to hit the target I wanted, so I pulled the emergency bomb release toggle on the pilot's pedestal. This salvoed the entire bomb load at one time. With the bombs gone, I could then get a course to take us home. We took the same route back to Benghazi that we had flown to Ploiești. We saw a few enemy fighters in the area, but they did not bother to attack us. After another long flight, we arrived safely back to the base.

Because of Compton's wrong turn and the chaos that ensued, the 376th's target, the Romana Americana refinery, codenamed White I, was not attacked, and suffered no damage. This was Compton's main target; he missed it, and so did everyone else. Further, this was a "political target" —it was explicitly marked to be destroyed to show that "American" refineries were not to be spared.

A few days after the attack, the Romana Americana refinery was at full production, and the Germans accused the Americans of preserving their refinery. Propaganda minister Joseph Goebbels joked that he was going to send a plane up to bomb the American refinery and leave all others intact.

—◦—

Killer Kane's leadership and steadfastness brought the 98th BG through flames, explosions, and the miasma of an inferno, and for this, he will be mightily rewarded.

Hail Columbia is a flying wreck; the Number 4 engine is cooked, trailing a trace of gray smoke. A flying cripple she is, with too many bullet holes and flak impacts to count.

Several B-24s pass Kane's ailing ship on their way home, the pilots and crew members shaking their heads. They give Kane a farewell salute, sharp, sad.

He returns the salute, sharper than theirs.

CHAPTER 21

And This They Did for Country

Turning and turning in the widening gyre
The falcon cannot hear the falconer;
Things fall apart; the centre cannot hold;
Mere anarchy is loosed upon the world,
The blood-dimmed tide is loosed, and everywhere
The ceremony of innocence is drowned;
The best lack all conviction, while the worst
Are full of passionate intensity.

—WILLIAM BUTLER YEATS

PLOIEȘTI—SUNDAY, AUGUST 1, 1943

THIS SUNDAY WAS NOT THE SAME IN PLOIEȘTI AS THE LAST. AS BRIGHT as some Sundays might be, from this point on, Sundays here would always sit under a shadow. Minds and hearts will forever pay homage to this date, and will call it Black Sunday.

In the years to come, Sundays for most in Ploiești will be filled with the dread dropped here from the unexpected. Memories of this Sunday will never vanish with the speed of the young fliers who left this place a torn, baneful ruin of wreckage and mourning. Their propellers left tears in their turbulence and took tears with them, to be held in their own chalice of grief, unlike any other afflictions they have had, or will ever have again.

The flyboys did not enjoy this day.

They doubted this day. They dreaded this day.

This day has been marred by them, yes, but they have been marred, too, forever wounded by doubts about their courage or bravery or duty to country. It was not the Romanians or the Germans who suffered and cried alone this day, no. The givers of the pain will have to live with the guilt of not seeing who they hurt—the faceless on the ground. They will have to live with the pain of not knowing where bombs dropped through black clouds hit targets they could not see. They will have to live with the pain of buddies they loved who are forever gone, and only sensed.

They will always ask the same questions: Was this right? Was this immoral? What has this done to my life, this tidal wave? Can I live with this for the rest of my time without pain?

The entire country of Romania had been shattered by a scattered force of young, scared American flyboys, a surprise to the citizenry, a shock to the world, but no surprise for *Generalleutnant* Alfred Gerstenberg. He knew it would come upon him.

Ploiești was a landscape from an apocalyptic horror dream, with columns of flames and black smoke thick enough in some areas to diminish the power of the sun—Black Sunday it is. Black Sunday it will be. Thick, oily, toxic smoke clotted lungs and throats, burned eyes, covered skin with greasy soot.

Some of the delayed bombs popped off long after the Americans had flown away—some bombs when they were supposed to, others untimely, their American fuses disrupted or mangled or inappropriately assembled in American factories. Romanian and Luftwaffe armaments personnel set out to defuse the bombs that did not detonate. Some got killed in the attempt.

In a top-secret memo from the Office of Strategic Services, titled "U.S. Army Forces in the Middle East, No. 4832, dated August 5, 1943, Results of the Ploiești Raid," states, in part:

> *By Monday [August 2, 1943], the following casualties were reported:*
> *In Ploiești—400 dead and 500 injured.*
> *In Baicoi—15 dead and 50 injured.*
> *In Campina—27 dead and 16 injured.*
> *65 Aviators are reported to have been captured.*

The report is dated four days after the attack, and subsequent, more accurate body counts would presage higher figures to come, once all the facts were in.

Over the target, the deluge of American bombs and gunfire that came down, from wave after tidal wave of B-24s, lasted twenty-six minutes from the first plane, the *Brewery Wagon* of the 376th, to one of the last from the 44th BG piloted by Charles A. Salyer flying Battleaxe from D Section of the last wave of the 98th. From the 179 B-24s that had left Benghazi for the Battle of Ploiești, 163 of the most tenacious B-24s, with an assortment of daffy, vain, sexual, outrageous, corny, sacrilegious, wholly politically incorrect names on their stumpy noses, bombed the refineries and cracking plants, as they were instructed to do.

Romanian fire brigades and occupation forces moved quickly to quench fires. As soon as the last bomber vanished, the Luftwaffe and Romanian forces started tramping through cornfields and riverbeds in the Praha valley for miles and miles, up and down slopes and hills with old Cajvana trees and the scent of sweetgrass, on the hunt for downed planes and surviving crewmen and body parts.

They found a lot of both, and numerous dead Americans.

The hills and roads and stone fence lines were beset with once-formidable heavy American bombers, crushed and torn. If the "Rosie the Riveters" in US towns who had built these twisted aircraft with their own hands had seen them here, the sight would have made them weep.

Near some heaps of metal and bodies, cows and bleating sheep and goats went about lazily, foraging. Many planes and surviving crewmen were found in a variety of grotesque settings. Some still strapped in their seats. Some at their gun stations. Some whole, some in parts. Some of the B-24s made successful wheels-up belly landings; others rested, smoldering, with burnt and mangled corpses tangled and dangling in the wreckage, indistinguishable from spars and burned tubing exuding a noxious odor and still smoldering.

In one Romanian town, ordinary villagers worked for three hours to cut an airman free from twisted metal, where he sat in a noxious pool of aviation fuel, his skin seared, vomiting from the fumes.

Thirty-five husks of planes dotted the vast Wallachian Plain (sometimes referred to indistinctively as the Danubian Plain). Wounded Americans were scattered, crying and moaning among the twisted airframes, bleeding, burnt, in shock. Pleading for something to diminish their pain.

Now, Gerstenberg had a new challenge: What to do with American prisoners? One hundred thirteen Americans had been captured and now were prisoners of war. Gerstenberg had to figure out how to treat them accordingly. An effort was made to keep them in Romania, instead of shipping them to prisoner-of-war camps in Germany, where they would face certain dire circumstances.

While searches for planes and bodies went on around the fields and city of Ploiești, German fighters were up, baring their fangs, sharks seeking to snag a departing B-24 before the entire battle had ended and they lost their opportunity. They smelled blood that afternoon, the German boys did. They wanted to duke it out with the Americans, to see who among them was better.

Pickings would not be sparse, because the egress routes leading away from the smoking refineries were filled with predictably tattered, shot-up bombers, limping and stuttering their way back. So as the Americans departed hell, they had to face other potential harsh conclusions. Many could not defend themselves; they had spent all their ammunition coming to the target, and all they had to defend themselves were empty brass shell casing inches high on the fuselage floor.

The Luftwaffe pilots knew this, of course.

Killer Kane in *Hail Columbia* was among the fortunate to get this far, although he still had a long way to go. He ordered his boys to form up behind him, to follow him, their leader. To protect him. He'd get them someplace safe.

The Sandman was the first plane behind Kane.

John Palm and Bill Love, who had escaped the *Brewery Wagon* wreck just minutes ago, sat dazed, a short distance away from their wreck, in a rustic field of short grass and flittering butterflies—dazed mostly because they could not comprehend how they had survived the carnage smoldering behind them. And John Palm, half unconscious, still clutched his leg, thinking: Maybe some doctor with magician's skills can stitch it back together and everything will be all hunky-dory again, once I get home with, perhaps, just a limp.

Palm remembered: "After a while, here come a line of skirmishers," people partial to the Americans and on uneasy terms with the Luftwaffe. "I whipped out my .45, cocked a round in the chamber, and started to aim," and Bill Love shot his hand out and shouted, 'Sir! Don't do that!' He startled me, because he'd never called me 'sir' before. Right behind the skirmishers was a line of Luftwaffe guys with weapons. Rocky [Rockinson] went and got one of the German officers and brought him over to us. They were going to take us away, but the skirmishers, they wouldn't have it. The skirmishers got me into a balloon shack nearby; then, they got a truck. Five hours later, I was in a Romanian hospital. A doctor amputated the remaining leg and fixed it up good. The rest of the guys went to a jail in Bucharest. It was a hell of a day."

<hr />

Flying in a four-ship formation, Bob Sternfels had *The Sandman* 200 yards behind Killer Kane's ship, *Hail Columbia*. *The Sandman* was not doing well. The smoke trailing the Number 4 engine had thickened, and the ship was losing altitude.

"Suddenly," Bob said, "I see an object fly out of the right waist gunner's window, then more objects fly out of the left side. I'm not sure, but I think one of them was the honey bucket. The boys inside were throwing out anything they could get their hands on to lighten the load and keep them airborne."

Bob had his hands full on the throttles and mixture controls. *Hail Columbia* had difficulties maintaining altitude because she was flying too slowly.

Bob said, "I dropped my flaps, let the landing gear down and that slowed me enough to stay behind Kane."

After they tossed the machine guns out, *Hail Columbia* maintained speed and altitude.

Kane was aiming for landing at Cyprus, and his navigator, Norm Whalen, gave them an ETA.

At the precise time Whalen gave him, Kane saw Nicosia, the airfield on Cyprus; the airfield shot up a green flare, and Kane responded properly—they could land safely.

In his diary, Kane stated: "I was exhausted, too tired to fight the unbalanced engines. Therefore, I tried to stretch the glide and float the plane those last few yards."

It hit the runway too hard and the tail snapped up, then came down. Two wheels rolled off and bounced down the runway ahead of the ship. The struts dug in during the slide. Then *Hail Columbia* spun around to a halt. She had been flying for nearly fourteen hours.

Kane took a walk around *Hail Columbia*. Later, he wrote in his diary:

She was resting on the ground between two gravel pits. As her last act, she picked a safe spot to park. The nose wheel and the right main landing wheels had been sheared off just below the shock strut, leaving a heavy rod to scrape along the ground and hold up the wing. The prop had pulled loose from the damaged engine to leave the internal gears exposed. The engine had received a direct hit and had several cylinders broken, and the main case [had] cracked. The engine plane had been riddled by so many holes that it was a miracle no one had been killed. I counted over 20 holes by 20mm and 40mm shells. The smaller bullet holes were too numerous to count. Hail Columbia had earned her rest. Grand old gal that she was, she had taken deadly wounds but had brought us back safely. I had let her down at the last moment and increased her wounds. Yet she had been true to us in her last moments of life and picked a safe spot to die. I asked my crew to strip of her of the guns.

I patted her side for the last time and turned away so that the men could not see the tears in my eyes.

Kane's assessment of his cherished airplane was an indication of the severe beating the American boys had endured on Black Sunday. Of the five bomb groups, the highest loss was born by Kane's 98th Bomb Group:

42.5 percent of the B-24s that flew that day were lost. At this point in the mission, no one yet had a full understanding of the significance of the "wrong turn" and what went awry.

The next day, Bob Sternfels and John Kane had a big breakfast. They needed it; they had to fuel up *The Sandman* by hand, using cans, carrying them to the wings and pouring the fuel in, then refilling the cans, pouring the fuel in—there were no fuel pumps.

Kane flew as a passenger that day with Bob Sternfels piloting *The Sandman*. They flew to Palestine.

When they landed, Bob was met with a big surprise: "The headline in a newspaper had a photograph of *The Sandman* coming out of the smoke at Ploiești. The caption said that most of the German's oil supply had been knocked out. I had no idea if that statement was accurate."

<hr />

On the return trip from Ploiești to Benghazi aboard the *Teggie Ann*, Colonel Compton asked General Ent "if he were going to initiate court-martial proceedings against Kane for not following orders."

"I don't think we should. We did not stick to the mission plan either."

Years later, in retrospect, Compton said, "I am still angry with Kane for not keeping up with us and permitting a single massive strike on the refineries."

Eight days after Black Sunday, on August 9, 1943, General Order No. 53 awarded Col. John Riley Kane the Medal of Honor for "conspicuous gallantry and intrepidity at the risk of his own life above and beyond the call of duty." The Medal was bestowed on him by General Brereton on September 7, 1943, at the Gezira Sporting Club in Cairo, Egyot.

A total of 1,456 Distinguished Flying Cross awards were presented; 56 individuals were awarded the Distinguished Service Cross for bravery. The third-highest award, the Silver Star, went to 41 airmen.

Col. Keith Compton was awarded the Distinguished Flying Cross.

<hr />

General Brereton did not immediately issue a casualty report. But seven days after the mission, he crafted a confidential memorandum to

Washington, DC, in which he provided the best figures available at that time:

The losses in aircraft and crewmen are 54 aircraft lost and 34 damaged, 446 crewmen killed or missing in action, and 54 wounded. Of the 54 aircraft lost, 41 were lost or missing in action in Axis territory due to enemy action; 5 were lost from other causes, including 1 which crashed on landing at friendly bases after being damaged; 7 are interned in Turkey; and 1 landed in the sea off the Turkish coast. Losses due to enemy action were 30 percent of initial sorties. Approximately 20 aircraft and crews were lost in the vicinity of the target. It is believed that the majority of the remainder may have belly-landed in Axis territory, and that the crews are safe, although in Axis territory. Of the 11 returning from the mission, 11 landed in Cyprus, 8 in Sicily, and 4 in Malta. The remainder returned to home bases.

After Ploieşti, Bob Sternfels flew thirteen more missions as command pilot of *The Sandman.*

After one of those missions, to Wiener Neustadt in August, Bob was awarded the Silver Star and promoted to captain, and on October 2, 1943, he was given command of the 345th Bomb Squadron. On December 11, Bob took *The Sandman* on one more mission to distant targets. After he returned, another mission was posted for his aircraft and Bob was off on R&R (rest and recuperation).

Then, on December 19, another crew took the *The Sandman* on a mission to Augsburg, and it was reported missing in action.

"After enjoying the Bari, Italy, area for a few days," Bob said, "I received unexpected news—I was ordered to return to Lecce per orders from the CO of the 98th Bomb Group. When I reported to him, I was informed that *The Sandman* did not return from a mission to Augsburg, Germany. I was devastated."

His ship, his beautiful bird, ugly as she was, was part of him from the moment he'd first seen her in Topeka, Kansas, receiving her like a new car. She captured his heart; this often happens to men with their airplanes.

As Ernest Hemingway said, nothing, no man, no woman, can take the place of an airplane in a fighter pilot's heart. It becomes a permanent part of your soul, your life. It stays with you forever. They are always faithful to you, and they give you the best that they have; they give themselves. Yes, it is an unrequited love, and if you are not a fighter pilot or bomber pilot with a plane that's yours, you will never have any notion of what this relationship is all about. They accept each other, pilot and plane, then meld into one. And if the plane gets shot at, she will stay with you as long as she can, as long as her spars and engines and metal parts will allow, because she knows that you depend on her. She is faithful and depends upon you to keep her from harm.

When Bob first saw the nameless *Sandman* that first day on that gloomy factory ramp in Topeka, Kansas, he thought she was an ugly bird. He hated the color; he wanted an olive-drab finish and thought of asking Maintenance to paint her olive-green. He never did. He accepted *The Sandman* for what she was—a formidable warbird, the best America had to offer, with machine guns and the latest American technology.

Bob flew the then nameless *Sandman* from that factory, down through Florida, Puerto Rico, and South America, then across the Atlantic, landing in Libya. He never mentioned it, but Bob knew the value of what the United States of America had placed in his hands: a quarter of a million dollars' worth of American bomber. They trusted him with her. Bob Sternfels respected that, and in return, he would give his respect.

A wild journey for a young man from Detroit, twenty-three years old, who almost killed himself jumping from a garage roof with his mother's "parachute," an umbrella, clinging to the wish that he could someday fly into a dream like the one represented by that Eastern Airlines plane that flew over his head that day. *The Sandman* took Bob into history, to Ploieşti, and she took the gunfire and abuse of the enemy. But she endured.

Where was *The Sandman* now?

Her loss saddened him. After all, both of them had wanted to go home together.

On December 21, Captain Sternfels borrowed another B-24 and flew his own search for *The Sandman*.

He found nothing.

On August 2, 1943, Monday, the Protector received a telephone call from Adolf Hitler.

After his congratulatory remarks, the Führer handed the phone to Göring, who offered heartfelt thanks and his own congratulations. He said he felt justified in sending whatever materiel Gerstenberg asked for. Göring was delighted to have been handed a victory by Gerstenberg, because Göring's standing with Hitler was faltering. Gerstenberg was deeply flattered that Hitler himself had called.

Woldenga and Gerstenberg walked through the ruins at the refineries on Monday. In looking over the carnage, Woldenga told Gerstenberg that the 500-pound bombs had been too small; the Americans should have used bigger ones. They noted the unexploded bombs lying about. While they surveyed the area ten thousand Slav captives were busy at work, clearing the rubble and connecting bypass pipelines so the refineries could start running again, as quickly as possible.

Some German ordnance workers were taking a guess at which threaded part on the fuse would disarm the unexploded bombs. It was tricky work, but within twenty-four hours they had disarmed about one hundred bombs.

Woldenga showed Gerstenberg maps and charts taken from a briefcase found on one of the Liberators. The Protector admired the Americans' ingenuity and thought the plan was masterful. (Naturally, he had no notion whatsoever that most of the Plan, as it was intended, had not been successfully carried out, but rather had been haphazardly ad-libbed, totally muddled.)

"Extraordinary," said Gerstenberg, reviewing the charts. "It shows a very special effort on the part of the Americans. Excellent planning." Then he added, "I am certain the Americans will come again, despite what happened to them. Their bases are moving closer. They have a foothold in Sicily; southern Italy may be next. I have to remind Göring that he promised me Me 110s. We need more aircraft, more guns, more troops. We lost about a hundred flak personnel yesterday."

Gerstenberg sent out an order stating that all Americans' remains were to be buried with full military honors. Both Germans and Americans were given funerals en masse, with trumpets blaring, military honor guards, and volleys from rifles. Villagers stood about, tipping their hats as coffins passed by. Some wept, and not from the caustic smoke in the air.

As soon as Gerstenberg and Woldenga left the site, the defusing work continued.

A 500-pound bomb was spotted lodged in a rafter, and a Romanian fireman volunteered to defuse it. He was denied permission, but he persisted.

Up the ladder he went, gripping the fuse on the hulking nose.

"It's bent," he shouted down. "I'm going to turn it the other way." He reached for his pliers.

"No, don't—that might set it off," someone said from the safety of a nearby brick wall.

The explosion was heard two miles away.

It took ten minutes for the air to clear the shower of debris.

The only thing they found was the tongue from the fireman's shoe.

CHAPTER 22

The Sandman Redux

*Yes, you have been away a very long time. Oh, centuries and centuries;
so long," she said, "that I am sure I'm dead and buried, and this dear
old place is heaven.*

—EDITH WHARTON
THE AGE OF INNOCENCE

DECEMBER 19, 1943

Livinallongo Valley, Italy

HAUPTMANN (CAPTAIN) WALTER HAGENAH, A 24-YEAR-OLD LUFTWAFFE
fighter pilot, had six aerial victories on 19 December 1943. Today he was
searching for number seven. Competent, blond, handsome, Hagenah had
been up in the air in a heavily armed Focke-Wulf Fw 190A for forty-five
minutes—a patient, dangerous falcon, circling the Livinallongo valley for
B-24s. He would linger another five minutes because he was at minimum
levels for fuel and ammunition. Then, he would return to base and sleep
for the rest of the afternoon; or, celebrate first, then nap.

Hagenah knew the route the bombers used to fly back and forth to
Germany and Austria, and he'd received a report that several B-24s and
B-17s had bombed the Augsburg and Innsbruck area. On this day the
Germans had shot down eleven B-24s and B-17s in just thirty minutes.
Sometimes the American planes would fly this route in tight, disciplined
formations; other times, they would be scattered and wounded. Some-
times a straggler would pass this way, either alone or escorted.

Now the remnants were heading home, flying toward Hagenah's perch; his patience and calculations gave him confidence. At 12:03 p.m., against a dazzling, bright-sapphire winter sky, Hagenah spotted a pink-colored B-24, alone, lumbering over the village of Colfosco, Italy. He charged his guns, dove down on the bomber, and fired a long effective burst. He got lucky: A wingtip on the B-24 flashed a lively orange. The explosion tore the right wing from the outboard engine mounting, leaving the bomber floundering. It tipped right where the wingtip had ripped away, then nosed over and became invisible, consumed by a globe of orange fire and charicoal black smoke. It was Hagenah's seventh victory; he was joyful. He turned and headed back to base. He would end the war with seventeen victories.

At that instant, the same hour, the same second, down in the village of Colfosco, Angela Castlunger, fourteen at the time, was observing the disorderly return of American bombers. Angela was walking down a flight of wooden stairs and flopped into the snow. Behind the bombers, a mile or so, came a straggler. Then, she saw something horrible: A Luftwaffe fighter fired his cannons at the foot-dragger—Angela didn't know the name or model of the bomber. A bright orange flash came off the wing. She saw the gray gun smoke trails from the fighter's cannons and heard their pounding clatter. Then the bomber came down in long tongues of flames and smoke, threatening her village, constructed of wood.

Filomena Pitschieder was a little older. When she looked up at that same moment, she also saw the horrible flames. She watched as a large metal object ripped off the aircraft and fluttered down like a leaf, shattering the wooden bell tower of the village church. The bomber went straight down, a long plume of fire shaped like a teardrop, and disappeared behind Mount Ciampac, into the Livinallongo valley, specifically the Pordol pass in Northern Italy. This area is considered part of the Italian Alps, in the Dolomites, and the exact location is close to the village of Corvara, about 100 air miles east of Bolzano.

Hours later, several members of the local militia made a backbreaking trek through the thick snow to the wreckage site and recovered the crewmen's mutilated remains; they did so with centuries-old reverence and heartfelt sorrow. At the time, they mistakenly thought there were eleven crewmen's bodies, because there were so many parts about, but there were actually only ten, the usual number of crew members on a B-24.

The remains were carted respectfully in wooden wagons pulled by two, stout dray horses, used for humping field plows and such, taken to the village of Corvara. There the parish priest, Don Fortunato Daporta, performed a religious ceremony, almost a funeral, and the airmen were buried in a common grave in the church's graveyard. These remains, according to Herb Harper, historian of the 98th Bomb Group, were disinterred and brought to Site E at the Zachary Taylor Cemetery in Louisville, Kentucky. Death dates for all are recorded as December 19, 1943, six days before Christmas. Luftwaffe records for that day indicate that *Hauptmann* Hagenah scored his seventh victory in Italy, 80 kilometers south of Innsbruck.

Not all pieces of the aircraft were discovered or recovered; Germans and villagers scavenged for the aluminum and melted it down to sell. For a long time, many of them wore shoes cut from the tires of the B-24, and wore the jackets, pants, and vests of the crew until they wore out.

On October 20, 2001, Giorgio Pietrobon, a retired schoolteacher whose hobby was to identify USAAF and German aircraft wreckages, hiked to the site with several villagers who showed him where the plane had crashed in flames on December 19, 1943.

(At the time of his visit, Pietrobon was saddened to learn that the dog tags found on all the remains had been attached to room keychains at the local hotel, as a "tourist attraction." Once the tags wore out, they were tossed away without the identities noted. A discomfiting end for men who had died for their country.)

At the wreckage site, Pietrobon was able to reconstruct how the crash occurred (two other crashes also occurred in the area). Although English is not his native language, Pietrobon wrote that "First the impact with a slight slope, then violently skating down against some rocky tips, diving down in the ravine and then the blaze. Pieces of iron scrap is still visible." A hike through the area today with the help of local villagers would probably reveal the remains of several other USAAF and Luftwaffe aircraft yearning for identification and final rites. It was impossible at that time for Pietrobon to identify a single plane.

Two days later, on October 22, 2001, Franceso Mersa, a farmer, contacted Pietrobon and said he had a piece of metal he thought Pietrobon might be interested in. The piece he gave Pietrobon—which he misleadingly referred to in Italian as a "plate" (*piatto*)—was aluminum, factory spray-painted a sand or pinkish color at the Kansas factory.

Pietrobon took the piece home in his hands as he would carry a wounded sparrow. It had a large grease stain and other marks, and some indication of fire, but he used gasoline and a rag and buffed until the numbers came alive once again. After sixty years, the numbers popped clear and fresh as the day they'd initially been painted.

The piece measured 25 inches long and 5 inches wide; it still had the Dzus spiral cam fasteners attached. Named after their inventor, William Dzus (pronounced "Zeus"), these proprietary quarter-turn lock fasteners are often used to secure metal-skin panels on cars and aircraft, and prevent loosening under vibrations.

Pietrobon set out to ID this part, in order to connect it with a specific bomber. From there, he would try to identify the crewmen who flew the plane that day. He already had the date the plane crashed, the site where it crashed, and a piece from the plane with a distinct part number. He turned to the Internet, which was starting to expand at this time, visiting several US Air Force websites. He attached a picture of the part showing the relevant numbers to his e-mails, and asked for any information.

Al Blue of San Diego happened to see Pietrobon's posting. Blue has the distinction of having a complete record of all 19,000 or so B-24s manufactured by Consolidated Aircraft. He answered Pietrobon's e-mail and said the number on the cowling belonged to a famous B-24, the one pictured flying over the flames and smokestacks in Ploieşti, Romania, with the left wing slightly dipped during the attack on the refineries.

Could this definitively be the bomber Bob Sternfels had been searching for, for sixty years, *The Sandman*?

In 2002, Bob received an e-mail from Al Blue stating that he had received an e-mail from a man in Italy, Giorgio Pietrobon, who said he had in his possession a piece of aircraft aluminum—a strip of an engine cowling—with numbers stenciled on the underside. The numbers were:

B-24D NO. 1479
ENGINE NO. 1-R.H.

This was the part the farmer had given Pietrobon, the piece he'd carried home like a sparrow and buffed clean.

Blue had gone into his extensive records and matched those part numbers to a B-24D, Army Air Force Serial Number 42-40402 .

That serial number belonged to *The Sandman*.

After nearly sixty years, *The Sandman* had been found in the valley of Livinallongo, Italy, waiting, we would like to imagine, to once again be in the hands of Bob Sternfels.

The numbers would prove that this piece was assembled in a plant in Topeka, Kansas, where B-24s were manufactured, one part of thousands of parts and pieces that made up a B-24 with the Serial Number 42-40402.

USAAF records would show that 42-40402 had flown from its birthplace in Kansas on training flights around the United States, day and night, then left Kansas, flew to Florida, down into Puerto Rico and the Caribbean, across the Atlantic to Egypt, then to Benghazi. There, it endured withering sandstorms, survived a flash flood, and produced two loaves of bread baked inside its oven-like temperature. The sun had faded its sand-colored fuselage into what many thought was too delicate a pink hue for a bomber. It flew multiple missions to and from targets in Italy and Austria.

That aircraft in the Livinallongo valley was undoubtedly *The Sandman*. Waiting for Bob.

Now for the names of the crew.

Pietrobon was given permission to go through 1943 files in the Colfosco municipal office that might show the names of crewmen who had been found in aircraft wrecks. He soon found that the documents had been destroyed in a fire. Although his hopes of finding a list of the deceased had been diminished, Pietrobon did not give up. His quest continued with determination.

He met with Francesca DeCarlino, head of the cabinet of the government commission of the city of Bolzano. DeCarlino presented Pietrobon with a definitive list of names of the crewmen that had flown the mission and happened to encounter *Hauptmann* Walter Hagenah over the Livinallongo valley, a couple of minutes before he was going fly back to his base to take a nap:

1/Lt John W. Viers, Pilot, Louisiana
2/Lt William M. Smyser, Co-pilot, New Jersey
2/Lt Stanley W. Napierala, Navigator, Buffalo, New York
T/Sgt Paul L. Jacobson, Bombardier
T/Sgt Theodore N. Hagberg, Engineer, Michigan
T/Sgt William O. Marshman, Radio Operator, Massachusetts
S/Sgt S. A. Freeze, Asst/Engineer, Texas
S/Sgt Forest D. Hundley, Gunner, Alabama
S/Sgt Curtis C. Washburn, Gunner, Texas

The last crew to fly *The Sandman* are buried together at Site E in Zachary Taylor Cemetery in bucolic horse country, Louisville, Kentucky. Their death dates are engraved on each individual headstone: December 19, 1943, six days before Christmas.

Bob quickly established an e-mail relationship with Giorgio Pietrobon, eventually asking if he could "borrow" the piece: "It would mean a lot to me, Pietro," wrote Bob, "if I could have that piece of my airplane sit on my mantle for a while. Not only have I flown 31 missions in that plane, but she was part of the raid on Ploieşti."

Pietrobon turned him down.

More time passed, and Bob contacted Pietrobon again, saying, "Look, I'm not getting any younger. It would mean a lot if I could just borrow it, have the piece in my hands before I died."

Pietrobon politely declined again.

Then, in 2006, we contacted Pietrobon to see if our efforts would dislodge the sentimental, historic piece, telling him how much it would mean for Bob to have a piece of the bomber that was such an integral part of aviation history—and his life.

Pietrobon, at this point, certainly knew who Bob Sternfels was—that he was the pilot of *The Sandman*, which made history through the picture taken from *Chug-A-Lug*. He certainly had to know how much the piece would mean to Bob. Pietrobon had dozens of other pieces of the aircraft, although none had identity numbers on their parts. Further, there were additional remains of *The Sandman* up there on the slope; they are most certainly still there today.

"No, sorry," wrote Pietrobon.

It seemed from Pietrobon's e-mails that the piece from the cowling of *The Sandman* was definitive proof of his years of laborious efforts to find parts of Luftwaffe and USAAF aircraft and meticulously ID and record their location. It seemed this hard evidence of his meticulous sleuthing hobby validated his efforts—proved that he was a military aviation historian. At the same time, Pietrobon had his own fifteen minutes of fame: An Italian producer did a piece on Pietrobon and his discovery for Italian television (it has never appeared on US television).

The effort to obtain the part from Pietrobon went no further—a sad ending for a warbird that had served her country—that against all odds had survived Ploieşti.

We had struck a tall, insurmountable Italian wall. The attempt to convince Pietrobon that this historic piece was more meaningful to Bob than anyone else came to a halt.

Afterword

We learn from history that we do not learn from history.
—Georg Wilhelm Friedrich Hegel,
German philosopher

History has clarity when viewed with coffee on Monday mornings.

Tidal Wave has few "blame" stones left unturned, and multiple fingers point in various directions, impulsively reaching many false conclusions. Almost all noted studies, books, and articles on Ploieşti use the word "failure" liberally—mainly directed at two prime players: Col. Jacob Smart and Col. Keith Compton. That's easy to do, as many of the writers don't want to be thought of as disparaging the courage and heroism of the boys that flew and died that day. Especially since no one living today was in *Teggie Ann*'s cramped cockpit on Black Sunday with Gen. Uzal Ent, Col. Keith Compton, and Capt. Harold Wicklund. None living among us today were present in the freshly painted conference rooms of the new Pentagon during the formative planning stages of Tidal Wave. All in the Pentagon knew that curtailing Hitler's oil supply would have a debilitating effect on his war efforts. Some thought and said that a successful attack on Ploieşti would shorten the war. It didn't. This notion was wishful thinking. During World War II, many similar utterances were applied to various battles and operations. Military minds were always seeking the magic pill—the ease of convenience. It is the American way.

For years, several fallacious "theories" of Tidal Wave went unabated.

The first false theory stated that *Wongo Wongo* was the leading B-24 for the 376th Bomb Group and had the lead navigator aboard, Robert F. Wilson. So, when *Wongo* suddenly rolled over and slammed inexplicably into the Mediterranean Sea an hour into the flight, killing all on board, the role of the lead navigator passed to Harold Wicklund, and the mission leader became Col. K. K. Compton. (Note: Compton and Ent had no idea that *Wongo* had crashed, because she was behind and off Compton's right wing when he dropped from the formation—and there was mandatory radio silence. So, when others in the formation saw *Wongo* go in, Compton was deprived of that information because of the radio silence edict.) The navigator in *Wongo Wongo*, Robert F. Wilson, was *not* the "Lead Navigator." The initial "Mission Lead Navigator" assignment went to Capt. Harold Wicklund, highly experienced, highly regarded, and flying with Compton in the nose aboard the *Teggie Ann*. Wicklund was also the Group navigator for the 376th Bomb Group. General Ent was Mission Commander—the ranking air force officer flying the mission that day. Ent would not be flying in any other B-24 except the flagship, *Teggie Ann*, flown by Mission Leader Compton, and leading the entire attack.

The second fallacy: Compton, piloting the *Teggie Ann*, was solely responsible for the wrong turn. In a year 2000 interview with Bob Sternfels—which did not receive widespread exposure, because at that point, Tidal Wave was fifty-seven years in the past—Compton said *he* was responsible for the wrong turn at Targoviste. Wicklund said no, *he* was responsible: "I gave Colonel Compton the wrong time to turn to the target. I did not correct him during the turn. I simply made a mistake," Wicklund told Sternfels. It should be noted, too, that nowhere is there a record of Wicklund conveying to Compton "the wrong turn" time.

Often, the public refuses to accept simple explanations for an event, and then conspiracy theories blossom. Each man—Wicklund *and* Compton, it seems—was coming to the other's rescue in the spirit of military brotherhood. Compton wanted to show that he was the "captain of the ship" (the attack force) and alone was responsible for a significant error; Wicklund would not have that.

It should also be noted that careers were at stake here, particularly that of the twenty-seven-year-old Compton, a full colonel, who, naturally, was seeking the star of a brigadier general, and had been tapped for such a rank. If he screwed this up, that could have ended the dream. Unless the error was massively egregious, the brotherhood would remain walled and silent.

These conflicting accounts between Wicklund and Compton will never be fully resolved to everyone's satisfaction; it is too simple for many people and too complex and mysterious for others. Again, none among the living were on the flight deck that day. At best, Compton and Wicklund were *both* responsible for turning at Targoviste instead of Floresti, the correct IP; one checking the other might have avoided the wrong turn. This they did not do. Either way, the decision to turn when they shouldn't have had disastrous consequences and flipped the mission upside down; it would never recover.

Nearly six decades after Black Sunday, Compton expressed his frustration to Sternfels in the same year 2000 interview. He said: "I can't believe where some of these ideas came from that appear in books on the Ploieşti Mission. They are simply not true! I believe that it is time for everyone to know the truth and the background on the mission, and what was actually happening on the flight deck during the run-up to the IP, and afterward."

———

Jacob Smart, then a colonel, had no experience flying a B-24, as Bob Sternfels learned on July 15, 1943, when he took the colonel up on his first bombing mission. More notable is the fact that he had no combat experience whatsoever—that is, up until his first combat mission in *The Sandman*, also on July 15, 1943, which is noted in Sternfels's pilot's logbook (seen here in this book). Smart had been a flight instructor years before, which did not include heavy bomber time. The first time he flew a combat mission was two weeks after his check ride in the States, when he climbed aboard Bob Sternfels's aircraft and was asked, "Colonel, do you want to fly the aircraft today?" Smart said no. A wise move, since he only had about an hour's worth of flight time logged in the B-24.

Smart took his position that day, standing between Bob and the co-pilot, Tony Flesch. After takeoff, Bob, a first lieutenant, had had to rebuke Smart, a colonel, to not touch the controls. In this case, Smart was fortunate, because Sternfels logged "four holes" in his logbook on the July 15 mission. Smart must have felt satisfied with that, as it was an "honest and true" combat mission: They were shot at, dropped bombs, and made it home, with "battle damage." At this point, the Ploieşti mission was two weeks away.

It wasn't that Smart was incompetent—far from it. He was a brilliant tactician who went on to earn four stars in the new US Air Force. He just had no grasp of the nuances of a B-24, a high-altitude bomber that in his Plan, he designated to fly 50 feet off the ground, and in close, dangerous formation with other B-24s, wingtip to wingtip. When Smart went heavy-bomber shopping in 1943, there were no other aircraft qualified for the mission—it was the B-24 or nothing. Essentially, Smart was asking a Mack truck and its driver to perform like a Ferrari with a Formula One driver at the wheel. Thus, he had no other choice.

Pilots initially thought the idea was crazy, but in rehearsals, many found it to be fun, because they were never allowed to fly that low. Smart, it seems, did not know that such low-level flying obscures landmarks that pass in a blur. Or, maybe he did know and just ignored it, because target information, or lack thereof, could have derailed the whole Plan.

Furthermore, flying below 100 feet made it impossible for crewmen to parachute out, even though in desperation, they did so during Black Sunday and many perished in the process. The Stricklind parachutes would not deploy in time before they hit the ground. Sadly, this was borne out several times during the raid. And some crew members smashed into B-24s, causing death to themselves and fatal destruction to the aircraft.

Despite this, the boys who flew that day did their best to fly according to Smart's Plan—which was quite extraordinary, considering none had ever flown this type of low-level mission called for in Operation Tidal Wave. It helps if you know how the chain saw behaves before you pull the starter cord.

In a memo Smart wrote sometime in August 1943, after the attack, his opening sentence is off-putting—"Unfortunately, the operation was not carried out exactly as planned"—and the rest of the memo, rife with errors. He inaccurately and confusingly describes which navigator was the lead, and what Colonel Compton's position was in the 376th Bomb Group. Compton was flying at the head of the 376th, not "buried" in the second or third wave in the Group, as some have noted.

There was a reluctance to publish Smart's entire memo here for fear it would only add to the confusion of the lead-ship and mission-navigator issues. Upon reflection and careful consideration, this author decided it should be read, for the sake of overall understanding, objectivity, and clarity. It is a historical document that is extremely relevant to Tidal Wave, because the memo initiated much of the confusion inherent in the operation's history:

> *Unfortunately, the operation was not carried out exactly as planned. The 5 Groups proceeded to Corfu in the designated manner, the 376th Group leading, Col. Compton commanding, with Gen. Ent aboard. The remaining Groups following in this order: the 93rd, with Lt. Col. Baker commanding; the 98th, with Col. Kane commanding; the 44th, with Col. Johnson commanding; the 389th, with Col. Wood commanding.*
>
> *Upon reaching the turning point north of Corfu, and with an altitude of 10,000 feet, the leader of the 376th Group—who was also the leader of the entire formation—spun into the sea. [Note: This was* Wongo Wongo, *which was not the B-24 leading the group.] We have no possible explanation as to what caused this airplane to crash. Upon striking the water, it immediately caught fire and burned very rapidly.*
>
> *Gen. Ent, the commander of the entire striking force, and Col. Compton, the commander of the 376th Group, who were flying in one of the following elements [Note: This is false: Compton and Ent were* leading *the entire Group], did not know that the plane that went into the ocean was that of the leader of the entire formation. [Note: This is false;* Wongo Wongo *was not the leader—Compton was—and yes, they were unaware of* Wongo *falling out of formation and crashing.] Leadership of the 376th Group and, consequently, of the entire striking force, then became the responsibility of the second in command of the leading squadron. [Note: Compton was always the leader, and never assumed the responsibility of second in command.]*

If one of the three men—pilot, co-pilot, navigator—flying in the *Teggie Ann* that day had been monitoring the Command Channel, they would have heard about *Wongo Wongo*'s crash, and later on in the mission, they would have heard people shouting *"wrong turn, wrong turn!"*

Because Compton was unaware of these two radio calls, the radio silence had morphed into a friend of the enemy. Further, from the time Compton and Wicklund discovered the wrong turn, it took Compton six minutes to turn toward Ploieşti. This was not time spent on contemplating how difficult it was to turn such a large force; it was "meditative" time in which Compton, by his own words, was trying to sort out a plan. How would either incident affect the outcome of the mission? Only a soothsayer can say. But, of course, there can be plenty of speculation.

Unquestionably, all of these details can be confusing, and that leads to misunderstanding.

Tidal Wave was one of the most intricate, complex missions ever flown: There were five Groups merged from two air forces—the 8th AF and the 9th AF, each with a specific number of B-24s, each with a Group Leader—about 179 planes, initially, flying in a variety of formations with commanders who had their own ideas about what settings to use to best fly the B-24, flying complicated routes, and with two key Group commanders—the 98th Bomb Group with Kane, and the 376th Bomb Group, with Compton—who clashed on procedures and had personalities that were polar opposites. Each Group had a specific target to hit. Because of the wrong turn, many of the targets were hit twice, a waste of time, and lives.

The combat experience levels of the pilots and crews flying that day were varied. To expect perfection in holding formation with many aircraft over seven hours en route to the target reveals Smart's lack of knowledge and experience.

No contradiction of Smart's memo, his words considered "gospel," was published until half a century after the mission had ended. Smart's memo hung out there for decades, engendering misunderstanding and confusion. The question is, why did Smart get the details wrong in such an important, historic memo? What does it say of his perception and judgment? If he'd made an ad-libbed speech and gotten some of the details wrong, okay. But he had had time to compose his words, think about them, check the facts, and then set them to paper, for history to see. Shouldn't he have known that he was memorializing his thoughts and had to get them down correctly?

Why didn't Smart draft the memo and give it to Compton and Ent to vet, for veracity? That question will never be answered and will remain indelibly intertwined in the fabric and folklore of Tidal Wave's mysteries. We do know that it added to the fallacies of the mission, and those fallacies have been perpetrated for years.

In the end, Colonel Smart was the father of Tidal Wave. Anything he said or wrote would be taken as dogma. Instead, this memo misled, confused, and obfuscated the facts, casting doubt on the men who flew the mission.

Hopefully, this book will set the record right.

On paper, the Smart Plan was sound and feasible, with acceptable losses. However, this view was disputed in 1983 by one historian: "It was painfully obvious how unrealistic it was to think five formations of lumbering bombers could sneak up on a heavily guarded area more than 1,300 miles, deep in enemy territory."

—⁓—

Smart assembled his attack force from two Groups: the 8th Air Force, stationed in England, and the 9th Air Force, which came to Libya from the United States. These Groups had their own "styles" of flying in formations, their own traditions, and their own flying experiences, which, naturally, were often at odds. Melding the two together would prove problematical and a detriment to the mission. Often heard between them was the statement: "Well, we don't do it that way."

There was no security at the bases the B-24s were stationed at in Benghazi. Three German Wehrmacht spies were left behind when Rommel left Africa. They worked diligently and surreptitiously, noting the movements of the bomb groups. Undoubtedly, they paid local Libyans to help them in their spying efforts. While speculation and rumors have indicated that the Germans knew the target was Ploiești when they took off on August 1, this has never been proven.

Smart's plan had an attack force of 179 bombers—this number dropped for a variety of reasons, mostly mechanical—to fly 1,700 miles from Benghazi to Ploiești and return. This was to be part of the "surprise." A force of 179 bombers flying anywhere in 1943 would have had a difficult time surprising anyone unless they flew at ground level, but there were serious mountains in the flight plan. And the Germans had erected a new radar site in Athens around the same time the Americans arrived in Benghazi—unknown to Smart and his planners before August 1.

Until Ploiești, the US Army Air Force had been clinging to the belief that any target could be taken out through a single strike. Ploiești taught the Air Force that this was not the case. As the war progressed, planners came to realize that hitting a target hard, once, was not the answer—that a series of follow-up bombings would be necessary. The Germans, in particular, had an excellent repair record. Knock them out one day, and a few days later, they would be up and running again.

At the Casablanca Conference, when Gen. Hap Arnold ordered Smart to "make it [the attack] happen," Smart went to work with enthusiasm and diligence—another career-making assignment. The order, after all, came down from President Roosevelt. Naturally, Smart set out to please his commanding officer, who, at that time, held the five-star rank of general of the army and general of the air force, the most superior officer in the armed forces.

Smart was a career officer with a big future ahead, and despite his age, thirty-nine, was starting to show that he would fit in well in the "new" US Air Force that would be formed on September 18, 1947, as a separate branch of the armed forces. He had an analytical mind, was a team player, a graduate of the US Military Academy, and had a "dream" regarding Ploiești, which he noted on the piece of paper that outlined his Tidal Wave plan. Many thought he was nuts—that the plan was based on "stunt" flying.

Tidal Wave had an inherent disadvantage with its two conflicting personalities—Kane and Compton—and their conflicting procedures that were obvious in the rehearsal stage of the mission. This difference in flying methods would adversely affect the outcome of the attack on the refineries at Ploiești. And no differences could have been more pronounced than those between Killer Kane and K. K. Compton. These two opposite personalities lived on different planets, with "new school" and "old school" flying techniques glaringly in opposition. When they got in the air that day, these differences would prove fatal. Instead of hitting their targets as assigned, the Groups came in scattered, disorganized. After the mission, back at an airfield in Benghazi, Compton and Kane almost came to blows. They had to be physically separated, each blaming the other for the deadly chaos that had ensued.

From the minute Tidal Wave took off from Benghazi on August 1, the strike force was on the radar scopes of the Germans in Athens, thus blunting the much desired and toted surprise element. The plan's structure and cohesion began to crumble. Sadly, Compton and General Ent had no idea that they had been detected. If they had, what would they have done? Would they have turned back? How would they have deviated from the basic elements of the Smart Plan?

There are several possible answers to this question. Picking one with certainty would be impossible. The German forces were strong and daunting, not thoroughly understood by Smart, and now all they had to do was wait for the Americans to appear in their gunsights. Gerstenberg's *eine falle*—his trap—had been primed and was waiting.

Criticism has been heaped on Jacob Smart for rejecting a photoreconnaissance mission using a British de Havilland Mosquito. He was afraid the Mosquito would spoil the surprise he was after. In rejecting the offer, Smart seemed to not consider the HALPRO mission, which Gerstenberg said was an indication that the Americans were anxious to bomb the oil wells. In France, Germany, and elsewhere in Europe, the deft "Mossie" had been effectively taking pictures of potential bombing targets for years. When the Mosquitos were flying, Germans knew that they were taking photographs for target analysis; it was no surprise. The Germans were doing the same.

The addition of the Tokyo tanks, although there was no other alternative to add fuel, caused many aircraft to catch fire, explode, and crash. Tokyo tanks were installed in specific locations in all the B-24s' wings to add the necessary fuel to make the round-trip from Benghazi to Ploiești. One tank was also added to the bomb bay of each plane, and this was problematic, as its installation displaced bombs. And when the bomb-bay doors were open, the Tokyo tank was exposed, vulnerable to bullets and shrapnel. It did not take a very significant strike on this tank (nor many gallons of gasoline inside it) for it to explode and envelop the aircraft in a massive ball of fire. If a B-24 took a hit in a Tokyo tank, it was almost certain to crash.

Many pilots chose to use the 400 gallons in the tank prior to reaching the target, thus avoiding the danger of explosion from ground fire. Many aircraft were seen going down in flames that emanated from the bomb bay's Tokyo tank. There was nothing that could be done about this; despite the inherent danger attached to installing these tanks, the B-24s needed the extra fuel to complete the mission.

An interesting question: What if Smart *had* used the Mosquito for photo recon? He would surely have seen the comprehensive defense system interlaced throughout Romania, especially in the Ploieşti area. Would it have changed the specifics of his plan? Would he have canceled the mission?

It seems quite possible that knowing what the defenses were—their number, locations, the types of guns and cannons—would have influenced the mission, changing it or postponing it for reconfiguration. The question will remain unanswered forever.

After the fliers left Ploieşti, almost before they landed back at Benghazi, the "reviews" were coming in. Americans almost always seem to need reviews to affirm their successes. Sometimes—many times—the facts become obscured in the hastiness often associated with journalism.

New York Times reporter A. C. Sedgwick did his best to write a piece immediately after the attack, which put him at a disadvantage, as it would be weeks before all the facts rolled in.

A slightly inaccurate, shallow article by Sedgwick appeared in the August 2, 1943, issue of the *New York Times*:

PLOIEŞTI SMASHED
300 Tons Rain on
Major Gasoline Source of
Reich Air Force
RAID MADE AT LOW LEVEL
Delayed-Action Bombs Enable
2,000 Fliers to Get Away,
Leaving Great Fires

. . . the raid "may materially affect the course of the war." Brigadier General Uzal Ent led the mission, and Colonel Keith Compton was quoted, saying, "We got them completely by surprise." General Lewis H. Brereton was "among the anxious crowd" waiting to welcome General Ent. Captain Harold Wicklund said, "I saw some smoke and we did a lot of damage, but [it] all happened so quickly." Particularly notable were the comments of some of the aircrews who said that the Rumanian [sic] peasantry had shown the greatest friendliness. Rumanian [sic] girls were said to have waved "a great welcome." A Rumanian [sic] soldier, gun on shoulder, was described as completely unconcerned.

Sedgwick did not write about the "wrong turn" or the body count or the number of aircraft lost, or the Romanians and Luftwaffe killed on the ground. It was a different time in American journalism, less vicious; and, more probably, these facts were unknown at the time Sedgwick wrote his piece. But the article was brimming with a sense of joy, an understanding of the American can-do spirit prevalent during the war years—one of unity, patriotism, and teamwork that would sadly never again prevail across the nation as such.

Any objectivity or facts seemed to have been distanced from the event in the *Times* piece. It was another great battle the Americans had endured, and it seemed to have rung with the success and tradition of the American fighting man.

The *Stars and Stripes* newspaper showed the totemic picture of *The Sandman*, one wing down, coming over the smokestacks of a refinery, raging flames and smoke below her belly. The headline above the photo read: "As Liberators Blasted Axis Oil Supply."

If you look closely, you can make out the letters of *The Sandman*'s name painted on the nose of her right flank.

That's the image we are left with: A single bomber flying through smoke and fire, surviving, heading to another mission.

Could we ask for more?

Only time's passage would reveal the answer.

Coda

In our sleep pain which cannot forget
falls drop by drop upon the heart,
in our own despair, against our will,
comes wisdom through the awful grace of God

—AESCHYLUS

ON AUGUST 2, 1943, THE DAY AFTER THE PLOIEŞTI ATTACK, THE US
Army Air Force unwittingly transitioned to a future with expectations for
dominant US airpower, becoming a branch of their own—separate, lean,
and agile, as it is today. The visionaries of the interwar years had no idea
how Ploieşti's radical thinking could positively affect the air force. From
the so-called Ploieşti "failure" evolved significant lessons that taught the
ability to adapt on the fly, to be flexible, and to "think outside the box."

Despite its issues, the Ploieşti attack became a blueprint for future
missions. No longer was high-altitude bombing *de rigueur*. Low-level
bombing was a "game-changing phenomenon," demonstrating the
potential for surprise and stealth. Low-level training took two weeks
in the desert. Other challenges were quickly overcome—for example,
installing extra fuel tanks to give the bombers an extended range. New
three-dimensional targets maps were created to show key pinpoints at the
targets. Fuse settings on bombs were reconfigured so the bombers could
leave the area before they exploded. The top-secret Norden bombsight
was abandoned for one used by fighter planes.

These changes forced the development and adaptation of new
technologies for these new methods and systems, eventually leading to
smart bombs, pilotless drones, satellite imaging—all of which would be
embraced throughout the US Air Force. As a result, today's US airpower
has the capability to quickly react to any threat, anywhere on the planet.
This new thinking and approach helped lead to our modern-day US Air
Force, the most potent in the world.

In this sense, the attack on Ploieşti was not a failure, but, rather, a hard-earned, valuable lesson.

No one sacrificed their lives in vain.

———

Conclusions concerning achievements and faults for the attack were put down in an air force report, the previously quoted September 30, 1943, Informational Intelligence Report from the Office of the Assistant Chief of Air Force, Intelligence. In Section VIII, Conclusions of Commanding General, Ninth Air Force, there are notable conclusions drawn. Here, in part, are the more salient words:

> Anticipating that the enemy air warning system would pick up the formations after *crossing the Danube, in any case, hindsight suggests that a decision to break radio silence and reassemble the entire formation at the Danube might have resulted in greater success and fewer losses* [emphasis added].
>
> The decision of the commander to execute an attack from the south after his formation had been lost and missed its IP was unsound. *It resulted in wrong targets being bombed, destroyed coordination, and sacrificed the benefits of thorough briefing and training of the crews* [emphasis added]. Each individual crew had been assigned an individual target and trained to recognize it from models and photographs based on an approach from the northwest.
>
> Although tactical errors and erroneous decisions are pointed out above, *no blame is attached to any commander or leader participating in the mission for decisions which were made on the spot under the stress of combat* [emphasis added]. On the other hand, the IX Bomber Command is deserving of the highest praise for its excellent staff procedure and leadership displayed in the planning, training, and execution of this most difficult mission.

While readers should draw their own conclusions from this report as well as newspaper and magazine articles, and the like, it would appear that anyone involved in either planning Tidal Wave or flying the mission that day had not been blamed for poor judgment.

However, Prussian general and military theorist, Claus von Clausewitz, stated, "Many intelligence reports in war are contradictory; even more are false, and most are uncertain."

A plethora of military historians, writers, and pundits have precipitously deigned the mission a "failure"—a superficial, harsh, and expedient word choice used to ill-define an exceedingly complex and deadly operation; the critics, however, did not fly, nor did they plan the raid. They did not see *Wongo Wongo* crash at sea, killing all on board. They did not hear *Kickapoo* explode on takeoff or smell the charred flesh, nor did they examine the "stress of combat"—the mindset of the moment. And they certainly did not see or hear cries of shredded airmen over the target or witness the lacerated bodies entangled in the twisted carnage on the ground, nor heard the brutal clatter of machine guns and cannonade. Thus, their hasty criticism comes quick and is paid for inexpensively. Their eyes and ears did not see what the men of Black Sunday saw, nor did they have to endure any portion of the bloodiest air battle in history.

No one was there except those that had died and those that had persevered.

"Failure," as they hastily termed the Black Sunday mission, has had a diminutive influence that places a carapace on the valiant efforts made by those that died and those forever wounded. Spilling one's blood in combat for country and freedom is not failure. Sacrifice was made. Sacrifice was achieved. Honor bridged bravery.

But not as such that baseball games are won with scores kept, but instead by valor and effort given so that we may endure.

Therein lies no space for failure then nor now.

When the bombers returned to the airfields at Benghazi that evening, most of the boys sequestered themselves, alone and in small groups, pensive, woeful. Some looked to the stars as if answers would glitter and fall and elucidate all that had befallen them that day. But it was not easy. There was no magic for them to grab in the sanctified darkness. There were too many hardstands, empty and joyless, that no longer bore the names of buddies' airplanes on their portly noses. Laughter did not skim the chilly sand. That emptiness would not go away. What they recalled was, instead, a racket of chaos and cannon fire and falling, failing bombers and men dying. The twisting, tumbling B-24 fireballs far out-glowed the exuberance of the twinkling stars, their shine bleak and diminishing, making the boys feel the iciness of ineffable ache. Sadness was theirs and would not be repulsed with their tears. They were exactly where they were. They were not beyond this.

Many of the B-24s that returned to Libya were irreparably damaged, would never fly again, and would be used as spare parts. Several with severe battle damage touched down in Cyprus, Malta, and Sicily. Two could not make landfall—they crashed-landed in the Mediterranean Sea. According to Smart's plan, the estimated time for the force to return was 8:00 p.m. Benghazi time. The first B-24 touched down at 8:20 p.m., the last at 9:10 p.m.—that aircraft had been in the air for 14 hours and had less than one hundred gallons of fuel in its tanks.

By midnight many B-24s were still unaccounted; it would be another two days before all reports were collated, and even then, incertitude would prevail. Five-hundred and sixteen men failed to return to their bases at Benghazi. One-hundred and thirty-two had been captured. A final analysis—as of this writing—for the losses on Tidal Wave shows that 308 American boys were killed. Of those, 124 remain missing. Several wounded during the mission reached their airfields in Libya but died in hospital because of their wounds. The dying began as soon as the Tidal Wave became airborne with the crash of *Kickapoo* on takeoff; occurred during the flight to Ploiești; on contact with the *Flak Zug*, during the battle; and after the gunfire rested. *Exterminator*—the crew's picture is on the back cover of this book showing them dressing for a mission—was damaged but managed to start home. On the way, it entered a cloud bank and crashed into another B-24 also limping home. Twenty-one airmen were killed in the collison (there was a spare pilot aboard *Exterminator* flying as an observer).

After the mission, the airbases exuded a funeral sadness. Most of the men, according to Bob Sternfels who walked among them at this bleak moment, felt that they had been deluded—that leadership had let them down; that they had not done their best in planning the mission. A lot of them had never believed in Tidal Wave from the first day they had learned about it, and the results of the mission provided plentiful proof of their skepticism, they said. Nevertheless, they had done their duty to each other and their country. But mostly to each other. Look at them now standing in the darkness raising a middle finger salute to leadership's cruel roll of the dice.

Nothing upon their return that day could annul their profound ache. Nothing. All of them, from the pilots upfront to the shooting gunners in the rear, could unlock their sorrow and loss and delusion, and allow it to escape forever. Their hearts and their honesty would not let their tears diminish and should not. Deep, wistful loneliness had modified them and would never leave them for all their years left. Never. On the vast shadows of the sand, they stood sullen on the tears of each other, numbed, muted, and no star would brighten so others could see what they saw and suffered. No star would allow their anguish to evaporate. Not even the power of the next day's brassy sun. But though they did not know it yet, nothing would diminish their bravery.

That haunting stanza from a long-ago distance came to them in a tidal wave, the suicidal *Battle of Balaclava* written in 1854 by Alfred, Lord Tennyson, would wail on and on, over and over and over, haunting and with heartbreaking rhythm:

> "Forward, the Light Brigade!"
> Was there a man dismayed?
> Not though the soldier knew
> Someone had blundered.
> Theirs not to make reply,
> Theirs not to reason why,
> Theirs but to do and die.
> Into the valley of Death
> Rode the six hundred.

In the many years following Black Sunday, at reunions and round-tables, the aging men continued voicing their criticism and doubt, always praising and holding dear those who had participated and those who died not in vain.

Maj. Gen. Lewis Hyde Brereton, the commanding general of the 9th US Air Force, and overall commander responsible for Operation Tidal Wave, was one of five officers to serve in all branches of the US Air Force and its progenitors—the US Army Air Corps, the US Army Air Force, and the US Air Force. He was the only officer to do so on continuous active duty. While many considered him a capable commander and effective leader, they didn't believe he was a great general. Brereton was in that significant middle ground of competent but unspectacular American officers who brought victory in World War II. Between Ploiești and retirement, Brereton held many notable positions in the new US Air Force.

Lt. Gen. Lewis Brereton died on July 20, 1967, of a heart attack while in Walter Reed Army Medical Center, after undergoing abdominal surgery ten days earlier. He is buried at Arlington National Cemetery.

Generalleutnant Alfred Gerstenberg, the Protector, never wrote an autobiography or had a book written about him. He should have. He was a historic figure in the Luftwaffe, in military aviation. He was the leading air defense personality of World War II, and many lessons could have been learned from his tactics. Between World War I and World War II, he served in numerous significant Luftwaffe organizations. When the Versailles Treaty forbade Germany to have an air force, Germany accepted Stalin's offer to train German pilots in Russia, and Gerstenberg headed the project. Secretly, he trained many future German aces, both in Germany and in Russia, and learned to speak Russian fluently. He deserves to be in the pantheon of distinguished air force generals to serve his country. Gerstenberg always preferred to remain an enigma, and that served him well at Ploiești.

After Tidal Wave, Gerstenberg continued to serve in Romania until August 23, 1944, when the country switched sides and went with the Allies. Gerstenberg assembled four thousand men and led them in an attempt to enter Bucharest to occupy critical points and stop the Russians. He knew he faced formidable odds, and had to call upon the *Brandenburgers*, a German elite unit that was a forerunner of today's special forces and Navy Seals. The attempt failed. Gerstenberg's troops were encircled by Russian troops, and on August 30, 1944, the general threw out the white flag and surrendered to the Soviet Army. The Russians knew who he was, knew that he spoke fluent Russian, and were respectful of his capabilities. The Russian troops immediately drove to the oil fields and refineries in Ploiești. They met with no resistance. When they arrived at the facilities, they found them shut down, like a ghost town.

Gerstenberg was held in captivity in Russia. The Russians attempted to convince Gerstenberg to lecture and pass on his skills to the Russian Air Force, but he refused. He was kept in Russia until October 1955, after which he returned to his hometown in Garmisch-Partenkirchen, Germany. He died there in January 1959 from tuberculosis, at the age of sixty-six.

The attacks on Ploiești continued after Tidal Wave, between April 1944 and August 19, 1944. The task for the bombing was passed on to the 15th Air Force. The 15th suffered mightily. They flew nineteen traditional high-altitude missions: 5,479 sorties, 223 bombers lost, almost 1.2 million tons of oil production destroyed. Ploiești became known as the "graveyard of the bombers."

Maj. Gen. Uzal Girard Ent was a West Point graduate, class of 1924, and served as commanding general of the 9th Bomber Command, 9th Air Force, until December 1943. He received the Air Medal for his participation in Tidal Wave. Some of the men who flew the mission on Black Sunday did not understand why, saying Ent was mostly a passenger on K. K. Compton's aircraft.

After Tidal Wave, Ent became chief of staff and then commanding general of the 2nd Air Force, based at Colorado Springs, Colorado. In September 1944, General Ent selected Lt. Col. Paul Tibbets to put together an organization and train them to drop the atomic bomb from B-29 bombers on Hiroshima and Nagasaki, Japan.

Ent had the reputation of being a dangerously incompetent pilot. In October 1944, during his takeoff roll in a B-25 at Fort Worth Army Airfield, Texas, Ent, apparently confused, thoughtlessly pulled the landing gear "Up" handle before the B-25 had reached flying speed. The plane settled down on the runway at 125 mph with the partially retracted landing gear. Another version of the story has Ent singing to himself on takeoff; the co-pilot, thinking that Ent had signaled for the landing gear to be retracted, pulled the "Up" handle. The inevitable crash caused one of the propellers to strike the runway pavement. It cartwheeled off the engine, bounced off the runway, sliced through the fuselage and the pilots' cockpit, and severed Ent's spinal cord, leaving him paralyzed from the waist down. Ent learned to walk again using braces, but his disability forced him into retirement in 1946, with the rank of major general. Complications from his back injury led to Ent's death at Fitzsimons General Hospital in Aurora, Colorado, on March 5, 1948.

Lt. Gen. Keith Karl "K. K." Compton rose to the rank of lieutenant general before retirement. In 1951, Compton strapped himself into a North American F-86 Sabre jet at Murdoc Field, Edwards Air Force Base, California, in an attempt to break the transcontinental speed record. Compton was successful, hitting 553.76 mph in 03:27:00.0, setting the speed record and winning the Bendix Trophy. He served in several essential positions after Tidal Wave. After serving as the Air Force Strategic Air Command's vice chief of staff at Offutt AFB, Nebraska, he retired in 1969. An accomplished golfer, Compton won the US Golf Association's Senior Amateur Championship in 1978. He died on June 15, 2004, at the age of eighty-eight, in San Antonio, Texas. He is buried at Arlington National Cemetery.

Despite Col. John R. "Killer" Kane's many achievements, including receiving the Medal of Honor, he did not rise above the rank of colonel. After Black Sunday, Kane moved from three base commander positions to attending the National War College and another series of similar positions. Kane was unquestionably not a team player, and this held him back from promotion to brigadier general, despite having won the Medal of Honor. Kane had retired from active service in 1954; and for reasons hard to discern, he left without a pension and had to tend bar in Pennsylvania. Influential air force friends got him reinstated into the air force, where he spent just enough time to get his pension, fully retiring in 1956. John Kane was eighty-nine and living in a veterans' nursing home in Pennsylvania when he died on May 29, 1996. He is buried at Arlington National Cemetery.

On his twenty-ninth mission, May 10, 1944, one month before D-Day, as commanding officer of the 97th Bomb Group, Col. Jacob E. Smart was piloting a B-17 Flying Fortress at 15,000 feet on a mission to bomb aircraft factories near Wiener Neustadt, Austria. At that altitude, his B-17 was slammed by an antiaircraft shell, violently fracturing the aircraft and blowing pieces of it through the sky—including Smart.

In midair at 15,000 feet, descending like an anvil amid the falling wreckage, and several dead crewmen, Smart was miraculously thrown clear of the chaos. He managed to grab the D-ring on his chute despite the wounds he had received from the explosion. He yanked the D-ring— many thanks to the Switlik Parachute Company in Trenton, Jersey—and the chute blossomed pillowy white above him.

One of seven survivors, Smart landed on a rural patch of Austrian farmland, plopping down among a few drowsy milking cows, their bells pinpointing his presence. They eyed him suspiciously, then continued foraging.

Smart was captured by the German *Polizei* and became a *Krieger*, short for *Kriegsgefangener* (prisoner of war), in Stalag Luft III, 100 miles southwest of Berlin. Stalag Luft III was the same POW camp that would become renowned in the classic World War II film, *The Great Escape*, starring Steve McQueen. In the film, Virgil Hilts, the McQueen character, does a herculean leap riding a Triumph Bonneville TT Special motorcycle painted to look like a German military bike, in an attempt to evade his enraged German captors. Smart achieved no such artful feat during his imprisonment.

Before his captivity, Smart had been sent to a German hospital for treatment of the shrapnel wounds he suffered when blown out of his B-17. He was given excellent medical treatment. One night at the hospital, he was mysteriously approached by two men who asked him if he would help them assassinate Adolf Hitler. In a circuitous way, he declined.

In captivity for eleven months, he was quickly identified by the Abwehr, German intelligence, as General Arnold's aide.

Ja—that colonel, from the Casablanca war council. The colonel standing against the right frame in the photograph. The one with all the secrets and codes, no doubt.

From there, it was a snap for the Abwehr to deduce that Col. Jacob E. Smart was one of the chief logistical planners for the invasion of Europe.

Mein Gott! The Germans had struck the mother lode. They had a thick dossier on Hap Arnold and his extraordinary background, and this colonel in their camp was his aide. *Wie fortuitous!*

Das Lagerkommandant passed the news along to Hansen's successor in Wünsdorf who would urge them to press Smart for all the details they could get. Georg Alexander Hansen was the former Chief of Division I who was executed for his participation in the July 20 plot to assassinate Hitler. They only had to unlock Smart's mind to determine how to get to what was inevitably one of the most complex, expert plans of World War II—the invasion of Europe.

At the time of Smart's capture, the invasion had been planned for May 1944, a detail Smart had burrowed in his head, naturally. But that date would change to June 5, 1944. And then, because of bad weather over the English Channel, it would ultimately move to June 6, to be known forever as D-Day.

Although these changes were unknown to Smart at the time of his capture, what he had in his head could save Germany. His captors went at him full force—until the camp was liberated on April 29, 1945, by the 14th Armored Division of Gen. George Patton's 3rd Army.

So the Germans got nowhere. And Smart endured.

He would remain a prisoner until Germany's unconditional surrender on May 8, 1945, after which he made his unceremonious exit and resumed his eminent US Air Force career, heading toward a four-star rank.

Smart held many valuable posts in the air force after Ploiești. Flying in the Korean War, he was wounded. After retiring from the air force in 1966, General Smart held several high positions at the National Aeronautics and Space Administration, where he worked on the Hubble Space Telescope project, among other things. He retired from NASA in the mid-1970s.

When he went home to Ridgeland, North Carolina, Smart was greeted by three marching bands marching down a street that had been named after him. He eventually wrote a book about what local people did during World War II, and helped set up a local historical museum.

Gen. Jacob Edward Smart died on Sunday, November 12, 2006, of congestive heart failure at the age of ninety-seven, in the same house, and the same bed, where he was born.

—⁓—

Robert W. Sternfels was promoted to captain in October 1943. Upon promotion, he took command of the 345th Bomb Squadron. He holds the Silver Star, the Distinguished Flying Cross, and the Air Medal with clusters. He flew fifty combat missions (Ploiești counted as two). In January 1944, he was promoted to major, returning to the United States in April 1944. Shortly after, Bob flew a war-weary B-24 from Casablanca to Atlantic City on R&R with his navigator, Capt. O. K. "Ozzie" Parker, a native of Vineland, New Jersey, a short distance from Atlantic City.

Parker arranged a double date, where Bob met Gwendolyn Charlesworth, a friend of Nancy Barker's.

Bob told Parker after the date, "I'm going to marry that girl a month from now."

"Gwenie?"

"No, your date. Nancy."

One month later, Bob and Nancy were married in Trinity Episcopal Church, Vineland, NJ.

After an assignment at the Pentagon, they moved to Wilmington, Delaware. In December 1945, Bob and Nancy moved to California. There, they built their own home in Laguna Beach, and Bob resumed working at the Kerr Dental Products Company. He became a vice president and area manager.

— ⁓ —

On a bright, sunshiny afternoon in 2007, in Laguna Beach, California, Bob Sternfels answered the doorbell. A UPS man handed him a package. Sternfels knew the driver, and after they had chatted for a minute, Bob took the package inside.

The bulky box had a return address in Italy. Bob opened it. The sun filtered through the windows and shone gold on the contents, as if to illuminate a long-ago mystery.

Bob's hands reached inside, back into history. He took out an envelope that had his name scrawled on it. He opened it and read the handwritten note:

> Penso che te lo meriti più di me.
> Tu amico!
> Giorgio Pietrobon
> I think you deserve this more than I do.
> [Your friend,
> Giorgio Pietrobon]

There, inside the package, Bob Sternfels saw something he had not seen since the last time he'd looked over his shoulder at *The Sandman*: a strip of pinkish metal with a serial number, as bright as the last time he'd seen it in Benghazi. It was a piece from *The Sandman*'s right engine nacelle—the piece that Pietrobon had found years ago, and was reluctant to relinquish.

The Sandman had come home. She was back in Bob's good, trusted hands again.

Today, the remnant is in a showcase at the Commemorative Air Force Museum in Mesa, Arizona. It sits among other parts of *The Sandman* that

Giorgio Pietrobon ultimately sent to Bob: a piece of a tire, a part of one engine's manifold, a portion of a flap, and a lot of memories.

———

Bob Sternfels died in his sleep on the morning of January 24, 2018. He was born on Halloween, October 31, 1920, in Detroit, Michigan.

I regret that he never got to read this book, which he so selflessly and graciously helped to bring alive. I so much wanted him to because he put much faith and energy into helping it come alive. He read a little more than half of it, and I still have notes he made in the margins that straightened me out on a lot of the mysteries of the B-24, and the complexities of the Ploieşti attack plan that only Bob was privy to. He was a patient, thorough man, much loved by all who knew him.

Bob was one of the leading experts in the world regarding Operation Tidal Wave.

First, he lived it as a pilot. He suffered through it. He lost many friends (excluding the spiders and scorpions and desert rats at Benina). There was no question that on August 1, 1943, he was going to die. As long as I knew him, he never understood how he had survived. The only thing he attributed it to was that it "just was not my time to go."

Bob did extensive research on the "wrong turn." He interviewed everyone on the *Teggie Ann*'s flight deck who flew the mission that day: Keith Compton and Harold Wicklund. Although General Ent had passed away before Bob started his interviews, he did interview Ent's son. There were multiple interviews conducted over the years with others who flew the mission. After some time, Bob crafted a presentation that he delivered to anyone who wanted to hear about Tidal Wave. He had a lot of attentive listeners over the years: at air force associations, reunions held for pilots at air force bases throughout the country, and numerous colleges and high schools. He was also featured in Lt. Col. Oliver North's television series *War Stories*: "Liberators: The B-24 Bomb Boys," which related highlights of Tidal Wave.

Bob was an honest, objective critic of Tidal Wave. His criticism was not mere idle talk, but encompassed valid points made by other critics who shared his opinions. There were many of the mission's critical details he could never comprehend, multiple details overlooked. He never understood why the air force had appointed Smart as the mission planner—someone who had no combat time and no experience flying the B-24, except for a "one-hour check ride" a week before the mission. Bob witnessed this firsthand when he took Smart up on his very first combat mission. Smart, Bob felt, had to have known the mission would never be a surprise, and the notion of refusing aerial photoreconnaissance was, in Bob's words, "ridiculous and untenable."

Some time ago, in one of the dozens of e-mails we exchanged over the years, in which I asked Bob many questions about Ploiești, I got back a lucid, detailed response. At the time he was approaching 90.

But what stands out in that e-mail is the last sentence, a genuine indication of what a cheerleader Bob was and why I cherished him as much as I did from the first day I met him sitting at the opposite end of a bar in Bermuda.

He wrote: "Write a good story . . . this one will be yours!"

I hope I have done that here.

Acknowledgments

Abundant thanks and heartfelt appreciation to:

Nancy Scheer-Lupiano, Robert Sternfels's niece, who introduced me to Bob many years ago when the scent of Bermuda grass and violets layered the air, on a romantic harbor where the wonder of this began, and the journey took flight. And for researching and putting up with dozens of phone calls, conversations, texts, and e-mails through the years regarding Bob Sternfels and his family, and for her hope and support.

My children, Ali and Paul. Their encouragement amounted to a million cheers, always rooting for their dad. Love you more and more every moment, and my love knows no limits.

Paula, my sister, always encouraging and supporting. If I ever needed a booster shot, Paula had the magic dust in hand. Love you!

For BBB, Dr. Heather Bellizzi, LCSW, and her empathetic supply of advice, heartfelt concern, and bright laughter, and, most of all, for that big bright light she keeps hidden somewhere that has shone on paths past, present, and future, and whose wattage helped light the way. When crossing the precarious rope bridge above the chasm of doubt and futility, I only had to look behind me, and there she was, Heather, with a life preserver, a lanyard, and an abundance of smiles.

Dear Marian Moore. Elegant, amazingly bright, and a smart, artful writer. Encouragement from her—always heartfelt, I know—provided a startling amount of precious rocket fuel that made the final ascent much easier. Without Marian, there might have been much wallowing around page one.

To Rainer Gerbatsch, for patiently answering queries regarding the often perplexing and intricate German grammar, syntax, and translation: *Lieber Freund, Ihre Hilfe mit der oft schwierigen und verwirrenden deutschen Sprache hat die* Operation Tidal Wave *zu einem besseren Buch gemacht. Ich danke Ihnen von Herzen für Ihre Bemühungen und unsere dauerhafte Freundschaft. Vielen Dank!*

To Ed Timmes, IT man extraordinaire. I could not write a word unless the hard drives were driving, the external drives, externalizing, and the backups, backing. When the computer got obstinate, hands on hips, staring back at me with a harsh "no-no" glare, I texted Ed, and his skill got the train back on track. Word would be just a noun, deadlines would not have been met, and files would have ended up on the third ring of Saturn.

Mark Sternfels, Bob's son. He provided many personal photos of Bob's Benghazi experience that lent realism and honesty to a significant chapter in US Army Air Force history, as well as Bob's life. Mark's generous fingers always tapped out a rapid response to my often obscure questions.

Maryann Karinch of The Rudy Agency, my agent, for putting her faith in this writer's ability to make the long journey from concept to publication. Maryann made the trip smooth sailing. Every writer should be so lucky to have Maryann rooting for them with her distinct professionalism and heartfelt dedication to her writers. Thank you.

Finally, to my parents, whom I sorely miss—Judge Vincent A. Lupiano and Roselle S. Lupiano. Their parental examples, always astute, plowed the field and showed me the splendor of the English language, and all the nooks and crannies that make it so wonderous.

There are not enough words . . .

Bibliography

"Addison Baker." Wikipedia. June 2018. https://en.wikipedia.org/wiki/Addison_Baker.

"Alfred Gerstenberg." Wikipedia. https://en.wikipedia.org/wiki/Alfred_Gerstenberg.

Army Air Corps Library and Museum. "Ninth Air Force." Accessed July 2019. www
.armyaircorpsmuseum.org/wwii_9th_Air_Force.cfm.

Army Air Forces in Europe—World War II. Accessed November 2019. http://www
.usaaf.com/9thAF.html.

Baldwin, Hanson W. "Ploieşti Raiders Flew Amid Fires," "Ploieşti Raid Worth Cost."
New York Times, August 5, 1943: 1, 4.

Bender, Roger James. *Air Organizations of the Third Reich: Luftwaffe*. San Jose, CA:
R. James Bender Publishing, 1997.

Bishop, Chris. *The Illustrated Weapons of World War II: A Comprehensive Guide to Weapons
Systems, including Tanks, Small Arms Warplanes, Artillery, Ships and Submarines.*
London: Ambers Books Ltd., 2018.

"B-24 Start-Up Procedure." Wikipedia. April 2010. www.461st.org/B-24_Manual
/B-24_Manual.html.

"Carl Gustaf Emil Mannerheim." Wikipedia. May 2020. https://en.wikipedia.org/wiki
/Carl_Gustaf_Emil_Mannerheim.

Carter, Kit C., and Robert Mueller. *The Army Air Forces in World War II: Combat Chronology 1941–1945*. Washington, DC: Office of Air Force History, 1973.

Chant, Chris. *From 1914 to the Present Day: The World's Great Bombers*. Edison, NJ:
Chartwell Books, Inc., 2005.

"Col. John R. 'Killer' Kane." This Day in Aviation: Important Dates in Aviation History.
www.thisdayinaviation.com/tag/colonel-john-r-kane/.

"Col. John R. 'Killer' Kane." Wikipedia. January 2020. https://en.wikipedia.org/wiki
/John_R._Kane.

Conley, Kevin. *Luftwaffe Field Divisions, 1941–1945*. New York: Osprey Publishing,
1990.

Davis, Larry. *B-24 Liberator in Action: Aircraft Number 80*. Carrollton, TX: Squadron/
Signal Publications, 1987.

Dugan, James, and Carroll Stewart. *Ploieşti: The Great Ground-Air Battle of 1 August
1943*. New York: Random House, 2002.

———. "Ploieşti: German Defenses and Allied Intelligence." *The Air Power Historian*,
Air Force Historical Foundation, Vol. 9, No. 1 (January 1962), 1–20. www.jstor
.org/stable/44512693.

8th Air Force Historical Society. "Perpetuating the Accomplishments and Heritage of
the 8th Air Force for Present and Future Generations." www.8thafhs.org.

"Ernst Udet." Wikipedia. March 2018. https://en.wikipedia.org/wiki/Ernst_Udet.

Feist, Uwe, and Edward Maloney. *Messerschmitt Me 109*. Fallbrook, CA: Aero Publishers, 1965.

Fili, William J. "The Siege of Ploieşti: The Truth about the Alleged Wrong Turn during Tidal Wave—The Awesome Low-Level Attack on Ploieşti." http://Ploieşti.net /page12.html. 2006.

Freeman, Roger A. *The Ploieşti Raid: Through the Lens*. London, England: Battle of Britain International Limited, n.d.

"German Railway Flak, from *Tactical and Technical Trends*." Lone Sentry. www.lone sentry.com/articles/ttt07/railway-flak.html.

Hamilton, Charles. *Leaders and Personalities of the Third Reich: Their Biographies, Portraits and Autographs*. San Jose, CA: R. James Bender Publishing, 1996.

Hill, Michael. *Black Sunday: Ploieşti*. Atglen, PA: Schiffer Publishing, 1993.

———. *The Desert Rats: The 98th Bomb Group and the August 1943 Ploieşti Raid*. Missoula, MT: Pictorial Histories Publishing Co., 1990.

"The Hitler and Mannerheim Recording in Finland, June 4, 1942." Military Story: Chronicles of War. March 2019. www.militarystory.org/the-hitler-and-mannerheim -recording-in-finland-june-4-1942-subtitles/.

"Hitler and the Mannerheim Recording." Wikipedia. https://en.wikipedia.org/wiki /Hitler_and_Mannerheim_recording.

"House Order of Hohenzollern." Wikipedia. November 2019. https://en.wikipedia.org/ wiki/House_Order_of_Hohenzollern.

Johnson, Frederick A. *B-24 Liberator: Rugged but Right*. New York: McGraw-Hill, 1999.

Kaplan, Philip, and Jack Currie. *Round the Clock: The Experience of the Allied Bomber Crews Who Flew by Day and by Night from England in the Second World War*. New York: Random House, 1993.

"Keith K. Compton." Military.wikia.org. May 2018. https://military.wikia.org/wiki /Keith_K._Compton.

"Keith K. Compton." Wikipedia. https://en.wikipedia.org/wiki/Keith_K._Compton.

Laing, Malcom. *Focke-Wulf F1 190A/F: Walk Around Number 22*. Carollton, TX: Squadron/Signal Publications, 2000.

Lupiano, Vincent dePaul, and Ken Sayers. *It Was a Very Good Year: A Cultural History of the United States: From 1776 to the Present*. Avon, MA: Adams Media Corp., 1994.

"Manfred von Richthofen." Wikipedia. May 2020. https://en.wikipedia.org/wiki /Manfred_von_Richthofen.

Mitcham, Samuel W., Jr. *The Rise of the Werhmacht: The German Armed Forces and World War II*, Volume 1. Westport, CT: Praeger, 2008.

Modrovsky, Robert J. *1 August 1943—Today's Target is Ploieşti: A Departure from Doctrine*. Maxwell Air Force Base, Alabama. 1999.

Newby, Leroy W. *Target Ploieşti: View from a Bombsight*. Novato, CA: Presidio, 1983.

New York Times. "U.S. Bombers Missed Ploieşti, Turks Hear." June 21, 1942: 5.

———. "81 Airmen Honored for Raids in Africa (John R. Kane Received DFC for Naples Attack)." January 6, 1943: 4.

———. "Brereton's Fliers Also Raided Rome, Report of July 19th Bombing." July 20, 1943: 4.

———. "Raid Losses Equal Germans' Output," "Oil Production Cut 40 Percent," "Turks to Release Americans." August 12, 1943: 5.

———. "2 Colonels Honored Over Raid on Ploieşti (Medals of Honor Awarded to John R. Kane and Leon Johnson)." August 20, 1943: 3.

———. "Wings Highest Award." August 21, 1943: 4.

———. "Six Who Raided Ploieşti Oil Fields Get Distinguished Service Cross (Awards to Keith K. Compton, Julian N. Bleyer, Delbert H. Han, Norman C. Appold, Herbert I. Shingler, Lewis N. Ellis)." October 1, 1943: 22.

———. "A Congressional Medal Hero Back Home (captioned photo of John R. Kane with his wife and son in Shreveport)." November 26, 1943: 5.

———. "Ploieşti Raid Leader Decorated in Britain (Leon Johnson presented with Medal of Honor)." November 26, 1943: 7.

"Order of Michael the Brave." Wikipedia. November 6, 2019. https://en .wikipedia.org/wiki/Order_of_Michael_the_Brave.

Pietrobon, Giorgio. *The Nephew of Uncle Pilot Is in Italy.* Treviso, Italy.

"Ploieşti." Wikipedia. January 2017. https://en.wikipedia.org/wiki/Ploieşti.

Rust, Ken. *The 9th Air Force in World War II.* Fallbrook, CA: Aero Publishers, n.d.

Sedgwick, A. C. "Ploieşti Oil Output Reported Cut 75%," "Ploieşti Bombing Group Honored." *New York Times*, May 9, 1944: 3.

———. "Big Rumanian [sic] Oil Field Bombed by 175 U.S. Planes in Long Flight." *New York Times*, August 2, 1943: 1, 3.

Sternfels, Robert W. "Colonel, "Don't Move the Controls." For file, 2010.

Stout, Jay. *Fortress Ploieşti: The Campaign to Destroy Hitler's Oil.* Haverton, PA: Casemate, 2003.

Sulzberger, C. L. "Reich Vulnerable in Oil of Romania." *New York Times*, February 17, 1943: 3.

———. "Col. Compton Named: K. K. Compton Appointed to Command 376th." *New York Times*, March 4, 1943: 6.

Swopes, Bryan R. "1 August 1943." This Day in Aviation: Important Dates in Aviation History. Accessed May 2019. www.thisdayinaviation.com/tag/9th-air-force/.

"Timberlake, Edward J. (Edward Julius), 1909–1990." National Archives Catalog. Accessed August 2, 2019. https://catalog.archives.gov/id/10613443.

"Tokyo Tanks." Wikipedia. March 2020. https://en.wikipedia.org/wiki/Tokyo_tanks.

United Press International. "Ploieşti Oil Raid Damage Big; Plane Loss Tops 20, Foe's 51 (reports of target damage, US losses)," "Gunner's First Combat Job Brings Down Enemy Plane" (David Rosenthal Bags Me 109, Bombers Over Ploieşti)." August 4, 1943: 1, 2, 4, 18.

"Uzal G. Ent." Wikipedia. January 2016. https://en.wikipedia.org/wiki/Uzal_Girard_Ent.

Valant, Gary M. *Vintage Aircraft Nose Art.* Osceola, WI: Motorbooks Internationl, 1987.

Vassiltchikov, Marie. *Berlin Diaries: 1940–1945.* New York: Random House, 1988.

von Kardorff, Ursula. *Diary of a Nightmare: Berlin, 1942–1945.* First edition, published by Rupert Hart-Davis, 1965.

"Walter Hagenah." Aces of the Luftwaffe. www.luftwaffe.cz/hagenah.html.

War History Online. "The Only Known Recording of Hitler's Normal Speaking Voice, as He Talks to Marshal of Finland Mannerheim." www.warhistoryonline.com/featured/recording-of-hitlers-normal-speakingvoice.html.

Way, Frank, and Robert W. Sternfels. *Burning Hitler's Black Gold*. Frank Way, publisher, 2002.

"Wilhelm Steinmann." Aces of the Luftwaffe. February 2018. www.luftwaffe.cz/steinmann.html.

"Wilhelm Steinmann." Military. Knight's Cross of the Iron Cross. https://military.wikia.org/wiki/Wilhelm_Steinmann.

Williamson, Gordon. *The "Hermann Göring" Division*. New York: Osprey Publishing, 2003.

———. *Knight's Cross with Diamonds Recipients: 1941–1945*. New York: Osprey Publishing, 2006.

"The World's First Oil Refinery: Ploieşti." Wikipedia. January 2017. www.worldrecordacademy.org/technology/worlds-first-oil-refinery-ploiesti-218277.

INDEX

Page numbers in *italics* refer to the photo insert.